Educational Path For ADHD

Fill Your Child's Needs and Triumph as a Parent by Creating a "Language Enriched Environment". Suited to Defiant, Lazy and Shy Children/ Release Anxiety and Achieve Results.

By
Positive-Parenting Education project
&
Saline Cure Meditation Team

© Copyright 2020 by Brain Training Academy - All rights reserved.

This document is geared towards providing exact and reliable information in regards to the topic and issue covered. The publication is sold with the idea that the publisher is not required to render accounting, officially permitted, or otherwise, qualified services. If advice is necessary, legal or professional, a practiced individual in the profession should be ordered.

- From a Declaration of Principles which was accepted and approved equally by a Committee of the American Bar Association and a Committee of Publishers and Associations.

In no way is it legal to reproduce, duplicate, or transmit any part of this document in either electronic means or in printed format. Recording of this publication is strictly prohibited and any storage of this document is not allowed unless with written permission from the publisher. All rights reserved.

The information provided herein is stated to be truthful and consistent, in that any liability, in terms of inattention or otherwise, by any usage or abuse of any policies, processes, or directions contained within is the solitary and utter responsibility of the recipient reader. Under no circumstances will any legal responsibility or blame be held against the publisher for any reparation, damages, or monetary loss due to the information herein, either directly or indirectly.

Respective authors own all copyrights not held by the publisher.

The information herein is offered for informational purposes solely, and is universal as so. The presentation of the information is without contract or any type of guarantee assurance.

Table of contents

Part 1: Theory and Activities

Chapter 1 Learn About Developmental Milestones
1.1 Healthy Bodies for your Kids
1.2 The proper height and Weight for your children
Chapter 2 Montessori Toddler Discipline
2.1 Best way to make your kids grow faster
2.2 How to Increase the Height of a Child
2.3 How to keep your toddler busy and Happy at the same time
Chapter 3 Naptime And Nighttime Training
3.1 Toddler discipline and proper upbringing
3.2 Timeouts is Not for Every Kid
3.3 Commandments Discipline for Toddler
3.4 Disciplining Your Toddler to make the right choice
Chapter 4 The Right Approach To Potty And Tantrums
4.1 General Knowledge of potty for children
4.2 Dealing with the emotions
4.3 Using motivation for the training
4.4 How will I know my toddler is ready to be potty trained?
4.5 How to know when its time for a child with special need
4.6 Potty Training Challenges
4.7 How to Use Positive Practice for Accidents
4.8 When to Get Help for Special Needs Kids With Potty Training Difficulties
4.9 Getting started with toilet training
4.10 After training is started
4.11 Potty Training Chairs
4.12 Starting the process
4.13 Pre-potty training
4.14 Step-by-Step Potty training
4.15 What Not to Do
4.16 How to Potty Train a Child with Special Needs as a mum
4.17 How to Potty Train a "Late" Bloomer

4.18 How to potty train your kid as a dad

4.19 A Real Dad experience

4.20 How to Potty train a kid as a grandpa

Chapter 5 How To Potty Train Your Kid In 3 Days

5.1 The First day Journey to the 3 days potty training

5.2 Constipation

5.3 The second day journey of the 3 days

5.4 When they finally get it right

Chapter 6 Build Empath With Your Child

6.1 How to Use Positive Practice for Accidents

6.2 Children Tantrums

6.3 Regression in potty Training

6.4 Addressing fear in the kids

6.5 Potty training Twins or multiple children

6.6 Help from daycare provider

6.7 Travelling and Errands during potty Training

Chapter 7 Introduction To ADHD

7.1 What exactly is ADHD?

7.2 What's really ADHD like?

7.3 ADHD Symptoms and Signs of Inattentiveness

7.4 ADHD Symptoms and Signs of Hyperactivity

7.5 ADHD Symptoms and Signs of Impulsiveness

7.6 ADHD Positive Aspects of Kids

7.7 Is it ADHD, Really?

7.8 Supporting an ADHD Kid

Chapter 8 Adhd Diagnosed Kids Treatments

8.1 Treatment Options for ADHD

8.2 ADHD Medications

8.3 Treatment for ADHD Begins at Home

8.4 ADHD Professional Treatment

8.5 ADHD Behavioral Therapy

8.6 ADHD Kid Treatment Supporting Tips

8.7 Praise Importance

Chapter 9 Causes Of ADHD

Chapter 10 Adhd Mindfulness Meditation & Hypnotherapy

10.1 What exactly is Mindfulness?

10.2 Is it Spiritual?

10.3 How will individuals with ADHD be improved by being mindful?

10.4 Working of Mindfulness Meditation
10.5 What if I cannot Concentrate?
10.6 Who can do Mindfulness Meditation?
10.7 How much it costs?
10.8 Researches About Mindfulness
10.9 Training of Mindfulness for ADHD
10.10 ADHD in Early Years and Mindfulness
10.11 Mindfulness Parenting by Parents
10.12 ADHD Kids Mindful Activities
10.13 Mindfulness Advantages for Kids
10.14 Kid's Mind on Mindfulness
10.15 Cognitive Traits Building
10.16 Other Remedies for ADHD Treatments
10.17 Hypnotherapy for ADHD Treatment
Chapter 11 Home And School-Based Mindfulness Activities For Kids
Chapter 12 Parenting Tips And Guidelines For Parents
12.1 ADHD Kid Raising Guidelines
12.2 How Parents Should Take Care of Themselves?
12.3 Managing Time A Survival Key For Parents
Conclusion

Part 2 : Bedtime Stories

Chapter 1 The Introduction To Bedtime Stories
1.6. Tips for Parents
Chapter 2 The Risky Ventures Of Zorian – An Adventurous Bedtime Story For Kids
Chapter 3 Bedtime Fairy Tales For Kids
3.1. A most Different Voyage
3.2. The Pig man
3.3. The Emperor's new clothes:
3.4. The Fir tree
3.5. The Snow Queen:

3.6. The real princess

Chapter 4 Bedtime Fables For Kids

4.1. The wolf and the dog

4.2. The Bear That Set Alone

4.3. The man and the wood

4.4. The wolf and the lamb

4.5. The dog & his shadow

4.6. The Lion's share

4.7. The Wolf and the crane

4.8. The man & the snake

4.9. The cock and the pearl

4.10. The City Mouse and the Village Mouse

4.11. The giddy Lion

4.12. The crow & the Fox

4.13. The Ass and the Lapdog

4.14. The Miller Mouse & Jack the Lion

4.15. The wolf and the kid

4.16. The Swallow and the Other Birds

4.17. The frogs desiring a king

4.18. The Hares and the Frogs

4.19. The woodman and the serpent

4.20. The Mountains in Labour

4.21. The bald man and the fly

4.22 The fox and the stork

4.23. The fox and the mask

4.24. The fox and the ox

4.25. The hart and the hunter

4.26. Androcles

4.27. The jay and the peacock

4.28. The Bat, the Birds and the Beasts

4.29. The belly and the members

4.30. The serpent and the file

Chapter 5 Hypnosis Bedtime Stories For Kids

5.1. Marlene Worry Warthog – Hypnosis story for kids

5.2. Pediatric Hypnosis and metaphorical approaches

5.3. Molly Macaw – A hypnosis bedtime story

5.4. Harry the hypno-potamus – A hypnosis story

Chapter 6 Bedtime Fables To Help With Learning
6.1. Tweety the bird
6.2. Daisy pumpkin's elephant shadow
6.5. Geire, the Wolf who tried to flee
6.7 The Teddy Bear War
6.9. Gigantic or super smart
6.13 Water In The Desert
6.14 Water In The Desert
6.15. The Ugly Duckling
6.16. Dinosaurs In My Bed
6.17.The Boy Who Cried Wolf
6.18 Little Albert and White Fluffy Bunny
6.19. A Queer Friendship
Chapter 7 Greek Mythological Stories
7.1. Zeus, King of the Gods
7.2. Poseidon, God of the Sea
7.3. Hades, King of the Dead
7.4. Hera, Queen of the Gods
7.5 Artemis, Goddess of the hunt:
7.6. Artemis, the huntress
7.7 Apollo, The God of Light:
7.8. Hephaestus, God of Fire and the Forge:
Chapter 8 Inspirational Bedtime Stories
8.1. Look after yourself – Five little chickens
8.2. Kids can make a difference – Goldilocks and four bears
8.3. Seeking happiness – an inspirational bedtime story for kids
8.4. Feed what you want to grow – An inspirational bedtime story for kids
8.5. Kids can make a difference – Trevor a boy in early teens
8.6. It's in the way you do it – An inspirational bedtime story:
8.7. Do what you can do.
8.8. Make the most of what you have been given
References

Part 1 "Theory and Activities"

Introduction

Parents play a key role in toilet training. Parents need to provide their child with direction, motivation, and reinforcement. They need to set aside time for and have patience with the toilet training process. Parents can encourage their child to be independent and allow their child to master each step at his or her own pace. WHEN TO BEGIN TOILET TRAINING YOUR CHILD There is no right age to toilet train a child the approximate time is between 15 months to 30 months.

Readiness to begin toilet training depends on the individual child. In general, starting before age 2 (24months) is not recommended. The readiness skills and physical development your child needs occur between age 18 months and 2.5 years.

Potty training might seem like a daunting task, but if your child is truly ready, there's not much to worry about. "Life goes on and one day your child will just do it," says Lisa Asta, M.D., a clinical professor of pediatrics at University of California, San Francisco, and spokesperson for the American Academy of Pediatrics. "When kids want to go on the potty, they will go on the potty. Sometimes that happens at 18 months, sometimes it doesn't happen until close to age 4, but no healthy child will go into kindergarten in diapers." So don't stress—your child will ultimately get on the potty and do his thing, but you can help guide the process along. If you're ready to make diapers a thing of the past in your house, experts recommend following these seven easy steps.

Your child will show cues that he or she is developmentally ready. Signs of readiness include the fol-lowing:

- Your child can imitate your behavior.
- Your child begins to put things where they belong.
- Your child can demonstrate independence by saying "no."

- Your child can express interest in toilet training (e g, following you to the bathroom).
- Your child can walk and is ready to sit down.
- Your child can indicate first when he is "going"(urinating or defecating) and then when he needs to "go."
- Your child is able to pull clothes up and down (on and off).
- Each child has his or her own style of behavior, which is called temperament.
- In planning your approach to toilet training, it is important to consider your child's temperament.
- Consider your child's moods and the time of day your child is most approachable.
- Plan your approach based on when your child is most cooperative.
- If your child is generally shy and withdrawn, he or she may need additional support and encouragement.
- Work with your child's attention span.

Plan for distractions that will keep him or her comfortable on the potty chair. All this and many more on how to get your kid on potty will be explain in this ebook.

Chapter 1

Learn About Developmental Milestones

Skills such as taking a first step, smiling for the first time, and waving "bye-bye" are called developmental milestones. Developmental milestones are things most children can do by a certain age. Children reach milestones in how they play, learn, speak, behave, and move (like crawling, walking, or jumping).

During the second year, toddlers are moving around more, and are aware of themselves and their surroundings. Their desire to explore new objects and people also is increasing. During this stage, toddlers will show greater independence; begin to show defiant behavior; recognize themselves in pictures or a mirror; and imitate the behavior of others, especially adults and older children. Toddlers also should be able to recognize the names of familiar people and objects, form simple phrases and sentences, and follow simple instructions and directions.

Positive Parenting Tips

Following are some of the things you, as a parent, can do to help your toddler during this time:

Mother reading to toddler

Read to your toddler daily.

Ask her to find objects for you or name body parts and objects.

Play matching games with your toddler, like shape sorting and simple puzzles.

Encourage him to explore and try new things.

Help to develop your toddler's language by talking with her and adding to words she starts. For example, if your toddler says "baba", you can respond, "Yes, you are right—that is a bottle."

Encourage your child's growing independence by letting him help with dressing himself and feeding himself.

Respond to wanted behaviors more than you punish unwanted behaviors (use only very brief time outs). Always tell or show your child what she should do instead.

Encourage your toddler's curiosity and ability to recognize common objects by taking field trips together to the park or going on a bus ride.

Child Safety First

Because your child is moving around more, he will come across more dangers as well. Dangerous situations can happen quickly, so keep a close eye on your child. Here are a few tips to help keep your growing toddler safe:

Do NOT leave your toddler near or around water (for example, bathtubs, pools, ponds, lakes, whirlpools, or the ocean) without someone watching her. Fence off backyard pools. Drowning is the leading cause of injury and death among this age group.

Block off stairs with a small gate or fence. Lock doors to dangerous places such as the garage or basement.

Ensure that your home is toddler proof by placing plug covers on all unused electrical outlets.

Keep kitchen appliances, irons, and heaters out of reach of your toddler. Turn pot handles toward the back of the stove.

Keep sharp objects such as scissors, knives, and pens in a safe place.

Lock up medicines, household cleaners, and poisons.

Do NOT leave your toddler alone in any vehicle (that means a car, truck, or van) even for a few moments.

Store any guns in a safe place out of his reach.

Keep your child's car seat rear-facing as long as possible. According to the National Highway Traffic Safety Administration, it's the best way to keep her safe. Your child should remain in a rear-facing car seat until she reaches the top height or weight limit allowed by the car seat's manufacturer. Once your child outgrows the rear-facing car seat, she is ready to travel in a forward-facing car seat with a harness.

1.1 Healthy Bodies for your Kids

Give your child water and plain milk instead of sugary drinks. After the first year, when your nursing toddler is eating more and different solid foods, breast milk is still an ideal addition to his diet.

Your toddler might become a very picky and erratic eater. Toddlers need less food because they don't grow as fast. It's best not to battle with him over this. Offer a selection of healthy foods and let him choose what she wants. Keep trying new foods; it might take time for him to learn to like them.

Limit screen time and develop a media use plan for your family.external icon For children younger than 18 months of age, the AAP recommends that it's best if toddlers not use any screen media other than video chatting.

Your toddler will seem to be moving continually—running, kicking, climbing, or jumping. Let him be active—he's developing his coordination and becoming strong.

Make sure your child gets the recommended amount of sleep each night: For toddlers 1-2 years, 11–14 hours per 24 hours (including naps)

1.2 The proper height and Weight for your children

Baby growth charts for boys and girls are an important tool health providers use when it comes to comparing your child's growth to other kids her age. But for the average parent, they can be a little confusing to decipher.

To make it easier for you to get informed, we had experts breakdown the information you really want to know about your child's physical development. Here's a simple look at average height and weight growth at every age:

Baby Height and Weight Growth

Birth to 4 Days Old

The average newborn is 19.5 inches long and weighs 7.25 pounds. Boys have a head circumference of about 13.5 inches and girls measure in at 13.3 inches, according to the National Center for Health Statistics.

A baby drops 5 to 10 percent of his total body weight in his first few days of life because of the fluid he loses through urine and stool, says Parents advisor Ari Brown, M.D., author of Baby 411.

5 Days to 3 Months

Babies gain about an ounce a day on average during this period, or half a pound per week, and they should be back to their birthweight by their second-week visit. Expect a growth surge around 3 weeks and then another one at 6 weeks.

3 Months to 6 Months

A baby should gain about half a pound every two weeks. By 6 months, she should have doubled her birthweight.

7 Months to 12 Months

A child is still gaining about a pound a month. If you're nursing, your baby may not gain quite this much, or he may dip slightly from one percentile to another on the growth chart.

"At this point, babies may also burn more calories because they're starting to crawl or cruise," says Tanya Altmann, M.D., a Los Angeles pediatrician and author of Mommy Calls. Even so, by the time he reaches his first birthday, expect him to have grown 10 inches in length and tripled his birthweight and his head to have grown by about 4 inches.

Toddler Height and Weight Growth

Age 1

Toddlers will grow at a slower pace this year but will gain about a half a pound a month and will grow a total of about 4 or 5 inches in height.

Age 2

A kid will sprout about 3 more inches by the end of her third year and will have quadrupled her birthweight by gaining about 4 more pounds. By now, your pediatrician will be able to make a fairly accurate prediction about her adult height.

Preschooler Height and Weight Growth (Ages 3-4)

A preschooler will grow about 3 inches and gain 4 pounds each year.

You may also find that your child starts to shed the baby fat from his face and looks lankier, since kids' limbs grow more by the time they are preschoolers, says Daniel Rauch, M.D., associate professor of pediatrics at Mount Sinai School of Medicine, in New York City.

Kids Height and Weight Growth (Ages 5+)

Starting at 5 years old, kids will begin to grow about 2 inches and gain 4 pounds each year until puberty (usually between 8 and 13 for girls and 10 and 14 for boys). Girls often reach their full height about two years after their first period. Boys usually hit their adult height around age 17.

Happiness in POWERFUL

What Makes a Child Happy?

We all want the same things for our kids. We want them to grow up to love and be loved, to follow their dreams, to find success. Mostly, though, we want them to be happy. But just how much control do we have over our children's happiness?

Happy toddlers don't just happen...they're molded by parents who care!

Bubbling giggles, chubby feet and colorful facial expressions all make-up a happy toddler!

It thrills my soul to see a content, obviously well-loved toddlers, explore their new world.

Their enthusiasm about daily life is contagious

But some toddlers don't enjoy the blessings of a home that's filled with encouraging words, bundles of hugs and wheelbarrels full of kisses. Instead, they face daily criticism and harshness.

Have you ever heard a mother or father yell "Shut-up!" to their toddler?

Unfortunately I have. I absolutely shutter and my teeth clench when I hear those anger-filled words. Instead of tearing toddlers down, we should be encouraging them!

Our focus should be creating happy toddlers — not creating sad, frustrated, misunderstood toddlers! I'll admit it.

Sometimes it is crazy-easy to snap at toddler because you're trying to get other work done and they interrupt you once again.

Be present in your toddler's life. Don't push your munchkin away when you are answering an email. Instead take a few moments and address her needs or wants. Take time to play with your toddler every day. Make tents together, color pictures, go on walks, bake together, try these simple toddler activities or whatever your child enjoys doing — do it! My youngest child enjoys swinging on our large patio swing. I try to make a "date" with him everyday for this special time. We are making memories!

Set goals. Are you making dinner soon? Ask your toddler to help set the table. Do you clean your room in the morning? Ask your little one to help you make your bed. By giving toddlers responsibilities you are letting them know they have an important place in the family. When a child successfully completes a goal, like chores, he begins to develop security and an "I can do it!" attitude.

It is my three-year-old son's task to open the door for visitors after they leave our home. He enjoys it so much! When he runs back to us, he always has an upbeat spirit and can't wait to help out in another area!

Establish boundaries. Definite boundaries help a child understand what is acceptable in your home and what is not. If she does not know the rules, she can become paranoid and insecure of messing up. Make your rules reasonable and make sure you stick to them! If rules are not enforced, they are worthless.

Examples of acceptable rules for toddlers:

- No whining or screaming.
- Say "please" and "thank-you."
- Pick up your toys after you play.
- Do not open the refrigerator.

As your child obeys these rules, she will feel confident that she is able to obey "house rules."

By establishing clear boundaries, you are promoting even more security for your toddler!

Praise often. Criticism and negativity comes from everywhere in the outside world. Create a haven in your home by praising your toddler for jobs well-done, good attitudes or any positive characteristics you observe. Praising a child always adds extra dashes of happiness to the soul!

Use eye contact. When praising or correcting, get down on your toddler's eye level and speak one-on-one together. You are letting him know she is the focus of your thoughts and energy. When he asks for a drink, squat down and ask him if he want juice or milk. Take these special short conversations to interact with your child in order to build his confidence in your unbiased love.

Smile often. It's so easy to lose our smile when we're busy in daily tasks and life, isn't it? But a toddler finds much happiness in seeing a smile on mom's face. When a toddler sees that smile, the entire world seems like a peaceful, happy place...and the toddler knows that mom really does love and care for him! Our face speaks a thousand words!

Listen. Nothing says, "You don't really matter," like someone not listening to what you are saying. When your toddler gets excited about something and wants to show and tell you about this new discovery, really listen and pay attention. Comment on their discovery. Don't just say, "Uh...yeah. That's neat. Now, go and play!" Your toddler knows when you're really listening and when you're just trying to shoo her away.

Laugh!. Go ahead, let your hair down and be super silly with your toddler. Sing silly songs with them, talk in funny voices — anything to get a smile or laugh from your kiddos. Adding some silliness and fun to your toddler's day is the perfect way to build them up!

Celebrate victories! Did your toddler finally get the potty-training deal?! :) Did your toddler learn to successfully and routinely nap?! Those are HUGE milestones and should be celebrated! Celebrate with just an ice cream cone, a trip to the park or some stickers! Keep it simple so it's always convenient to celebrate a new milestone in your munchkin's life.

If your toddler is struggling with napping successfully, we have an awesome super-loaded course for that! Yay for a toddler naps ,right?!

Chapter 2

Montessori Toddler Discipline

"The first idea that the child must acquire, in order to be actively disciplined, is that of the difference between good and evil; and the task of the educator lies in seeing that the child does not confound good with immobility, and evil with activity, as often happens in the case of the old-time discipline." Maria Montessori

A Montessori approach to discipline consists of a delicate balance between freedom and discipline. Like any part of Montessori education, it requires respect for the child.

I'd like to share some Montessori articles that give more insight into Montessori discipline, which by nature is a form of gentle/positive discipline.

As a parent, your greatest ally is the child's own desire to grow, to learn, to master her own emotions, and to develop her own character. By keeping calm and respecting your child and her desires, you can help her on her own quest for inner discipline. By setting clear expectations and supporting your child's active thought and reflection, you can support the sense of personal autonomy she is naturally seeking as she follows her own unique path to physical, emotional, and intellectual independence.

Validate a child's emotions.

Of course, sometimes a child is going to want to take an action that is not permissible. A preschool-age child doesn't always understand why he is allowed to make some choices, but not others. Why can he choose what he has for dinner, but not when he has dinner? Why can he choose what to wear to school, but not whether he has to go to school in the first place? As an adult, you can help the child master himself in these frustrating moments by acknowledging his emotions. "You really wanted to wear your boots today! You are not in the mood for shoes! You're sad and mad about it." Be sure to allow your child time to experience the disappointment, and remember to save any reasoning or discussion until the initial emotion has run its course.

Montessori also encouraged teachers to talk with children about their behavior. To quote Dr. Montessori herself:

...if he shows a tendency to misbehaves, she will check him with earnest words...

Many people misinterpret the Montessori method to be a permissive method that allows children unlimited freedom. In reality, the freedom is within limits that are carefully enforced through guidance by the teacher. Common consequences in a Montessori classroom include:

- Putting a material away that's not being used properly
- Cleaning up a mess or a spill
- Staying close to the teacher

You can use these same consequences in your home.

Natural Consequences

When it comes to discipline, parents often feel the need to impose consequences and punishments on the child, rather than letting things run their course. However, this teaches your child to fear getting caught by a parent, teacher or authority figure rather than learning the natural consequences of their actions.

But, what are natural consequences?

In part, it's helping your child see what will happen as a result of their choices and actions, and letting it happen. Like what? For example, your child chooses to skip lunch. You allow them to skip lunch, but save their plate for later and when they ask for a snack, they can finish their lunch. Or your child leaves toys out and doesn't want to clean up. You can explain that leaving toys on the floor is dangerous for others because they might step on them and the family needs a clean place to live. Then, you can clean up the toys together, ensuring your child helps. Rather than feeling threatened with punishment, your child learns to see how their actions affect themselves and others.

An easy way to implement this technique is by narrating what you see and helping your child predict the future. This also works well with aggressive behaviors like biting and hitting, and of course tantrums. You can say for example "I see you're angry. You want to hit me." However, in these cases, you may need to intervene to prevent children from getting hurt and say things like "I won't let you hurt your brother".

Montessori encouraged the use of control of error in materials and classroom activities. Natural consequences are the control of error of life. For example, Montessori encouraged the use of real glass dishes so that if children weren't careful or had an accident, the dishes would break. She believed this natural consequence was valuable for children to experience so that they could change their behavior in the future.

2.1 Best way to make your kids grow faster

Most parents would love for their children to be tall and strong, as it has been widely regarded as a sign of good health. Parents usually go to great lengths to ensure that their children grow up healthily, and their height is treated as an indication of their overall health condition by most parts of the society.

Genes have the most say in determining the height of the child – however, it is not the only factor which influences it. Many external factors, like living conditions and a healthy diet, can influence the height of children quite a lot. Therefore, it is possible for parents to improve the chances of their children grow up to be tall and strong, through simple methods. Let us take a look at the top 10 ways to make your child grow taller.

2.2 How to Increase the Height of a Child

There are many ways a parent can influence the height of their child, and here's a list of the top ten ways.

1. A Balanced Diet

The most important aspect of how to increase your kid's height is to ensure that he gets proper nutrition. The food he consumes has to be healthy so that he grows up to be tall. A balanced diet has to include proteins, carbohydrates, fat and vitamins in the correct proportion – loading up on only one of these can have a detrimental effect. You must also ensure that the child keeps away from junk food most of the time – this includes food like burgers, aerated sweetened drinks and fried items in general. Lean proteins have to be had aplenty, along with leafy vegetables and items rich in minerals like calcium and potassium. Simple carbs like pizza and cakes have to be avoided for the most part. Zinc has been found to have a huge effect on the growth of the child, so zinc-rich foods like squash seeds and peanuts must also be added to their diet. A balanced diet not only provides the right nutrients to increase your child's height but it will also make him stronger in every sense.

2. Stretching Exercises

Stretching exercises, even if they are simple ones, can have a huge impact on the height of your child. Introducing your child to stretching exercises from a young age will facilitate the process of height growth. Stretching helps elongate the spine and also improves the posture of your child at all times. The exercises can be simple ones. Make him stand on his toes with his back against the wall and stretch the muscles in his leg while reaching up simultaneously. Another simple exercise for stretching involves the child sitting on the floor with his legs wide apart, and reaching to touch the toes of both legs with his arms.

Stretching exercises to grow taller

3. Hanging

Hanging has been recommended for decades now, for parents who want their children to be taller. Hanging from bars also helps the spine elongate, which is an important part of becoming taller. Apart from regular hanging, you can also encourage your child to do pull-ups and chin-ups. Both make the muscles of the arm and the back stronger and are great exercises to help him keep fit.

4. Swimming

Swimming is another healthy habit, one which helps your child stay active and enjoy it, too. Swimming is a full-body exercise, meaning that it works all the muscles in the body to great effect. Swimming for a long time can help your child lose any extra fat present, making him healthier as a whole. The exercise involves a lot of stretching forward, which strengthens the spine and lays the groundwork for a tall, healthy body. Swimming is also a highly enjoyable activity- no child has ever said no to playing in the water!

5. Jogging

Jogging is an amazing exercise, not just for children- it has a range of benefits for grown-ups too. Jogging strengthens the bones in the leg and also increases the quantity of HGH, the growth hormone, which is required for any growth in the body. To make it even more fun, you can maybe join in with your child and make jogging be an activity you do together!

6. Sleep

The importance of sleep can never be stressed upon enough, not just for children – for adults, too. Skipping sleep occasionally does not affect the growth of your child in the long term- however, you have to ensure that the child gets a good 8 hours of sleep on most nights, in order for him to be taller and stronger. This is because the growth hormone in children, HGH, is released only when the child sleeps. This plays a direct role in making your child taller, so skipping sleep constantly is definitely a bad idea.

7. Posture

To increase your child's height, it is integral that he has a proper posture. Slumping or slouching can put unnecessary stress on the spine which can have many negative affects on the body. Additionally, poor posture can alter the shape of your child's spine which can compromise his growth. Make sure that your child practices good posture not only to increase his height but also to prevent any long term health issues. Remind him to sit and stand up straight every time you see him slouching.

There are many ways to make your child grow taller, but all of them work only when complemented by the other activities on the list. A good diet must be accompanied by regular exercise and sound sleep- else, you do not get what you want. Therefore, take care of your child the right way, and make him grow tall and strong.

2.3 How to keep your toddler busy and Happy at the same time

We all know that watching TV and playing video games isn't good for our kids. No parent is proud of how much time their kids spend in front of a screen but what are we supposed to do?

Sometimes, we just need to get things done. We need to clean the house or cook food or just take a few minutes for ourselves. It's hard to think of other things that could keep a kid distracted long enough to actually accomplish anything.

There are options, though. Sure, they take a bit more energy than just plopping a child in front of a screen, but encouraging your child to do something constructive just might be worth the extra effort.

We all know that watching TV and playing video games isn't good for our kids. No parent is proud of how much time their kids spend in front of a screen – but what are we supposed to do?

Sometimes, we just need to get things done. We need to clean the house or cook food or just take a few minutes for ourselves. It's hard to think of other things that could keep a kid distracted long enough to actually accomplish anything.

There are options, though. Sure, they take a bit more energy than just plopping a child in front of a screen, but encouraging your child to do something constructive just might be worth the extra effort.

Create a game box

Fill a box full of things your child can play with alone – things like coloring books, playing cards, or easy puzzles. When you need to keep your kids busy, give them the box. They might resist at first, but the more you do it, the more they'll accept "game box time" as part of their routine.

Have them make their own cartoon

Instead of watching cartoons, have your children make their own. Give them a piece of paper and some crayons, and ask them to draw you a hero and a bad guy. When they're done, let them come back and tell you their hero's story.

Let them help you

If you're cooking or cleaning, let your kids help. Give them a job they can handle. For young kids, that might be stringing beans or setting the table. For older kids, that might be slicing vegetables, sweeping the house, or taking out the recycling.

Give them an important mission

Give your child a task, and make it a really big deal. Tell them they need to draw a picture for Dada, or that they need to make a block fort for Grandma. If they think it's an important job, they won't complain about working on it independently.

Generate an idea box

Brainstorm ideas with your children about what they can do to overcome boredom. Write down their suggestions, and put them in an empty box. Then, the next time they're bored, have them pick out one of their own suggestions. Given that it was their idea, they'll be more willing to actually do it.

Offer creative toys

Any toy that lets a child create is sure to keep them distracted for a long time. Invest in Legos, puzzles, and Play-Dough. Not only will your child be able to play with them for hours, but they'll build up their spatial reasoning, too.

Design a treasure hunt

Hide something like a coin or a sticker somewhere in the house. Give your kids a clue, and let them run wild trying to find it. If you make it a bit tricky to find, you'll build up their resilience – and their ability to find things without begging for your help.

Let them play outside

Don't forget how your parents kept you busy. Just give your child a ball and a stick, and let them run wild. If you're worried about their safety, just keep them in sight of the window. They'll be fine.

Send them to a friend's house

Work out a deal with another parent on your street. When you need some time, send your kid over to play with their kid. To be fair, you'll have to let them send their kid over sometimes, too. When two kids play together, they keep themselves distracted.

Build a fort

Give your child a few pillows and a blanket, and challenge them to turn the couch into a fort. No child will turn down the chance to make a secret base – and they'll be much more likely to play independently once they're inside.

Make a sculpture

Give your child a few pipe cleaners and a piece of Styrofoam – or any other child-friendly items you might have on hand – and ask them to make a sculpture. Anything will do, but favorite heroes are a winning suggestion.

Listen to an audiobook

If your child's too young to read independently, pick up audio versions of their favorite books. Let them sit down and turn the pages while listening to a friendly voice read to them. Or, if you can't find a recording, use your phone to make one yourself.

Play with locks and bolts

Hand your child a lock and a key or a nut and bolt and let them play with it. Young kids, especially, will be mesmerized by the act of unlocking something – and they'll develop their motor skills while they're at it. Give them a mixed bag, and see if they can figure out which lock goes with which key.

Chapter 3

Naptime And Nighttime Training

Naptime

Yes it's ok to put your child down for a nap during training. I personally have found that most kids will not have an accident if you have them go pee before the nap and then just as they wake up. Make sure you stay close though so you know when your child wakes.

Nighttime

Do not give your child anything to drink when they are getting ready for bed. In fact, it's best to stop the liquids 2 to 3 hours beforehand. Take them to the toilet at least twice before tucking them in to bed for the night. If nothing happens in the bathroom, maybe read a book together for a few minutes and try again. Remember what I said about "trying" don't keep them on the toilet. Having them clear their bladder is important. Once your child has released twice you can put them in bed. Do not use a diaper (you shouldn't have any).

If your child has a hard time waking up dry and they are older than 22 months, the following procedure may help:

- Wake the child 1 hour after he or she has gone to sleep
- Take them to the toilet and return them to bed
- In the morning, wake the child 1 hour before they normally arise

Take them to the toilet This helps the child realize two things:

1.It is ok to get up to go pee

2. It is also expected If your child is in a crib, you can still follow these steps.

You just need to keep an ear open for them. If you hear your child stirring, or whimpering, they may need to pee. You do not need to do the above steps if your child usually wakes up dry. Your child may wet the bed at night. Don't be alarmed or upset.

This is halfway to be expected – we're giving them lots of liquid. Don't make a big deal of it – don't reprimand or scold. Just change the sheets. Remind the child to tell you when he needs to go pee, and that they need to keep their underwear dry. Again, don't be negative; don't say "Bad, No," etc.

This will be the end of a busy and perhaps frustrating day. Do not worry. It will click; your child will "get it", if not tomorrow, then on the third day. Be sure to keep a positive and loving attitude with your child, even if you have to change sheets in the middle of the night.

A tip for parents with older children: To help your child to go to the bathroom before bed and to stay dry during the night you can try using a chart system with the following on it:

Bedtime Routine:

- go pee
- put on night clothes
- read a book
- brush teeth
- go pee again
- keep bed dry all night

Let your child know that if he gets a star by each one he will get a prize in the morning.

Remind him that he's got to get up and go pee if he's got to go. A special tip, that works for even the hardest of cases. The following has been used even with long time bed-wetters to help them overcome bed wetting... Once your child goes to sleep, make a bed up on the floor without him knowing. Now throughout the night you will say to him "be sure to tell mommy when you have to go pee". Anytime during the night when you hear him start to move and stir around, say to him "Do you have to go pee? Make sure tell mommy when you have to go pee".

What this does is allows you to see how often your child is stirring in his bed and will help him remember that he's suppose to pee in the potty not in his bed.

3.1 Toddler discipline and proper upbringing

Have you ever found yourself in deep negotiations with your 2-year-old over whether she can wear her princess costume to preschool for the fifth day in a row? Have you taken the "walk of shame" out of the local supermarket after your toddler threw a temper tantrum on the floor? There may be comfort in knowing you're not alone, but that doesn't make navigating the early years of discipline any easier.

Toddlerhood is a particularly vexing time for parents because this is the age at which children start to become more independent and discover themselves as individuals. Yet they still have a limited ability to communicate and reason.

Child development specialist Claire Lerner, director of parenting resources for the nonprofit organization Zero to Three, says, "They understand that their actions matter -- they can make things happen. This leads them to want to make their imprint on the world and assert themselves in a way they didn't when they were a baby. The problem is they have very little self-control and they're not rational thinkers. It's a very challenging combination."

What do you do when your adorable toddler engages in not-so-adorable behavior, like hitting the friend who snatches her toy, biting Mommy, or throwing her unwanted plate of peas across the room? Is it time for...timeout?

Timeout -- removing a child from the environment where misbehavior has occurred to a "neutral," unstimulating space -- can be effective for toddlers if it's used in the right way, says Jennifer Shu, MD, an Atlanta pediatrician, editor of Baby and Child Health and co-author of Food Fights: Winning the Nutritional Challenges of Parenthood Armed With Insight, Humor, and a Bottle of Ketchup and Heading Home With Your Newborn: From Birth to Reality.

"Especially at this age, timeout shouldn't be punitive. It's a break in the action, a chance to nip what they're doing in the bud."

Timeouts shouldn't be imposed in anger, agrees Elizabeth Pantley, president of Better Beginnings, a family resource and education company in Seattle, and author of several parenting books, including The No-Cry Discipline Solution. "The purpose of timeout is not to punish your child but to give him a moment to get control and reenter the situation feeling better able to cope." It also gives you the chance to take a breath and step away from the conflict for a moment so you don't lose your temper.

3.2 Timeouts is Not for Every Kid

Some experts insist that timeouts work for all, but Shu and Pantley disagree. "For some kids who just hate to be alone, it's a much bigger punishment than it's worth, especially with young toddlers," says Shu. "They get so upset because you're abandoning them that they don't remember why they're there, and it makes things worse." She suggests holding a child with these fears in a bear hug and helping her calm down.

You can also try warding off the kind of behavior that might warrant a timeout with "time-in." That means noticing when your children's behavior is starting to get out of hand and spending five or 10 minutes with them before they seriously misbehave. "It's like a preemptive strike," Shu says. "Once they've gotten some quality time with you, you can usually count on reasonably OK behavior for a little while."

Toddler Discipline Dos & Don'ts

Shu says a good stage to initiate timeouts is when your toddler is around age 2. Here are a few guidelines.

- Do remove your child from the situation.
- Do tell him what the problem behavior was.
- Use simple words like "No hitting. Hitting hurts."
- Don't berate your child.
- Do place her in a quiet spot -- the same place every time, if possible. For young toddlers, this may have to be a play yard or other enclosed space.
- Don't keep him there long -- the usual rule of thumb is one minute per year of age.
- Do sit down with your child after timeout is over and reassure her with a hug while you "debrief" by saying something like, "We're not going to hit anymore, right?"
- Don't belabor what the child did wrong. Instead, ask her to show you how she can play nicely.

3.3 Commandments Discipline for Toddler

Children aren't born with social skills it's human nature for them to start out with a survival-of-the-fittest mentality. That's why you need to teach your toddler how to act appropriately and safely -- when you're around and when you're not. In a nutshell, your job is to implant a "good citizen" memory chip in her brain (Freud called this the superego) that will remind her how she's supposed to behave. It's a bit like breaking a wild horse, but you won't break your child's spirit if you do it correctly. The seeds of discipline that you plant now will blossom later, and you'll be very thankful for the fruits of your labor. (Just don't expect a tree to grow overnight.) Here are the commandments you should commit to memory.

1. Expect rough spots. Certain situations and times of the day tend to trigger bad behavior. Prime suspect number 1: transitions from one activity to the next (waking up, going to bed, stopping play to eat dinner). Give your child a heads-up so he's more prepared to switch gears ("After you build one more block tower, we will be having dinner").
2. Pick your battles. If you say no 20 times a day, it will lose its effectiveness. Prioritize behaviors into large, medium, and those too insignificant to bother with. In Starbucks terms, there are Venti, Grande, and Tall toddler screwups. If you ignore a minor infraction -- your toddler screams whenever you check your e-mail -- she'll eventually stop doing it because she'll see that it doesn't get a rise out of you.
3. Use a prevent defense. Sorry for the football cliche, but this one is easy. Make your house kid-friendly, and have reasonable expectations. If you clear your Swarovski crystal collection off the end table, your child won't be tempted to fling it at the TV set. If you're taking your family out to dinner, go early so you won't have to wait for a table.
4. Make your statements short and sweet. Speak in brief sentences, such as "No hitting." This is much more effective than "Chaz, you know it's not nice to hit the dog." You'll lose Chaz right after "you know."
5. Distract and redirect. Obviously, you do this all day. But when you try to get your child interested in a different activity, she'll invariably go back to what she was doing -- just to see whether she can get away with it. Don't give up. Even if your child unrolls the entire toilet-paper roll for the 10th time today, calmly remove her from the bathroom and close the door.
6. Introduce consequences. Your child should learn the natural outcomes of his behavior -- otherwise known as cause and effect. For example, if he loudly insists on selecting his pajamas (which takes an eternity), then he's also choosing not to read books

before bed. Cause: Prolonged picking = Effect: No time to read. Next time, he may choose his pj's more quickly or let you pick them out.

7. Don't back down to avoid conflict. We all hate to be the party pooper, but you shouldn't give in just to escape a showdown at the grocery store. If you decide that your child can't have the cereal that she saw on TV, stick to your guns. Later, you'll be happy you did.

8. Anticipate bids for attention. Yes, your little angel will act up when your attention is diverted (making dinner, talking on the phone). That's why it's essential to provide some entertainment (a favorite toy, a quick snack). True story: My son once ate dog food while I was on the phone with a patient. Take-home lesson: If you don't provide something for your toddler to do when you're busy, she'll find something -- and the results may not be pretty.

9. Focus on the behavior, not the child. Always say that a particular behavior is bad. Never tell your child that he is bad. You want him to know that you love him, but you don't love the way he's acting right now.

10. Give your child choices. This will make her feel as if she's got a vote. Just make sure you don't offer too many options and that they're all things that you want to accomplish, such as, "It's your choice: You can put your shoes on first, or your coat."

11. Don't yell. But change your voice. It's not the volume, but your tone that gets your point across. Remember The Godfather? Don Corleone never needed to yell.

12. Catch your child being good. If you praise your child when he behaves well, he'll do it more often -- and he'll be less likely to behave badly just to get your attention. Positive reinforcement is fertilizer for that superego.

13. Act immediately. Don't wait to discipline your toddler. She won't remember why she's in trouble more than five minutes after she did the dirty deed.

14. Be a good role model. If you're calm under pressure, your child will take the cue. And if you have a temper tantrum when you're

upset, expect that he'll do the same. He's watching you, always watching.

15. Don't treat your child as if she's an adult. She really doesn't want to hear a lecture from you and won't be able to understand it. The next time she throws her spaghetti, don't break into the "You Can't Throw Your Food" lecture. Calmly evict her from the kitchen for the night.

16. Use time-outs -- even at this age. Call it the naughty chair or whatever you like, but take your child away from playing and don't pay attention to him for one minute for each year of age. Depriving him of your attention is the most effective way to get your message across. Realistically, kids under 2 won't sit in a corner or on a chair -- and it's fine for them to be on the floor kicking and screaming. (Just make sure the time-out location is a safe one.) Reserve time-outs for particularly inappropriate behaviors -- if your child bites his friend's arm, for example -- and use a time-out every time the offense occurs.

17. Don't negotiate with your child or make promises. This isn't Capitol Hill. Try to avoid saying anything like, "If you behave, I'll buy you that doll you want." Otherwise, you'll create a 3-year-old whose good behavior will always come with a price tag. (Think Veruca Salt from Charlie and the Chocolate Factory.)

18. Shift your strategies over time. What worked beautifully when your child was 15 months probably isn't going to work when he's 2. He'll have read your playbooks and watched the films.

19. Don't spank. Although you may be tempted at times, remember that you are the grown-up. Don't resort to acting like a child. There are many more effective ways of getting your message across. Spanking your child for hitting or kicking you, for example, just shows him that it's okay to use force. Finally, if your toddler is pushing your buttons for the umpteenth time and you think you're about to lose it, try to take a step back. You'll get a better idea of which manipulative behaviors your child is using and you'll get a fresh perspective on how to change your approach.

20. Remind your child that you love her. It's always good to end a discipline discussion with a positive comment. This shows your child that you're ready to move on and not dwell on the problem. It also reinforces the reason you're setting limits -- because you love her.

3.4 Disciplining Your Toddler to make the right choice

As a 2-year-old, Nathaniel Lampros of Sandy, Utah, was fascinated with toy swords and loved to duel with Kenayde, his 4-year-old sister. But inevitably, he'd whack her in the head, she'd dissolve in tears, and Angela, their mother, would come running to see what had happened. She'd ask Nathaniel to apologize, as well as give Kenayde a hug and make her laugh to pacify hurt feelings. If he resisted, Angela would put her son in time-out.

"I worried that Nathaniel would never outgrow his rough behavior, and there were days when I'd get so frustrated with him that I'd end up crying," recalls Lampros, now a mother of four. "But I really wanted Nathaniel to play nicely, so I did my best to teach him how to do it."

For many mothers, doling out effective discipline is one of the toughest and most frustrating tasks of parenting, a seemingly never-ending test of wills between you and your child. Because just when your 2-year-old "gets" that she can't thump her baby brother in the head with a doll, she'll latch on to another bothersome behavior —and the process starts anew.

How exactly does one "discipline" a toddler? Some people equate it with spanking and punishment, but that's not what we're talking about. As many parenting experts see it, discipline is about setting rules to stop your little one from engaging in behavior that's aggressive (hitting and biting), dangerous (running out in the street), and inappropriate (throwing food). It's also about following through with consequences when he breaks the rules—

or what Linda Pearson, a Denver-based psychiatric nurse practitioner who specializes in family and parent counseling, calls "being a good boss." Here are seven strategies that can help you set limits and stop bad behavior.

1. Pick Your Battles

"If you're always saying, 'No, no, no,' your child will tune out the no and won't understand your priorities," says Pearson, author of The Discipline Miracle. "Plus you can't possibly follow through on all of the nos.'" Define what's important to you, set limits accordingly, and follow through with appropriate consequences. Then ease up on little things that are annoying but otherwise fall into the "who cares?" category—the habits your child is likely to outgrow, such as insisting on wearing purple (and only purple).

"Keeping a good relationship with your child—who is of course in reality totally dependent upon you—is more important for her growth than trying to force her to respond in ways that she simply is not going to respond," says Elizabeth Berger, M.D., child psychiatrist and author of Raising Kids with Character. You may worry that "giving in" will create a spoiled monster, but Dr. Berger says this common anxiety isn't justified.

For Anna Lucca of Washington, D.C., that means letting her 2-1/2-year-old daughter trash her bedroom before she dozes off for a nap. "I find books and clothes scattered all over the floor when Isabel wakes up, so she must get out of bed to play after I put her down," Lucca says. "I tell her not to make a mess, but she doesn't listen. Rather than try to catch her in the act and say, 'No, no, no,' I make her clean up right after her nap." Lucca is also quick to praise Isabel for saying please and sharing toys with her 5-month-old sister. "Hopefully, the positive reinforcement will encourage Isabel to do more of the good behavior—and less of the bad," she says.

2. Know Your Child's Triggers

Some misbehavior is preventable—as long as you can anticipate what will spark it and you create a game plan in advance, such as removing tangible temptations. This strategy worked for Jean Nelson of Pasadena, California, after her 2-year-old son took delight in dragging toilet paper down the hall, giggling as the roll unfurled behind him. "The first two times Luke did it, I told him, 'No,' but when he did it a third time, I moved the toilet paper to a high shelf in the bathroom that he couldn't reach," Nelson says. "For a toddler, pulling toilet paper is irresistible fun. It was easier to take it out of his way than to fight about it."

If your 18-month-old is prone to grabbing cans off grocery store shelves, bring toys for him to play with in the cart while you're shopping. If your 2-year-old won't share her stuffed animals during playdates at home, remove them from the designated play area before her pal arrives. And if your 3-year-old likes to draw on the walls, stash the crayons in an out-of-reach drawer and don't let him color without supervision.

3. Practice Prevention

Some children act out when they're hungry, overtired, or frustrated from being cooped up inside, says Harvey Karp, M.D., creator of the DVD and book The Happiest Toddler on the Block. If your child tends to be happy and energetic in the morning but is tired and grumpy after lunch, schedule trips to the store and visits to the doctor for when she's at her best. Prepare her for any new experiences, and explain how you expect her to act.

Also prepare her for shifting activities: "In a few minutes we'll need to pick up the toys and get ready to go home." The better prepared a child feels, the less likely she is to make a fuss.

4. Be Consistent

"Between the ages of 2 and 3, children are working hard to understand how their behavior impacts the people around them," says Claire Lerner, LCSW, director of parenting resources with

Zero to Three, a nationwide nonprofit promoting the healthy development of babies and toddlers. "If your reaction to a situation keeps changing—one day you let your son throw a ball in the house and the next you don't—you'll confuse him with mixed signals."

There's no timetable as to how many incidents and reprimands it will take before your child stops a certain misbehavior. But if you always respond the same way, he'll probably learn his lesson after four or five times. Consistency was key for Orly Isaacson of Bethesda, Maryland, when her 18-month-old went through a biting phase. Each time Sasha chomped on Isaacson's finger, she used a louder-than-usual voice to correct her—"No, Sasha! Don't bite! That hurts Mommy!"—and then handed her a toy as a distraction. "I'm very low-key, so raising my voice startled Sasha and got the message across fast," she says. A caveat: by age 2, many kids learn how to make their parents lose resolve just by being cute. Don't let your child's tactics sway you—no matter how cute (or clever) they are.

5. Don't Get Emotional

Sure, it's hard to stay calm when your 18-month-old yanks the dog's tail or your 3-year-old refuses to brush his teeth for the gazillionth night in a row. But if you scream in anger, the message you're trying to send will get lost and the situation will escalate, fast.

"When a child is flooded with a parent's negative mood, he'll see the emotion and won't hear what you're saying," advised the late William Coleman, M.D., professor of pediatrics at the University of North Carolina Medical School in Chapel Hill. Indeed, an angry reaction will only enhance the entertainment value for your child, so resist the urge to raise your voice. Take a deep breath, count to three, and get down to your child's eye level. Be fast and firm, serious and stern when you deliver the reprimand.

Trade in the goal of "controlling your child" for the goal of "controlling the situation," advises Dr. Berger. "This may mean re-adjusting your ideas of what is possible for a time until your daughter's self-discipline has a chance to grow a little more," she says. "You may need to lower your expectations of her patience and her self-control somewhat. If your goal is to keep the day going along smoothly, so that there are fewer opportunities for you both to feel frustrated, that would be a constructive direction."

6. Listen and Repeat

Kids feel better when they know they have been heard, so whenever possible, repeat your child's concerns. If she's whining in the grocery store because you won't let her open the cookies, say something like: "It sounds like you're mad at me because I won't let you open the cookies until we get home. I'm sorry you feel that way, but the store won't let us open things until they're paid for. That's its policy." This won't satisfy her urge, but it will reduce her anger and defuse the conflict.

7. Keep It Short and Simple

If you're like most first-time parents, you tend to reason with your child when she breaks rules, offering detailed explanations about what she did wrong and issuing detailed threats about the privileges she'll lose if she doesn't stop misbehaving. But as a discipline strategy, overt-talking is as ineffective as becoming overly emotional, according to Dr. Coleman. While an 18-month-old lacks the cognitive ability to understand complex sentences, a 2- or 3-year-old with more developed language skills still lacks the attention span to absorb what you're saying.

Instead, speak in short phrases, repeating them a few times and incorporating vocal inflections and facial expressions. For example, if your 18-month-old swats your arm, say, "No, Jake! Don't hit Mommy! That hurts! No hitting." A 2-year-old can comprehend a bit more: "Evan, no jumping on the sofa! No jumping. Jumping is dangerous—you could fall. No jumping!" And a 3-year-old can process cause and effect, so state the consequences of the behavior: "Ashley, your teeth need to be brushed. You can brush them, or I can brush them for you. You decide. The longer it takes, the less time we'll have to read Dr. Seuss."

8. Offer Choices

When a child refuses to do (or stop doing) something, the real issue is usually control: You've got it; she wants it. So, whenever possible, give your preschooler some control by offering a limited set of choices. Rather than commanding her to clean up her room, ask her, "Which would you like to pick up first, your books or your blocks?" Be sure the choices are limited, specific, and acceptable to you, however. "Where do you want to start?" may be overwhelming to your child, and a choice that's not acceptable to you will only amplify the conflict.

9. Watch Your Words

It helps to turn "you" statements into "I" messages. Instead of saying, "You're so selfish that you won't even share your toys with your best friend," try "I like it better when I see kids sharing their toys." Another good technique is to focus on do's rather than don'ts. If you tell a 3-year-old that he can't leave his trike in the hallway, he may want to argue. A better approach: "If you move your trike out to the porch, it won't get kicked and scratched so much."

Make sure your tone and words do not imply that you no longer love your child. "I really can't stand it when you act like that" sounds final; "I don't like it when you try to pull cans from the store shelves," however, shows your child that it's one specific behavior—not the whole person—that you dislike.

10. Teach Empathy

It's rarely obvious to a 3-year-old why he should stop doing something he finds fun, like biting, hitting, or grabbing toys from other children. Teach him empathy instead: "When you bite or hit people, it hurts them"; "When you grab toys away from other kids, they feel sad because they still want to play with those toys." This helps your child see that his behavior directly affects other people and trains him to think about consequences first.

11. Give a Time-Out

If repeated reprimands, redirection, and loss of privileges haven't cured your child of her offending behavior, consider putting her in time-out for a minute per year of age. "This is an excellent discipline tool for kids who are doing the big-time no-nos," Dr. Karp explains.

Before imposing a time-out, put a serious look on your face and give a warning in a stern tone of voice ("I'm counting to three, and if you don't stop, you're going to time-out. One, two, THREE!"). If she doesn't listen, take her to the quiet and safe spot you've designated for time-outs, and set a timer. When it goes off, ask her to apologize and give her a big hug to convey that you're not angry.

"Nathaniel hated going to time-out for hitting his sister with the plastic sword, but I was clear about the consequences and stuck with it," says Angela Lampros. "After a few weeks, he learned his lesson." Indeed, toddlers don't like to be separated from their parents and toys, so eventually, the mere threat of a time-out should be enough to stop them in their tracks.

12. Talk Options

When you want your child to stop doing something, offer alternative ways for him to express his feelings: say, hitting a pillow or banging with a toy hammer. He needs to learn that while his emotions and impulses are acceptable, certain ways of expressing them are not. Also, encourage your child to think up his own options. Even 3-year-olds can learn to solve problems themselves. For instance, you could ask: "What do you think you could do to get Tiffany to share that toy with you?" The trick is to listen to their ideas with an open mind. Don't shoot down anything, but do talk about the consequences before a decision is made.

13. Reward Good Behavior

It's highly unlikely that your child will always do whatever you say. If that happened, you'd have to think about what might be wrong with her! Normal kids resist control, and they know when you're asking them to do something they don't want to do. They then feel justified in resisting you. In cases in which they do behave appropriately, a prize is like a spoonful of sugar: It helps the medicine go down.

Judicious use of special treats and prizes is just one more way to show your child you're aware and respectful of his feelings. This, more than anything, gives credibility to your discipline demands.

14. Stay Positive

No matter how frustrated you feel about your child's misbehavior, don't vent about it in front of him. "If people heard their boss at work say, 'I don't know what to do with my employees. They run the company, and I feel powerless to do anything about it,' they'd lose respect for him and run the place even more," says Pearson. "It's the same thing when children hear their parents speak about them in a hopeless or negative way. They won't have a good image of you as their boss, and they'll end up repeating the behavior."

Still, it's perfectly normal to feel exasperated from time to time. If you reach that point, turn to your spouse, your pediatrician, or a trusted friend for support and advice.

Ages & Stages

Effective discipline starts with understanding where your child falls on the developmental spectrum. Our guide:

At 18 months your child is curious, fearless, impulsive, mobile, and clueless about the consequences of her actions—a recipe for trouble. "My image of an 18-month-old is a child who's running down the hall away from his mother but looking over his shoulder to see if she's there and then running some more," said Dr. Coleman. "Though he's building a vocabulary and can follow simple instructions, he can't effectively communicate his needs or understand lengthy reprimands. He may bite or hit to register his displeasure or to get your attention. Consequences of misbehavior must be immediate. Indeed, if you wait even 10 minutes to react, he won't remember what he did wrong or tie his action to the consequence, says nurse practitioner Pearson.

At age 2 your child is using her developing motor skills to test limits, by running, jumping, throwing, and climbing. She's speaking a few words at a time, she becomes frustrated when she can't get her point across, and she's prone to tantrums. She's also self-centered and doesn't like to share. Consequences should be swift, as a 2-year-old is unable to grasp time. But since she still lacks impulse control, give her another chance soon after the incident, says Lerner of Zero to Three.

At age 3 your child is now a chatterbox; he's using language to argue his point of view. Since he loves to be with other children and has boundless energy, he may have a tough time playing quietly at home. "Taking a 3-year-old to a gym or karate class will give him the social contact he craves and let him release energy," says Dr. Karp. "At this age, kids need that as much as they need affection and food." He also knows right from wrong, understands cause and effect, and retains information for several hours. Consequences can be delayed for maximum impact, and explanations can be more detailed. For example, if he hurls Cheerios at his sister, remind him about the no-food-throwing rule and explain that if he does it again, he won't get to watch Blues Clues. If he continues to throw food, take it away from him. When he asks to watch TV, say, "Remember when Mommy told you not to throw cereal and you did anyway? Well, the consequence is no Blues Clues today."

Chapter 4

The Right Approach To Potty And Tantrums

Potty training is teaching your child to recognize their body signals for urinating and having a bowel movement. It also means teaching your child to use a potty chair or toilet correctly and at the appropriate times.

When should toilet training start?

Potty training should start when your child shows signs that he or she is ready. There is no right age to begin. If you try to toilet train before your child is ready, it can be a battle for both you and your child. The ability to control bowel and bladder muscles comes with proper growth and development.

Children develop at different rates. A child younger than 12 months has no control over bladder or bowel movements. There is very little control between 12 to 18 months. Most children don't have bowel and bladder control until 24 to 30 months. The average age of toilet training is 27 months.

If you think your child is showing signs of being ready for toilet training, the first step is to decide whether you want to train using a potty or the toilet.

There are some advantages to using a potty – it's mobile and it's familiar, and some children find it less scary than a toilet. Try to find out your child's preference and go with that. Some parents encourage their child to use both the toilet and potty.

Second, make sure you have all the right equipment. For example, if your child is using the toilet you'll need a step for your child to stand on. You'll also need a smaller seat that fits securely inside the existing toilet seat, because some children get uneasy about falling in.

Third, it's best to plan toilet training for a time when you don't have any big changes coming up in your family life. Changes might include going on holiday, starting day care, having a new baby or moving house. It can be a good idea to plan toilet training for well before or after these changes.

Also, toilet training might go better if you and your child have a regular daily routine. This way, the new activity of using the toilet or potty can be slotted into your normal routine

4.1 General Knowledge of potty for children

You may (happily) have noticed that you're changing fewer diapers lately and your little one is usually staying dry during nap time. These, along with other signs, indicate that it's time to dive into the world of potty training. The key to potty training success is patience and an awareness that all tots reach this ever important milestone at their own pace. Different strategies work with different children, but these tips generally get the job done.

Since kids typically start potty training between 18 and 30 months, start talking about potty training occasionally around your child's first birthday to pique interest. Keep a few children's books about potty training lying around your house to read along with your child. And bring up the subject of the potty in conversation; saying things like, "I wonder if Elmo [or your child's favorite stuffed animal] needs to go potty" or "I have to go pee-pee. I'm headed to the potty." The idea is to raise awareness about going potty and make your child comfortable with the overall concept before he's ready to potty train.

If your child is staying dry for at least two hours during the day and is dry after naps, this could mean she's ready to give the potty a shot. Before you head to the bathroom, know that she can follow simple instructions, like a request to walk to the bathroom, sit down, and remove her clothes. Also make sure she's interested in wearing big girl underwear. Then consider if she's aware when she's wet: If she cries, fusses, or shows other signs of obvious discomfort when her diaper is soiled and indicates through facial expression, posture, or language that it's time to use the toilet, then she's ready to start the process.

Some children are afraid of falling in the toilet or just hearing it flush, If your child is comfortable in the bathroom, try a potty seat that goes on top of your toilet to reduce the size of the bowl's opening. If not, you can buy a stand-alone potty chair and put it in the playroom or child's bedroom, where he'll become comfortable with its presence over time. When he's ready to give it a try, experts suggest you move it into the bathroom for repeated use, so you don't have to retrain your child down the road to transition from going potty in other rooms. Also get a stepstool—if he's using a potty seat, he'll need it to reach the toilet and also to give his feet support while he's pooping. "People can't empty their bowels and bladders completely unless their feet are pressing down on the floor.

Even if your child seems ready, experts say to avoid potty training during transitional or stressful times. If you're moving, taking a vacation, adding a new baby to the family, or going through a divorce, postpone the potty training until about a month after the transitional time. Children trying to learn this new skill will do best if they're relaxed and on a regular routine. You might prefer to get potty training over with as soon as possible—maybe you're curious about the 3-day potty training trend. That's fine but do not always believe it, experts because you might find it frustrating not. "I often see parents who boast that they trained their 2-year-old in a weekend, and then say that the child has accidents four times a day, This is not the same as being potty trained. When kids are truly ready, they often will just start going on the potty on their own."

When you do decide it's time to start potty training, you'll want your child to go to the bathroom independently, day or night, so make sure she has transitioned out of the crib and into a big-kid bed. "Kids need access to a potty 24/7 if they're potty training so they can reach it on their own when they need it. Keep a well-lit path to the bathroom so your child feels safe and comfortable walking there during the night. Of course, if you think you're child isn't ready for a big-kid bed (or, let's face it, if you're not ready), there's no harm in keeping her in diapers at night for a while longer. Talk to your child's doctor about the best time to potty train your child; the answer will range greatly by child, though most kids should be out of diapers during the day by age 3. When you're ready to start training, let your child sit on the potty fully clothed when you are in the bathroom to get a feel for the seat. Then create a schedule: "The key is having times throughout the day where you ritualize using the potty so it becomes more of a habit," Dr. Swanson says. You might want to have him sit on the potty every two hours, whether he has to go or not, including first thing in the morning, before you leave the house, and before naps and bedtime. Tell him to remove his shorts or pants first, his underwear (or, if you're using them, training pants) next, and to sit on the toilet for a few minutes (allot more time, if you think he has to poop). Read him a book or play a game, like 20 Questions, to make the time pass in a fun way. Then, whether or not he actually goes potty, instruct him to flush and wash his hands. Of course, always praise him for trying.

It's not uncommon for a child who has been successfully using the potty for a few days to say he wants to go back to diapers. To avoid a power struggle or a situation where your child actually starts a pattern of withholding bowel movements, which can lead to constipation, you might agree to a brief break. But try to build in a plan to resume by asking your child, "Would you like to wear underwear right when you get up or wait until after lunch?"

When you're potty training, accidents are part of the process; some kids still have accidents through age 5 or 6, and many don't stay dry at night until that age (or even later). Never punish your child for wetting or soiling his pants; he's just learning and can't help it. In fact, doing so might only make your little one scared of using the potty, and that, in turn, will delay the whole process even further. Instead, when your child uses the potty successfully, offer gentle praise and a small reward. You might want to use a sticker chart—your child receives a sticker every time he goes potty; after he's earned, say, three stickers, he gets a small prize. "However, don't go nuts!" Dr. Goldstein says. "A lot of toddlers will react to excessive praise as they react to punishment—by getting scared and avoiding doing the thing that they were excessively praised or punished for." In other words, stick with stickers, a trip to the local park, or even a surprise cup of hot cocoa—no need to go on a shopping spree to Toys 'R' Us. Less tangible rewards, like finally living up to the promise of "being a big kid" are enough for some kids. Remind your child about the benefits of "being a big kid," like if he wore underwear, he would never have to stop playing in order to get his diaper changed.

So this should result to setting children up with good hygiene habits that will last a lifetime, washing hands should be a routine from Day 1, along with flushing and wiping, regardless of whether your child actually went in the potty. The Centers for Disease Control and Prevention recommends wetting hands with cool or warm running water, lathering up with soap, and scrubbing for at least 20 seconds. Make hand washing fun by buying colorful kid-friendly soaps, and make it last long enough by singing a favorite song, like "Happy Birthday to You" or the "ABC Song," so the bubbles work their germ-fighting magic. Yes, toilet training can be stressful—for the parents, that is! But if you follow your child's lead, it won't be stressful for him.

4.2 Dealing with the emotions

In this step-by-step guide, we are going to take you through some really in-depth training and information that my I have put together over the years on potty training. Additionally,

When it comes to potty training, most parents and most people think it begins with the child. The reality is that potty training is begins with you, the parent or the grandparent, the relative or the daycare worker.

When we get testimonials from our clients and they say, "Thank you, thank you, thank you," I always like to say, "No, thank you. You are the one that did the hard work, so you are the one that deserves the congratulations." With that being said, we are going to start with you, the parent, or you, the person who is going to be doing the training.

You must be prepared and know that this is going to be a trying time, for some parents more than others. This can be a very stressful time because it tends to be a very stressful situation. What I want to make sure you understand is that nothing that is going on with your child with respect to potty training is your fault.

You have not done anything wrong. It may be as simple as the information you have received (or lack thereof). As an adult, what you know is that kids are not born knowing what to do and we are not born knowing how to be parents.

Potty training, like many other lessons is something that is learned and you've taken the right steps in trying to acquire that information. So, the first step is to prepare yourself mentally for this project. Remember that your child has spent two or three years going to the bathroom in his or her diaper.

Now, you are going to ask them to do something that is completely out of the norm and, essentially erasing two or three years of habit. Saying that this is going to be a challenge may be an understatement as some children may battle and butt heads with you.

But being mentally prepared will help you in coping with the challenge itself. How do you get prepared? First, take your time, and get relaxed. Do whatever it takes to help you get into a relaxed state of mind. Its better if you can start the potty training process when have had a good amount of sleep. Being tired and trying to potty train makes it just that much more difficult.

You will also want to make sure your child is rested as well. This is just as stressful for them and being cranky while learning a new technique is not a good combination.

Also, practice counting to 10 and then counting backwards from 10. This is a practice that you will find calms you down during periods of frustration in the process. In addition to being relaxed, you will need to ensure that you have a good support system. Talk with your husband or your wife or friends, and make sure that everyone is on board with what you are going to do so you are all heading in the same direction and can be a sounding board for each other.

This is critical because if there isn't a support system, the person doing the potty training will have a more difficult time and experience feelings of their own relating to the responsibility, frustration, and in some cases, failure (at least in the short run).

If you are able to start this process on a weekend, it is highly suggested because you won't have the stress of work and you can have the dedicated focus needed to get this done right the first time. This can be applied to any period of time when you can get yourself a good three days to focus and concentrate.

4.3 Using motivation for the training

A lot of products out there will tell you that to motivate your child, you need to go to the store and pick up a toy or something like that. And while that's good, I want to give you something even better when it comes to motivation.

Here's the problem with giving them toys or saying, "I'm taking your toys away," and actually taking the toy away and hiding it so that they don't see it. When children are between the ages of 2 and 5, out of sight, out of mind, the average attention span at that age is about 7 minutes.

So, if you take the toy away it only takes 7 minutes before they never even realized they had a toy in the first place. So, that motivation does not go very far. What I like to do is instead is use fear of loss versus fear of gain.

Now, let me explain the difference to you between fear of loss and fear of gain. Most people even as adults think about it today. We work harder to prevent ourselves from losing things than we do to gain things. Fear of loss is a bigger motivator than fear of gain. So if you are saying, "If you behave, you will get..." or, "If you use the potty, you will get..."

Although it can be a good thing for motivation, I think you can get a better response by saying, "If you don't use the potty, you will lose this." In other words, if they don't use the potty, they're going to lose something.

Let me give you an example of one of the motivations we used to use with my youngest son. We had to "outsmart the fox" as I call it. I used to have to say something like, "Lorenzo, do you want to go to McDonald's?" And he'd say, "Yes, let's go to McDonald's." So, then I would say, "Okay, great. Go get your coat. Go get your shoes. Let's go to McDonalds."

He'd go get his stuff and we'd open the front door and get ready to walk out. And then I would say, "Oh, you know what Lorenzo, let's use the bathroom before we go because you don't want to have an accident at Ronald McDonald's house." So, what did I do it at that point? Using a fear of loss, I defuse the potty. At that point, losing McDonalds was way more important to him than the toilet. So, he went without any issues at all. Now, granted, going to McDonald's means you have to spend money, but there are other ways that you can use the same methodology inside the house. For example, you can use their favorite cookie or their favorite snack.

Let's say they like pudding. You might say, "Hey Lorenzo, do you want some pudding?" And the answer of course is going to be, "Yes." You then take the pudding, you put it on the table, you put the spoon in the bowl, you actually let them grab the spoon, get ready to take a bite and you say, "Wait a second, wait a second. Before you take that bite, let's go use the potty." At this point, the pudding and the reward are so real to the child that the potty is nothing. They'll use the potty just so they can come back and get that reward. You can do this with the toys as well.You can also do it with television. If it is a television program that they really like, then I would wait until the show is getting ready to start and I'd say, "Hey, let's go use the bathroom before we have an accident watching the show." If they said, "Oh the show is starting. I don't want to use the bathroom." Then, your answer is, "Well, we better go quickly if you want to see that show. Until we use the bathroom the show is not going to be on." Then, you can literally turn the television off. So, that is the way to motivate getting to the results. You don't want to use the same old, "I'm taking the toys away." You hide the toys and they don't see the toys for months, and to them, they never existed in the first place.

4.4 How will I know my toddler is ready to be potty trained?

If your little one isn't developmentally ready for potty training, even the best toilet tactics will fall short. Wait for these surefire signs that your tot is set to get started:

You're changing fewer diapers. Until they're around 20 months old, toddlers still pee frequently, but once they can stay dry for an hour or two, it's a sign that they're developing bladder control and are becoming physically ready for potty training.

▢ Bowel movements become more regular. This makes it easier to pull out the potty in a pinch when it's time.

▢ Your little one is more vocal about going to the bathroom. When your child starts to broadcast peeing and pooping by verbalizing or showing you through his facial expressions, potty training is on the horizon.

▢ Your child notices (and doesn't like) dirty diapers. Your little one may suddenly decide she doesn't want to hang out in her dirty diapers because they're gross. Yay! Your child is turning her nose up at stinky diapers just like you do and is ready to use the potty instead.

Kids are generally not ready to potty train before the age of 2, and some children may wait until 3 1/2. It's important to remember not to push your child before he's ready and to be patient. And remember that all kids are different. Your child is not developmentally lagging if he's far into his 3s before he gets the hang of potty training.

Potty training success hinges on physical, developmental and behavioral milestones, not age. Many children show signs of being ready for potty training between ages 18 and 24 months. However, others might not be ready until they're 3 years old.

There's no rush. If you start too early, it might take longer to train your child.

Is your child ready? Ask yourself:

- Can your child walk to and sit on a toilet?
- Can your child pull down his or her pants and pull them up again?
- Can your child stay dry for up to two hours?
- Can your child understand and follow basic directions?
- Can your child communicate when he or she needs to go?
- Does your child seem interested in using the toilet or wearing "big-kid" underwear?

If you answered mostly yes, your child might be ready. If you answered mostly no, you might want to wait especially if your child is about to face a major change, such as a move or the arrival of a new sibling.

Your readiness is important, too. Let your child's motivation, instead of your eagerness, lead the process. Try not to equate potty training success or difficulty with your child's intelligence or stubbornness. Also, keep in mind that accidents are inevitable and punishment has no role in the process. Plan toilet training for when you or a caregiver can devote the time and energy to be consistent on a daily basis for a few months.

4.5 How to know when its time for a child with special need

While parents often complain of difficulty potty training their children, for most families, potty training is a fairly easy experience. Even when there are problems or children show signs of potty training resistance, usually, they will eventually become potty trained.

Signs of Potty Training Readiness in Children With Special Needs

However, this is not always the case for children with developmental delays or disabilities, such as autism, Down syndrome, mental retardation, cerebral palsy, etc. Children with special needs can be more difficult to potty train.

Most children show signs of physical readiness to begin using the toilet as toddlers, usually between 18 months and 3 years of age 1, but not all children have the intellectual and/or psychological readiness to be potty trained at this age.

It is more important to keep your child's developmental level, and not his chronological age in mind when you are considering starting potty training.

Signs of intellectual and psychological readiness includes being able to follow simple instructions and being cooperative, being uncomfortable with dirty diapers and wanting them to be changed, recognizing when he has a full bladder or needs to have a bowel movement, being able to tell you when he needs to urinate or have a bowel movement, asking to use the potty chair or asking to wear regular underwear.

Signs of physical readiness can include your being able to tell when your child is about to urinate or have a bowel movement by his facial expressions, posture or by what he says, staying dry for at least 2 hours at a time, and having regular bowel movements. It is also helpful if he can at least partially dress and undress himself.

4.6 Potty Training Challenges

Children with physical disabilities may also have problems with potty training that involves learning to get on the potty and getting undressed. A special potty chair and other adaptations may need to be made for these children.

Things to avoid when toilet training your child, and help prevent resistance, are beginning during a stressful time or period of change in the family (moving, new baby, etc.), pushing your child too fast, and punishing mistakes. Instead, you should treat accidents and mistakes lightly. Be sure to go at your child's pace and show strong encouragement and praise when he is successful.

Since an important sign of readiness and a motivator to begin potty training involves being uncomfortable in a dirty diaper, if your child isn't bothered by a soiled or wet diaper, then you may need to change him into regular underwear or training pants during daytime training. Other children can continue to wear a diaper or pull-ups if they are bothered, and you know when they are dirty.

Once you are ready to begin training, you can choose a potty chair. You can have your child decorate it with stickers and sit on it with his clothes on to watch TV, etc. to help him get used to it.

Whenever your child shows signs of needing to urinate or have a bowel movement, you should take him to the potty chair and explain to him what you want him to do. Make a consistent routine of having him go to the potty, pull down his clothes, sit on the potty, and after he is finished, pulling up his clothes and washing his hands.

At first, you should only keep him seated for a few minutes at a time, don't insist and be prepared to delay training if he shows resistance. Until he is going in the potty, you can try to empty his dirty diapers into his potty chair to help demonstrate what you want him to do.

Tips for Potty Training Children With Developmental Delays

An important part of potty training children with special needs is using the potty frequently. This usually includes scheduled toileting as outlined in the book Toilet Training Without Tears by Dr. Charles E. Schaefer. This "assures that your child has frequent opportunities to use the toilet." Sitting on the potty should occur "at least once or twice every hour" and after you first ask, "Do you have to go potty?" Even if he says no, unless he is totally resistant, it is a good idea to take him to the potty anyway.

If this routine is too demanding on your child, then you can take him to the potty less frequently. It can help to keep a chart or diary of when he regularly wets or soils himself so that you will know the best times to have him sit on the potty and maximize your chances that he has to go. He is also most likely to go after meals and snacks and that is a good time to take him to the potty. Frequent visits during the times that he is likely to use the potty and fewer visits to the potty at other times of the day is another good alternative.

Other good techniques include modeling, where you allow your child to see family members or other children using the toilet, and using observational remarks. 4 This involves narrating what is happening and asking questions while potty training, such as "Did you just sit on the potty?" or "Did you just poop in the potty?"

Even after he begins to use the potty, it is normal to have accidents and for him to regress or relapse at times and refuse to use the potty. Being fully potty trained, with your child recognizing when he has to go to the potty, physically goes to the bathroom and pulls down his pants, urinates or has a bowel movement in the potty, and dresses himself, can take time, sometimes up to three to six months

Having accidents or occasionally refusing to use the potty is normal and not considered resistance.

Early on in the training, resistance should be treated by just discontinuing training for a few weeks or a month and then trying again. In addition to a lot of praise and encouragement when he uses or even just sits on the potty, material rewards can be a good motivator. This can include stickers that he can use to decorate his potty chair or a small toy, snack or treat. You can also consider using a reward chart and getting a special treat if he gets so many stickers on his chart.

You can also give treats or rewards for staying dry. It can help to check to make sure he hasn't had an accident between visits to the potty. If he is dry, then getting very excited and offering praise, encouragement, and maybe even a reward, can help to reinforce his not having accidents.

4.7 How to Use Positive Practice for Accidents

Another useful technique is positive practice for accidents. Dr. Schaefer describes this as what you should do when your child has an accident and wets or soils himself.

This technique involves firmly telling your child what he has done, taking him to the potty where he can clean and change himself (although you will likely need to help) and then having him practice using the potty. Dr. Schaefer recommends going through the usual steps of using the potty at least five times, starting when "the child walks to the toilet, lowers his pants, briefly sits on the toilet (3 to 5 seconds), stands up, raises his pants, washes his hands, and then returns to the place where the accident occurred."

Although you are trying to teach him the consequences of having an accident, this should not take the form of punishment.

4.8 When to Get Help for Special Needs Kids With Potty Training Difficulties

While it may take some time and require a lot of patience, many children with special needs can be potty trained by the age of 3 to 5 years. 3 If you continue to have problems or your child is very resistant, then consider getting professional help.

In addition to your pediatrician, you might get help from an occupational therapist, especially if your child has some motor delays causing the potty training difficulty, a child psychologist, especially if your child is simply resistant to potty training and a developmental pediatrician

When it's time to begin potty training:

Choose your words. Decide which words you're going to use for your child's bodily fluids. Avoid negative words, such as dirty or stinky.

Prepare the equipment. Place a potty chair in the bathroom or, initially, wherever your child is spending most of his or her time. Encourage your child to sit on the potty chair in clothes to start out. Make sure your child's feet rest on the floor or a stool. Use simple, positive terms to talk about the toilet. You might dump the contents of a dirty diaper into the potty chair and toilet to show their purpose. Have your child flush the toilet.

Schedule potty breaks. Have your child sit on the potty chair or toilet without a diaper for a few minutes at two-hour intervals, as well as first thing in the morning and right after naps. For boys, it's often best to master urination sitting down, and then move to standing up after bowel training is complete. Stay with your child and read a book together or play with a toy while he or she sits. Allow your child to get up if he or she wants. Even if your child simply sits there, offer praise for trying — and remind your child that he or she can try again later. Bring the potty chair with you when you're away from home with your child.

Get there

Fast! When you notice signs that your child might need to use the toilet such as squirming, squatting or holding the genital area respond quickly. Help your child become familiar with these signals, stop what he or she is doing, and head to the toilet. Praise your child for telling you when he or she has to go. Keep your child in loose, easy-to-remove clothing.

Explain hygiene. Teach girls to spread their legs and wipe carefully from front to back to prevent bringing germs from the rectum to the vagina or bladder. Make sure your child washes his or her hands afterward.

Ditch the diapers. After a couple of weeks of successful potty breaks and remaining dry during the day, your child might be ready to trade diapers for training pants or underwear. Celebrate the transition. Let your child return to diapers if he or she is unable to remain dry. Consider using a sticker or star chart for positive reinforcement.

4.9 Getting started with toilet training

The following tips may help you get started with potty training:

If there are siblings, ask them to let the younger child see you praising them for using the toilet.

It's best to use a potty chair on the floor rather than putting the child on the toilet for training. The potty chair is more secure for most children. Their feet reach the floor and there is no fear of falling off. If you decide to use a seat that goes over the toilet, use a footrest for your child's feet.

Let your child play with the potty. They can sit on it with clothes on and later with diapers off. This way they can get used to it. Never strap your child to the potty chair. Children should be free to get off the potty when they want.

Your child should not sit on the potty for more than 5 minutes. Sometimes children have a bowel movement just after the diaper is back on because the diaper feels normal. Don't get upset or punish your child. You can try taking the dirty diaper off and putting the bowel movement in the potty with your child watching you. This may help your child understand that you want the bowel movement in the potty.

If your child has a normal time for bowel movements (such as after a meal), take your child to the potty at that time of day. If your child acts a certain way when having a bowel movement (such as stooping, getting quiet, going to the corner), try taking your child to potty when he or she shows it is time.

If your child wants to sit on the potty, stay next to your child and talk or read a book.

It's good to use words for what your child is doing (such as potty, pee, or poop). Then your child learns the words to tell you. Remember that other people will hear these words. Don't use words that will offend, confuse, or embarrass others or your child.

Don't use words such as dirty, naughty, or stinky to describe bowel movements and urine. Use a simple, matter-of-fact tone.

If your child gets off the potty before urinating or passing a bowel movement, be calm. Don't scold. Try again later. If your child successfully uses the potty, give plenty of praise such as a smile, clap, or hug.

Children learn from copying adults and other children. It may help if your child sits on the potty chair while you are using the toilet.

Children often follow parents into the bathroom. This may be one time they are willing to use the potty.

Start out by teaching boys to sit down for passing urine. At first, it is hard to control starting and stopping while standing. Boys will try to stand to urinate when they see other boys standing.

Some children learn by pretending to teach a doll to go potty. Get a doll that has a hole in its mouth and diaper area. Your child can feed and "teach" the doll to pull down its pants and use the potty. Make this teaching fun for your child.

Make going to the potty a part of your child's daily routine. Do this first thing in the morning, after meals and naps, and before going to bed.

4.10 After training is started

The following tips may help you once the training is started:

Once your child starts using the potty and can tell you they need to go, taking them to the potty at regular times or reminding them too many times to go to the potty is not necessary.

You may want to start using training pants. Wearing underpants is a sign of growing up, and most children like being a "big girl or big boy." Wearing diapers once potty training has been started may be confusing for your child.

If your child has an accident while in training pants, don't punish. Be calm and clean up without making a fuss about it.

Keep praising or rewarding your child every step of the way. Do this for pulling down pants, for sitting on the potty, and for using the potty. If you show that you are pleased when your child urinates or has bowel movements in the potty, your child is more likely to use the potty next time.

As children get older, they can learn to wipe themselves and wash hands after going to the bathroom. Girls should be taught to wipe from front to back so that germs from bowel movement are not wiped into the urinary area.

Remember that every child is different and learns toilet training at his or her own pace. If things are going poorly with toilet training, it's better to put diapers back on for a few weeks and try again later. In general, have a calm, unhurried approach to toilet training.

Most children have bowel control and daytime urine control by age 3 or 4. Soiling or daytime wetting after this age should be discussed with your child's healthcare provider.

Nighttime control usually comes much later than daytime control. Complete nighttime control may not happen until your child is 4 or 5 years old, or even older. If your child is age 5 or older and does not stay dry at night, you should discuss this with your child's healthcare provider.

Even when children are toilet trained, they may have some normal accidents (when excited or playing a lot), or setbacks due to illness or emotional situations. If accidents or setbacks happen, be patient. Examples of emotional situations include moving to a new house, a family illness or death, or a new baby in the house. In fact, if you know an emotional situation is going to be happening soon, don't start toilet training. Wait for a calmer time.

4.11 Potty Training Chairs

Many parents ask, "Do I need a potty training chair to be successful in potty training?" The answer to that question is "yes" and "no". For even our own kids, I used potty training chairs for two and no potty training chairs for our third child.

Now, he was an advanced child. He was doing things that the other kids never did so he never even wanted to use the potty chair. Even today as a 6-year-old in kindergarten, he doesn't like doing things that the other kindergarten kids like to do.

He calls them "babies." But I will tell you this: having a potty training chair does several things for your child. First of all, it gives them flexibility. When they have a potty training chair, more than likely it is mobile, which means that it can be placed anywhere around the house including the TV room or the game room.

This increases the success rate of your child using the potty. The rationale? Well, as you might already know, if you're in any other room than the bathroom when you see kids doing a pee-pee dance or you realize that they've got to go, it's already too late. That pee or the bowel movement is almost on its way out the door.

But with a mobile potty chair, you can place it near their activities and in different rooms, so when the child feels the need to go, they don't have to rush all the way to the bathroom. They can simply get up and go in the vicinity of wherever they are.

Not only that, the act of running and holding for child that young is a very challenging thing. So trying to run to the bathroom from outside is almost asking for trouble. What you want to do instead is make sure that if you are going to use a potty chair, is that it's available and near. A potty chair is also great especially if you have a 2-story house and the bathroom is upstairs.

You can then put the potty chair downstairs and cut out that climb. And the way potty chairs are designed today, they're colorful, they are cute and kids love them. It just is a fun thing for them and they always get a sense of pride because it's their chair and nobody else's. What we used to do is put the potty chair in a laundry room because there was a door there. My son would be able to close the door so we couldn't see him and he would have his privacy.

4.12 Starting the process

There are three different times that you can start the training process.

Early — when the child is 2 or younger Middle — between the ages of 2 and 3, maybe 3 ½ Later — between 3, 3 ½ and older The optimal time for me is the age of 2.

And, I mean the day they turned 2 is when we normally like to start with potty training. With all the years that I have been in day care and all the children that I have potty trained, I started every single one the day they turned 2. Even our own kids, we started them at the age of 2.

Now, starting at a later time is okay and that is the case with most parents. But I want to explain to you the difference between starting at the age of 2 and starting later. The key difference in starting at the age of 2 is that the child hasn't developed all of their social skills yet and their ability to go out and have fun is limited.

At the age of 2 and somewhere between 2 and 3 is when they find their own voice. (You've heard of the terrible '2s'!?) They find their own voice and they find their own spirit and that's when they decide that they want to start doing their own thing. When you start earlier in the potty training process it is easier to get them to follow directions and it is just easier to get them to do what you want them to do versus them wanting to do what they want to do.

Now, girls can start even earlier than 2. Usually girls can start about 3 or 4 months before their 2nd birthday. Girls, as we know, even later on in life, are a lot smarter than boys and men, and I will be the first to admit that.

The earliest we've seen was a little girl in my class that was only 15 months that was potty training and doing a fantastic job. But some kids can start as early as 18 or 19 months, including boys. So, potty training earlier is great because it gives you the ability to control the process versus them being in control. When you start at that middle time frame, which is between 2 and 3 or 2 ½ to 3 or later than that, what happens is that child goes more into the independent stage.

That's where they're able to start making to some of their decisions which happens to often include the word "no". And thus what happens as a parent is you're not only dealing with potty training but you're also dealing with behavior as the result of a child that is looking to find their self and their voice. Starting late doesn't mean you did anything wrong, and it doesn't mean that you're not going to potty train.; All it means is that it's going to be a little bit more challenging and a little bit more work. And that's okay but it just means that it's going to take a little bit more time to get the child potty trained.

Now, the other thing that you want to realize is the later you start, the more years of behavior modification you're trying to reverse and that can account for some of that difficulty. In other words, when you start the potty training at the age of 2, you only have 2 years of pooping in their diaper or potty in the diaper to reverse. Whereas the later you start, let's say at the age of 3, you've got 3, 3 ½ years of pooping in their diaper or the potty behavior that you have to reverse. So, it's a very big difference starting earlier than later because it's a lot more habit that has to be broken and a new habit learned.

To drive this point home, just think about how hard it is to change a behavior or a habit in yourself. If you think it's hard for yourself, think about a child that doesn't have the same cognitive ability that you have. Trying to get rid of that behavior as early as possible is better because it's less work for the child. We want to keep in mind how hard that child actually has to work to do this. The key also is that we're looking at doing this in just 3 days through consistency. So, reversing years of behavior in just 3 days is even that much more challenging the older they are.

4.13 Pre-potty training

Pre-potty training is getting the child ready for what is about to come if you really want to potty train him within 3 days, or what it is about to happen. In other words, you set a time when you're going to start potty training. It's now February and you want to start potty-training in September or something to that effect. Before September comes around, there are things that you can do that will make the potty training process not only easier for yourself, but also easier for the child.

The first thing you want to do is sit your child down and explain what is expected of them. Sitting down is an important component of this.

You want to sit next to them or across from them and in a very loving and caring tone, you want to say, "I am going to explain potty training to you." And you want to say, "Potty training is when you go the bathroom (tinkle, pee or poopy) in the potty." Now in terms of the words that you use, you want to be consistent. If you call it "tinkle" then you want to continue using the word "tinkle". If you call it "poopy", then continue using the word "poopy".

As a young child, too many words are going to confuse them, so staying consistent with your terminology will help you enforce the concept and they will know exactly what it means. You want to be strong and direct.

By that I mean using words like, "Mommy is going to have you potty trained, and here's what you have to do for Mommy...poopy, tinkle, etc." Or, "When you have to go potty, you have to let Mommy know, and you have to sit on the toilet and then you go potty". Then, you physically walk them to the toilet and show them and say, "Here is where you go tinkle and poopy." This isn't being strict; it's being direct so that they know that you are in charge, and what is expected of them.

If you don't take it direct tone, kids are extremely smart. They can sense a lack of control and they might not follow your directions as well if you say, "Mommy would like" or, "It would be nice if you...".

Take them to the bathroom and get them use to seeing you in the bathroom. Let them sit down on the toilet. Let them get used to having the toilet touch their skin as well. Many parents don't realize this, but many children have a fear of being on the toilet as opposed to just being hard to potty train. So this might help them get over that fear so when the potty training begins, you don't have to battle two things.

One thing is to start using less absorbent diapers. Today, the diapers are so absorbent the child doesn't even realize that they are wet. And most kids do not like the feeling of being wet. So when they have on a less absorbent diaper, it helps them realize the act of letting go and releasing 'number 1'. But the wet feeling also starts to psychologically or subconsciously say to them, "When I get this feeling of letting go, I start to feel wet too, and I don't like that." You will also want to make sure that you change them frequently when they wet their diapers. This helps them get used to the feeling of being dry and staying dry. It also reinforces the feelings they have once they wet again.

It is also highly encouraged that you actually consider taking your child out of diapers while they are awake a couple of months prior to the actual potty training process. So, during nap time, you will use diapers, but during their waking hours, you will want them in big boy and big girl underwear. You will also want to make sure that this whole pre-potty training process is a loving experience because you want it to subconsciously erase some of the other negative connotations and fears that your child may have. It's important that you understand pre potty training is not a necessary step. It gives you an advantage if you are starting the potty training process early, but if you are like most parents, then you might have missed the stage or the time when you could have pre-potty trained. You can still pre-potty train if you prefer, no matter at which stage you are, but it's usually better if you can start as early as possible. Knowing what we know and from our customers, however, most parents usually has missed this stage to the degree that they can get the most effectiveness out of it.

4.14 Step-by-Step Potty training

In this section, I am going to teach you four stages to potty training. What you will notice and then appreciate is that these four stages can be applied to almost any other learned or practiced behavior which you are trying to alter or change.

The four stages of any behavior modification model include:

- Unconscious incompetence
- Conscious incompetence
- Conscious competence
- Unconscious competence

And now, I'll break these down to help you understand what they are and what you need to focus on during each one of these different stages.

Stage One: Unconscious Incompetence:

This is the "I do not know" stage, where your child's mind is thinking, "I do not know that going to the bathroom in my diaper is a wrong thing". In other words, the child has no idea that what they are doing is something they should not be doing. During stage one, when they don't know the difference, this is when it becomes your responsibility to educate them and get them to understand what they are doing is not something they should be doing.

This is where you are teaching the child that they do not need to be going to the bathroom in their diaper.

Stage Two: Conscious Incompetence

At this stage, the child has reached an understanding where they know what they're doing is something they should not do, but have no idea how to correct it. During stage two you are taking it to that next level where you are reinforcing the positive behavior by showing them where they are supposed to go to the bathroom—in the potty. So, now you're teaching the child where to go, how to go, and what to do.

Stage Three: Conscious Incompetence

Here, the child knows what they are doing is something they shouldn't be doing, they know what to do about it, but they are also not that great at it. They have to think about it. That is because the process is now occurring on the conscious level. It is during stage three that the child starts to understand on their own and they start to show you the signs that they can do this on their own as well. This is when you should be getting to the point of not having accidents anymore. Now, this is an area where most parents go wrong in that they get to stage three and they say, "My child is potty trained, there is nothing else that I have to do." In reality, this is where the real potty training begins. This is where you really want to be consistent to ensure they reach stage four and can consistently go to the potty by themselves. So, when you get to stage three, you have to make sure that you continue with consistency.

Stage Four: Unconscious Competence

And this is the fun stage. This is when the child gets to where they need to should know what they're doing and they don't have to think about it any longer. It is at stage four that your child can be officially considered 'potty trained.' Let's take a quick example to make sure the concept sinks in: If you are in stage three, you're not showing the child where to go potty anymore because they know where to go. What you're doing is being consistent with them going to the potty on a regular basis. During stage two you're not so much worried about consistency yet, you are more focused on helping them know where to go. Hopefully this description has given you a better understanding of how each stage develops and, better yet, what your actions need to be during each stage.

First Time Mom Potty Training

As a young mum who have no much experience about potty training; one of the best thing you can do to help your kid is to Be a positive potty model. When you go to the bathroom, use it as an opportunity to talk your child through the process. Use words he or she can say, like pee, poop, and potty.

If you plan to start your child on a potty seat, put it in the bathroom so it becomes familiar. Make it a fun place your child wants to sit, with or without the diaper on. Have your child sit on the potty seat while you read or offer a toy.

Also, tune in to cues. Be aware of how your child behaves when he has to pee or poop. Look for a red face and listen for grunting sounds. Take notice of the time when he pees and poops during the day. Then establish a routine in which your child sits on the potty during those times, especially after meals or after drinking a lot of fluid. This helps set your child up for success.

And use plenty of praise, praise, and more praise. Is your child motivated by verbal encouragement? Stickers on a chart? Small toys or extra bedtime stories? Check in with what feels right for you and use it to reward positive potty choices. Your good attitude will come in handy, especially when "accidents" happen.

4.15 What Not to Do

Sitting on the potty should be a want-to, not a have-to. If your child isn't into it, don't force it.

Just when you think your child has nailed it, accidents happen. It's OK to be frustrated, but don't punish or shame your child -- it won't get you closer to your goal. Take a deep breath and focus on what you and your child can do better next time.

Also, don't compare your son or daughter with other children. Some parents like to brag about how easy potty training went in their family. So if your neighbor says her kids potty trained themselves, smile and remember that the only right way is the one that works for you.

And if you a working mum, you juggle all your professional and personal responsibilities and, somehow, you make it look simple. Life is busy, though, and you've got a huge task to add to the to-do list: learning how to potty-train.

Helping your little one switch from diapers to the bathroom is a tough job — regardless of whether you're a stay-at-home or working parent. Because you fall into the latter category, you have to plan the process more carefully, so you are present for the majority of the transition. As you prepare for life without diapers, here are some tips to keep in mind to make it simpler for you as you balance your professional schedule and potty-train schedule.

1. Choose the Right Time

Parenting books will probably suggest the perfect time to start potty-training, but no two children are the same. Some little ones start using the potty at as young as 24 months, but that's rare. In most cases, children begin between 24 and 36 months, and the entire process can take up to eight months to perfect after that.

Still, you should be more focused on starting the process when your child shows they are ready for it. For instance, some kids will start to show interest in their siblings' or classmates' potty behavior, which can help you ease them into using the toilet, too. Also, if your child sleeps through nap time without wetting their diaper, they could be prepared to potty-train. To that end, staying dryer for longer also shows a little one has what it takes to wear big-kid underwear. Finally, your child might alert you when they must go, hide when they have to pee or poop, or tug at a dirty diaper.

Once you start seeing these cues, you should start thinking about beginning the process. There's no need to start too soon and put too much on your plate when you're already busy.

2. Invest in the Tools

Now that you know it's time to potty-train, you have to invest in the supplies you need to make it possible. For one thing, you'll need to pick up some underwear for your son or daughter. On a weekend or after-work trip to the store, bring your child along to help pick out their designs — they'll find it even more exciting to switch to underwear if they like the character or colors. Having the proper clothing and underwear, along with other potty-training supplies like extra bed sheets, flushable wipes, and soap you can keep your child comfortable and ready for anything.

However, mistakes happen! If they do make a mess, teach them to not put anything other than toilet paper or flushable wipes in the toilet! By preventing the flushing of wipes and the use of too much paper, you will minimize the amount of plumbing-related issues you will experience. When clogs do occur, knowing how to effectively use a plunger and when to call in a plumber can also save you a lot of grief.

3. Work with Teachers or Nannies

You can kick off your potty-training extravaganza over the weekend but, by Monday, you'll have to go back to work. Rather than halting your progress and popping your child back into diapers, work with their nanny or preschool teacher so everyone's on the same page about the transition. Chances are, your childcare provider will be more than willing to stick to the routine you've started, as well as any rewards system you have in place.

Think about it — it's beneficial for them not have to change diapers anymore, either. Make sure you pack plenty of dry clothes just in case, as accidents do happen. Then, once you pick up your child and go home, you can continue the training process yourself.

4. Reward Good Potty Habits

Experts have varying opinions on rewarding children for their successful use of the potty. Some say it's a great way to boost their accountability, while others think the feeling of being clean and dry is reward enough. It's up to you whether or not you'll incentivize the process with treats, stickers or a potty-training chart.

No matter what, it's vital that you verbalize how proud you are of your child as they use the potty. Even if their teachers take the reins during the day, shower them with praise as soon as you pick them up and hear updates on the process. It can be frustrating if your child fusses about using the toilet or if they suffer from accidents, but you can't let them see or feel this from you. With a supportive parent helming the transition from diapers to potty, children are more likely to try.

Start and Succeed

Once you've pinpointed the right time to start, invested in the right gear and enlisted the help of your child's teachers, you're ready to potty-train. You'll be surprised how these simple steps can make it so much easier to get the job done, even while you're working. Cheer your child to the finish line both of you will be freer and happier sans diapers, which is the best benefit of all.

4.16 How to Potty Train a Child with Special Needs as a mum

If you have a child with special needs, then you know that you may not be able to rely on the "typical" signs of potty training readiness. Kristen Raney from Shifting Roots shares her experience with potty training her son.

Potty Training a Child on the Autism Spectrum

First of all, don't read those stories about moms who potty train their children in three days!!! This will not work for our children and will cause you so much stress!! Remember through this process that you are a good mom doing the best you can for your child.

Most of the moms of autistic children I know were not able to potty train their children before four, many of them five, and some of them never. It just depends where your child falls on the Autism Spectrum and what their particular sensory issues are.

For context, our son would be considered to have Aspergers, but it's no longer a diagnosis and is now part of the Autism Spectrum. His body was ready to potty train around 2 1/2, but he had very intense fears about using the toilet. No bribe, game, song, or sticker chart in the world could get him to use it. He also was terrified to pee or poo in pre-K, daycare, or anywhere in public.

We started by getting him trained to pee on the potty, and he hit that milestone by 3 1/2. I don't remember how, because it was so stressful that I've erased that time from my mind. I think it involved making him pee in his diaper in the bathroom, and slowly transferring that idea to the potty. Once he got that, he had to ask for a diaper if he wanted to poo, and go in his diaper in the bathroom.

To get him trained all the way, it took a 90 minute battle of wills where I told him he could poop on the potty or on the bathroom floor, it was entirely his choice. It was terrible. He chose the potty, glared at me like I was killing him. We bought him a Thomas train for the next three times he went on the potty, and a fourth one for keeping it up for a week. Yes, this sounds completely excessive and terrible, but he was 4 1/4 and we were at our wits end.

I hope your journey is much less stressful than ours, but know that you're not alone! Don't take any flack from someone with a neurotypical kid who gives you grief about not having your child trained by now. You've got this mama!

4.17 How to Potty Train a "Late" Bloomer

Here's the thing. Out of all of my mom friends, not one of our kiddos potty trained at the same age/time. In my grandparent's era, children were toilet trained early (12-18 months). This had a lot to do with the needs of the adult, however, not necessarily the readiness of the child. Most American families are now waiting until their child is at least twenty-four months or beyond to introduce potty training. Keep in mind, that times are always changing!

An article by Healthy Children.org entitled "The Right Age to Potty Train", states that there is no exact right age potty train! Research over the past several decades indicates that there is no perfect age. Parents really need to look at the physical, mental, and emotional readiness of their child and go from there. These indicators could happen at vastly different ages.

Sumer Schmitt over at Giggles, Grace, and Naptime shares her experiences with potty training on "older toddler". Her son was nearly three and a half when he was fully potty trained. She shares her story of persevering through potty training and advises:

We, as moms, have heard it a million times. Don't compare. Don't compare your child to little Suzy down the street who was potty trained at 18 months. Or the story you read online about the 6 month old baby who is already doing elimination communication. Easier said than done, right? When you're in the thick of it though, it's hard not to get stuck in the comparison game.

Trust me, I get it. But, your child will potty train in his/her own time. Chances are, by the time your child reaches kindergarten, no one is even going to be talking about this milestone anymore. Just like they no longer talk about when your child first rolled over, sat up, crawled, or started walking. Those milestones are in the past and most children will all eventually catch up to one another.

Studies actually show that sometimes potty training later is better because your child will have a better developed vocabulary. Potty training may be easier and happen faster the later the age!

4.18 How to potty train your kid as a dad

As a father, either single father or not our child is more likely to understand potty use if he's no longer wearing a nappy. Training pants are absorbent underwear worn during toilet training.

They're less absorbent than nappies but are useful for holding in bigger messes like accidental poos. Once your child is wearing training pants, dress her in clothes that are easy to take off quickly.

Pull-ups are very popular and are marketed as helpful for toilet training. It isn't clear that they actually help. But you can try them to help your child get used to wearing underwear.

Generally, cloth training pants are less absorbent than pull-ups and can feel a little less like a nappy. Pull-ups might be handier when you're going out.

Wearing training pants is a big move for your child. If you celebrate it, the transition will be easier. Talk about how grown-up he is and how proud of him you are.

I've heard all the tricks stickers, bribing with toys, special underpants. But you have to pick something that's consistent with your parenting style. I didn't use rewards elsewhere, so I didn't want to start here. What did work: Lots of undivided attention, positive reinforcement, love, affection and pride when my kids were successful. Making a big deal about small steps of progress is key.

I didn't use any special stuff—no kiddie toilets, potty rings, or even pull-ups—because the local YMCA where my daughters attended didn't believe in them. We even had to sign a contract stating that we'd follow their potty training policy at home. I was instructed to just put the kids (they were around 2 1/2) on our regular toilet throughout the day when I thought they had to go. After a week and lots of "Yeah! You did number two!" and "Good for you! You made a wee-wee!" they were done, with barely any accidents. All told, I think they were just developmentally ready.

"The key is consistency," says James Singer, father of two, and a member of the Huggies Pull-Ups Potty Training Partners. "Whatever you do at home with your potty training plan, you also need to do elsewhere. For instance, if your child prefers to read a book while on the potty, talk to your daycare provider about sending in a favorite book. Keep in mind that daycare centers may be too busy to customize potty training to each child. In that case, ask them how they think they can help foster the success you have had at home and compromise. Then bring home something that works at daycare. If your child loves the soap they use at school, get some for home.

Boost the fun factor of using the potty with a Pee-Kaboo Reusable Potty Training Sticker. Slap a blank sticker onto the base of a portable potty, have your toddler pee in the potty, and then let him watch as an image of a train, flower, fire truck, or butterfly appears! After you empty, clean, and dry the potty, the image disappears, ready to be used again and again for up to six weeks. Too good to be true? We tested it on a formerly reluctant potty trainer, 2-year-old Gwenyth Mencel, who now shouts "Butterfly, butterfly!" when it's time to hit the potty.

Are you counting down the days to the toilet transition? Or maybe you've already dabbled in a few less-than-successful attempts? Either way, we heard one thing again and again: Your kid has to be good and ready. And don't worry, he will be someday. "No child is going to graduate high school in diapers," says Carol Stevenson, a mom of three from Stevenson Ranch, California, who trained each one at a different age. "But it's so easy to get hung up and worried that your child's a certain age and not there yet, which adds so much pressure and turns it into a battle." Once you're convinced your kid's ready to ditch the diapers (watch for signs like showing an interest in the bathroom, telling you when she has to go, or wanting to be changed promptly after pooping), try any of these tricks to make it easier.

4.19 A Real Dad experience

My wife, MJ, and I ran into the usual parent challenges when trying to potty-train our son. At first Will, then 2, was confused, then afraid, and next defiant. At 2 1/2 he still loved that diaper, and the mere sight of a toilet sent him into a tantrum. The most frustrating part was that I knew he was ready. He would stay dry the entire night, wake up, and pee into his diaper while standing right in front of us, grinning. It was a not-so-subtle reminder that if Will was going to learn, it would be on his own terms.

MJ and I spent countless hours trying to make the bathroom more appealing. We brought Will's stuffed animals in there, let him flip through his books while sitting on the potty (good training for when he's older, like Dad), and even threw Cheerios in the bowl to give him a target. Nothing worked.

At last we got Will to stand on the stool, lift up the seat, pull his pants down, and loom over the toilet. But he still wouldn't go. "Dad, it's not working," he'd say in the cutest way imaginable.

At first I urged him to keep trying. No go. So I turned on the faucet, thinking the sound of running water would make him feel like peeing. But I forgot that he doesn't like noise, so this move merely upset him.

Finally I had a eureka moment. "Hey, Bud, how 'about if Dad pees with you, and we race?" I said.

This clearly sparked Will's competitive spirit, because he brightened up and agreed to the challenge. I shifted his stool to the right so I could squeeze in next to him, and we prepared for our duel. I told him we'd fire on the count of three.

But my little cheater jumped the gun. I didn't even get to "two" before he let loose a stream into the toilet. Victory.

Will giggled and grinned with pride, and I silently awarded myself first place in the "Best Dad in the Universe" contest for solving the potty-training riddle. I smiled broadly at father and son sharing a moment, hitting a milestone (er, Cheerio), and having some genuine fun.

A little too much fun, as it turns out. Will became so excited and began laughing so hard that he started falling in mid-spritz. I was still peeing as well, so I did my best to keep him balanced, all the while making sure we hit the porcelain bull's-eye.

Will's left foot slipped off the stool. I was able to catch him somewhat with my hip and right hand, but not before he instinctively turned toward me. Yup, that's right he sprayed me. A good father would've taken the punishment. But I'm squeamish, so I jerked my body away from his shower. That caused my own pee to hit the wall and ricochet onto my poor son's back.

We both fell to the floor, shocked and disgusted. We were silent for a moment, until Will spoke.

"Dada?" he said quizzically.

"Yes, Bud?"

"You peed on me."

"To be fair, you peed on me first."

The two of us started cracking up belly laughs, guffaws, cackling, you name it - to such a degree that I would have peed myself right there if I hadn't just soaked my toddler. The racket attracted the attention of MJ, who came rushing over. When she turned the corner she stared at us: our soaked clothes, the yellow droplets slowly making their way down the wall.

I launched into an explanation. "Honey, you see, there was a pee race ..."

"I don't care," she interrupted, turning on her heels and walking away. "Just clean it up."

I did, and that day turned out to be a breakthrough. Will began using the toilet regularly (he asked me many times to race him again, but I never accepted) and was fully trained less than two months later. The bad news? He can't resist the urge to tell anyone and everyone about the time Dad peed on him.

4.20 How to Potty train a kid as a grandpa

Potty training is one of the more difficult endeavors we face as old parents. Every child is different and has their own unique challenges.

Unfortunately, it's a messy, stinky destination that you'll quickly want to conquer, but will seemingly get stuck in the mud (no pun intended). So why do some grand parents struggle so much with potty training? The answer may be in the diversity, or lack there of our teachings. The way I see it, the more activities you do to promote potty usage, the better your child's chance of success. You have to stack the deck in your favor. Some parents only do one or two things like buy pull-ups and attempt to put their child on the potty until they get frustrated from it not working. There is a better way. In fact, several different ways which should all be used in conjunction to make potty time a little less night marish and actually more successful!

Children are typically ready to potty train around the ages of 2 or 3 but maybe earlier if there are older siblings to learn from. Look for the signs.

Look out for signs that your child is ready. These include pulling their diaper on and off, going a while or whole nap with a dry diaper, telling you they're going, showing curiosity about the potty and what goes in it, and going number 2 the same time each day.

When starting, dedicate 1-2 weeks to potty training. This includes pausing play-dates, car rides, outdoor activities, and basically anything that brings your child out of the house. Once you start, there's no turning back. Make sure you're in it for the long haul...all or nothing.

Avoid pull-ups during the day as they give children a crutch to go, just like a diaper. Instead, let them be naked and rush them to the potty if they start to go while saying, "Make sure you go pee pee in the potty."

Put them on the potty every 15 to 30 minutes. A lot of kids also have a set time of day when they do their "number 2" business. Make sure to put your child on the potty for several minutes during this time of day and encourage them to go number 2.

Make it enticing and convenient for them to go by providing a smaller, fun themed potty that's not so intimidating to a toddler. My son had a fire truck potty that he loved and we kept it in the room he would play in.

Teach the process of going potty and washing hands with books! There are a ton of great books that you can read to your toddler while sitting on the potty.

Make a cool potty earning chart with fun stickers and rewards. My son received a sticker every time he went potty and after eight stickers he received a little cheap toy like a matchbox car. You can also reward with a few mini M&Ms when they're successful. Charts are a great way to be consistent.

Nighttime potty training usually comes later. We put nighttime pull-ups on our toddler for a good six months after he was day time potty trained. It wasn't until he started going the entire night without incident did we stop using them.

Try your best to stay calm, use positive reinforcement, and not get angry or frustrated when they have an accident. You don't want your child to be anxious or stressed with potty time. Don't make them feel bad for having an accident. They might not tell you when it happens the next time.

As stated earlier, potty training is one of the most difficult parts of being a parent. Consistency is your friend in this situation. Don't give up. Even with hard work, regression is possible and normal. Keep working at it until your little one is a potty pro.

Chapter 5

How To Potty Train Your Kid In 3 Days

The "Signs of Readiness"

I've heard people say that the child needs to show "signs of readiness" before you can potty train them for 3 days.

This is true. What most people don't understand is, "What exactly is a sign of readiness"? People often say that a sign of readiness is when the child starts showing interest in the toilet more than usual. In my opinion, this is an enormous misconception.

Children are curious creatures. As soon as they can crawl, they're out exploring their world. They inevitably find the toilet bowl and start playing in the water.

This is not "the sign" to look for (though it is if you want to prevent them from getting sick, hurt or causing other mayhem).

A necessary sign of potty training readiness is the ability for the child to frequently communicate his or her wants. I'm not talking about speech. I'm talking about gestures, behaviors, sounds, signing. If you can understand that a child wants something, and the child can direct you to the item, that is good enough.

Believe me, when a child is pulling your leg into the kitchen or bedroom, they know what they want, and they are effectively communicating with you! There is greater significance in this sign than you might think. What this behavior or attribute also means is that many children with Apraxia or speech, autism and other developmental problems can be potty trained using this method. Ultimately, the child learns that using the toilet is a good thing, something to be rewarded, and they will find a way to communicate their need to you. They like being rewarded.

A parent explained: My fifth child was diagnosed with Childhood Apraxia of Speech and was potty trained at 22 months old in under 3 days using 3 Day potty training method this is not an easy task. At the time his vocabulary consisted mainly of sounds - not actual words. If a child with apraxia can use potty at 22 month why did you think your own kid cant do that.

Secondly, your child must be able to go to bed without a bottle or cup, preferably two to three hours before bedtime.

There are a couple reasons why I say this.

1.I care about your child's dental health
2.It makes for easy potty training

What happens to you when you have a lot to drink just before going to bed? Late night visits to the bathroom! The same goes for your child. If you give them lots of fluid before bed, there's little chance they will wake up dry.

A few common questions I get from moms about this sign of readiness:

1.Our dinner is only an hour before bed, do I not give my child anything to drink? It is just fine for you to give your child something to drink with dinner. Just be sure that he's not getting tons just before he goes down for the night.

2.My child really enjoys his cup of milk before bed as it is part of our night time routine. Do I really need to stop this? No, you can continue as you have milk with your night time routine but try to decrease the amount. To do this maybe you can get him a smaller cup and then only fill it half way full. Also be sure to follow the night time routine outlined in this eBook.

3.My child wakes often during the night needing a drink, I don't want to tell him no because it's really dry where we live.You can go ahead and let your child have his "sips" of water during the night if he really needs this but there is no need for full cups of water. Being that your child does wake for drinks, he shouldn't have a problem also getting up to go to the bathroom.

Third, in order for this method to work for children under the age of 22 months of age, your child must be waking up dry. Check for dryness within half an hour of them waking up. Don't wait until they've been up for an hour or so. By then, they will have peed and you won't get an accurate indication of readiness. If your child is over the age of 22 months old he should be waking up dry but don't worry too much if he does not. Just be sure to follow the night time method outlined in the eBook to help him with waking up dry.

A few common questions I get from moms about this sign of readiness:

1. My child is 3 years old and still wakes up with a full diaper. Can I still potty training my child? Yes! As stated above, if your child or grandchild is over the age of 22 months and they still wake up wet, it's ok. Just be sure to follow the night time steps outlined in the eBook.
2. My first child is 5 years old and still wets the bed, I don't think my 2 year old will be able to be potty trained for nights. Can I just potty train for the days and use a pull-up or diaper for nights? Why would you want to? There is no need. You can easily potty train your child (even your older child) to wake up dry if you follow the method outlined in the eBook. It works!
3. My child is 18 months old and shows most the signs of readiness but doesn't wake up dry; can I still start potty training? Yes, just be sure to follow the steps outlined in the eBook for night time. I do recommend waiting until your child is 22 months of age because it can take longer than three days when they are younger than 22 months, but the choice is yours. It is my experience that children 22 months of age are at the ideal age to be potty trained. It is entirely possible that a 15 month old shows these signs. For me, if my 15 month old showed these signs, I would still wait until 22 months.

5.1 The First day Journey to the 3 days potty training

Day 1 is the day that we decide to start potty training. First of all, as mentioned earlier, make sure that not only you, but also your child and anyone else who's involved, gets a good night's rest. This is extremely important. It's very difficult to accomplish something when you are not only tired but the child is tired and everyone is cranky.

It is on this day that you get rid of the diapers and the child starts wearing big boy and big girl underwear fulltime... There are no more diapers in this process... Now, some of you are saying, "Well, maybe we'll go ahead and use pull-ups or padded underwear." What I like to say is, "A diaper is a diaper no matter what you call it or what you disguise it as." And subconsciously, if you put the diaper on the child, it gives them the wrong message.

Also, seeing as that we've already explained how difficult this process is for the parents or the potty trainer as it is for the child, not having the diaper makes the parent or the potty trainer more vigilant. You will pay more attention if you know that the child does not have a diaper on.

For example, if you know the child has a diaper and you are out and about somewhere in a store or going out shopping you might say to yourself, "Well, we don't have to find a bathroom right now. We're kind of in a rush. You've got a diaper on." But note that the one time you tell that child that it's okay to go potty in that diaper; you have opened Pandora's Box. You've just told them, "its okay". And they will continue to do that and you will hit a lot of regressions. So, we start with allowing them to pick their big boy or girl underwear and put it on. (This is something you might have done during the pre-potty training process).

Then, you're going to sit down with your child and explain the process to them again. You can say, "Here's what we are doing;

here is what Mommy expects; and here is what's going to happen." Then, you'll want to let them pick the spot for their potty chair.

You'll ask them, "Where do you want your potty chair?" We want to give them some control as well. If you have 2 bathrooms in the house, let them pick their favorite bathroom if they're going to be using the bathroom instead of the potty chair.

Then, you're going to take them to the bathroom. They are going to sit on the toilet and you are going to say, "Okay, Mommy wants you to use the bathroom." By this point, they should have seen you use the bathroom, so you can also say, "We want you to use the bathroom just like Mommy uses the bathroom." Don't be disappointed if nothing comes out. The act that getting them to sit there is a reward or it's an accomplishment all on its own. Once they get off the toilet, you're going to set a timer for 20 minutes.

Every 20 minutes for the first 3 days or for the first few days until they're trained, you are going to have them go and sit in the bathroom. When the timer goes off (and this is very important) it almost has to become a celebration in the house. Everybody can clap or say, "It's potty time. It's potty time. Let's go potty." And everyone can run to the bathroom.

Even with our older kids when we were potty training our youngest, would join into the celebration and run to the bathroom. And it was as if it was Cinco de Mayo or some big festivity in the house. That is very important because we're trying to make this a fun experience for the child.

Every time they go to the bathroom at those 20 minute intervals, you want to make sure they sit on the toilet for 3 to 5 minutes. This is not about them sitting on the toilet for hours; it's sitting on the toilet for 3 to 5 minutes. If they go right away and they pee or they do number 2, then they can get up right away.

Now, if they don't do either one then you want to make sure you wait the full 5 minutes with them sitting on the toilet. Note: At this point, we are not so much concerned about number 2. We want you and them to master number 1 first and then we'll move on. Now, even if they don't go, that is okay because the fact that you're getting them to sit down on the toilet is, again, an accomplishment all in its own.

But something that you want to see happen every single time they sit down on the toilet is for them to push. Even if they don't go number 2 or they don't do number 1, you want to make sure they push. So, you'll want to say, "Mommy wants to see you push. Now push." And some parents have told us, "Well, I can't tell when they're pushing." What you want to do is look at their stomach.

You can tell by the stomach muscle flexing whether they are pushing or not. You see, with a child, it is impossible for them to hold and push at the same time. So, you're almost tricking them into using the potty by asking them to push. So, no matter what—no matter where you go, no matter what time it is—the minute they sit on the toilet you want to make sure that they push and they push every single time.

Even if nothing comes out, as long as they push, that is a good thing because we want to get them used to using those muscles and pushing and moving whatever is inside of their system out. If you find they do not understand what pushing is, what you can do is just tickle their stomachs and the tickling sensation will cause them to contract their stomach muscles, which is a natural way to push.

The other thing that you want to start doing is giving them more fluids. Many people think that potty training is about not wetting themselves. That is not what potty training is about. Potty training is about recognizing when you have to go and knowing where to do it. So, one of the things that you're going to do to help them recognize that is giving them more fluids.

However, you do not want to give them more juice because sometimes the sugar and starches that are in the juice can cause constipation and other problems. Instead, you want to give them liquids like water and things that are going make them want to go potty. In addition to helping them potty, water also helps in the number 2 process as well, which we'll talk about later.

Now, sometimes what happens is that the child will sit for 5 minutes, they won't go, they'll get up and then they might wet themselves within a minute or two. So, here's what you do in that situation: shorten the amount of time that they sit on the toilet. Instead of sitting on the toilet for 5 minutes, let them sit on the toilet for 1 or 2 minutes, but you increase the frequency of how many times they go to the bathroom. So, instead of every 20 minutes, now it's every 15 minutes for 1 to 2 minutes. Another thing you'll want to do is ask them from the minute they get off the toilet and at least 3 or 4 times during that 20 minute timeframe, "Do you have to go potty? "Most of the time, they're going to tell you, "No," and that's okay.

You just want to get them used to hearing the words, "Do you have to go potty?" Then, when the 20 minutes are up and it's time to go potty, now the question is not, "Do you have to go potty?" Now, it's, "Time to potty." One is asking and one is telling. Hopefully you see and understand the difference between the two statements. It's very, very important especially for psychologically getting the child to want to go and use the toilet.

5.2 Constipation

Alright, let's start with holding. Some children will actually hold number 2. Sometimes they will hold number 2 for a day or two days. When it finally becomes too painful they will let it all out into the diaper. First of all if you find your child is holding it that long and all the other methods are not working, and then put a diaper on to let them go. Holding bowel that long is not good for them. This is one of the rare times we recommend putting on a diaper.

The thing to realize is...if they are holding it that long, then theoretically just by the nature of what potty training is, that says your child is potty trained and know what to do. For whatever reason they are afraid of the potty.

It's not an issue of potty training. It's an issue of being afraid or maybe going potty is too painful for them. If you find that their stool is hard, then it will lead to painful bowel movement. If they associate all bowels as painful then they would rather hold the stool then to let it go. So the things that you can do are give them foods that will cause them to go to the bathroom. Give them more liquids (preferably water, not soda or juice), more liquids in their system the easier for them to go number 2.

You want to also do other things. When they're sitting on the toilet try to take their mind off the potty. Some ways to do that would be to rub their stomach or their feet. In the scientific world this is called neuro-linguistic programming. Basically you are trying to get their mind off of something that they're afraid of. So by doing something that feels good to them, you are associating the toilet with something that feels good. Now they're not afraid of that anymore. You want to tickle them. When you tickle them, it forces them to push. You've heard me use the word push over and over so it's something that I'm going to stress.

Make sure they push. As long as they push you are doing good. They cannot hold and push at the same time. I cannot stress enough how important pushing is. If you feel they don't know what pushing is, then tickle their stomach and that will help them understand what pushing is. The other thing that you want to look at when it comes number 2 is constipation. There are a lot of things that cause constipation. Some causes of constipation are medical, while other causes are more mental. If you find your child is constipated, you want to do what I call the "bicycle trick". Don't ask how we had figured this out, but this works 100% of the times. What you do is you lay your child on their back. You should kneel in front of your child at the base of their feet.

Their feet should be almost touching your lap. Grab the base of their feet. Then rotate their legs as if they're riding a bicycle. Do this for about 10 minutes. Within 25 -30 minutes of doing this, the child will use the bathroom. We've told many parents to do this. Every parent I've told to try this, we've gotten a 100% success rate, whereas the child will end up using the bathroom within 30 minutes of doing the "bicycle trick".

So that is the constipation, and if you find the constipation lasting 4 or 5 days you may want to seek some form of medical attention for the child. That is not normal for them to be able to hold it for that many days.

5.3 The second day journey of the 3 days

Alright, so you've graduated from number 1. Your child is doing very well using number 1. Now, it's time for them to start using number 2. There is not much difference between training them from number 1 to number 2. As a matter of fact, I would go so far to tell you that number 1 is a lot harder than number 2, and the reason being that when they go number 1, they have to actually take action to hold it inside.

In other words, for them not to wet themselves, they have to actually squeeze the sphincter muscle and hold the fluids inside. Whereas with number 2, they don't have to do anything to hold it. They actually have to push it out so it is an action that is a lot less difficult than holding the number 1 is. This is behaviour. They have to actually take a step. They have to be proactive to go number 2 so they have a whole lot more control in the number 2 process than they do in number 1.

Now, again, one of the things that we want to make sure we do when they're sitting on the toilet is pushing. And, hopefully you understand how important the pushing strategy is. No matter how far along in the potty training process—whether they are two years old or whether they are four and a half—pushing is extremely important because that is how they are training themselves to go. This is especially true when it comes to number 2.

Now, some kids will want to go in number 2 in their diaper or a pull up. They will actually go and ask their parent for a pull up or a diaper to go number 2. Now, if this is the case for you, what you want to realize is the pull up then becomes a security blanket for the child.

In this case, what you might say is something to the effect of, "Okay, if you go number 2, then we'll put the pull up on." What that says is, "If you go number 2 first then we'll get the pull up." Now, something else I've had parents do is actually go get the pull up, let them put the pull up on only around their ankles. That way, they have their security blanket on, and they can feel it, and they can see it, yet they're sitting on the toilet. This allows them to use the bathroom and feel comfortable.

The other thing you want is to make sure that you give them is more fluids as I explained earlier. And you will also want to make sure to track their schedule. A lot of kids will go to the bathroom for number 2 at the same time or around the same time every day. With my youngest son, it was like clockwork. Within 30 minutes of him eating anything, he would go to use the potty and do number 2. So, we always knew after he ate that he was going to use the bathroom. Using a potty training journal is helpful.

If you don't have a potty journal and a potty chair or a potty chart, you can get yourself a potty training chart and journal to track when they go to the bathroom. Let's say you find that they go after dinner, which is around the time frame of 7:00 in the evening. Well, what happens is you're still using the same consistency as using number 1 which is every 20 minutes except now you are watching for 7 o'clock to come around because you know that they're going to be using the bathroom within a half hour.

At this point, what you want to do is time the bathroom use. You want to get them on the toilet but you also want to make sure that they stay on the toilet long enough to use the bathroom or use the bathroom to do number 2. their underwear again. It's going to help them make sure they use the bathroom the next time they go.

5.4 When they finally get it right

Alright, now you're taking them to the bathroom every 20 minutes and you go 3 days and you are not getting any accidents. Don't make the mistake that most parents make as I mentioned very early on. This is the stage when many parents decide that, "My child is potty trained and there was nothing left for me to do." This is the point in time where you want to be more consistent, more consistent, and more consistent.

This is when you want to make sure that you are still taking them to the bathroom every 20 minutes or you might change the interval from 20 minutes to 30 minutes. You might even feel comfortable waiting even longer than that - maybe 45 minutes. But don't let 45 minutes to an hour go by that you are not taking your child to the bathroom. Let me give you an example why this is. Your body has to get what's called "muscle memory." Remember at this point the child is only in stage 3 of potty training.

That's where they know what they're doing. They know what's wrong but they're thinking about it. It's not subconscious yet. At this point in time, the child is still thinking, "Should I go; should I not go? Where should I go? What should I do?" Think about it this way: Michael Jordan is one of the best basketball players that have ever played the game, yet even when he was scoring 30, 40, 50 points a game, he was still shooting and practicing for hours a day, taking 500 to 600 foul shots every single day. Even though he was the best there was, he was still practicing harder than anybody else.

That is the difference between regular athletes and professionals. The professionals, they practice harder than anybody else because when they get into a situation, they do not have to think about it, the body automatically reacts. So, that's why when your child is finally starting to get it, you have to then make sure you maintain the consistency.

Chapter 6

Build Empath With Your Child

How do you get them to start telling you? Basically the question is how do we get your child from Stage 3 to Stage 4? And Stage 4 is where they can go to the bathroom themselves. They recognize on their own, they don't need you to take them to the bathroom every 20 minutes. Basically, its complete autonomy and freedom for the child and complete autonomy and freedom for you... So, the question is, "How do we get to that stage?" With consistency. You have to be consistent.

Once they start to show you they are ready, you have to make sure that you are continually being consistent. The other thing you can do is you can play the game that I call the "let's race to the potty game." All you do is sit at the table with your child and you say, "Okay, let's see who can get to the potty first and whoever wins gets a prize." So, basically it's a race between you and the child, and, of course, you're going to let the child win (but they don't know that).

Then, you pick a good reward of something that they're going to enjoy or really like. To start the race they have to say the words, "Mommy, I have to go potty." That's the cue. It's like saying "1, 2, 3, set go." But instead of saying "1, 2, 3, set go," they say, "Mommy I have to go potty". Once they say that, the race begins, so the both of you run to the bathroom and the first one that gets to the bathroom wins the game. What this does is gets the child used to saying, "I have to go potty," and then the next steps are them going to the bathroom.

You want to practice this probably two or three times a day once you find that they are starting to be more consistent with no accidents. You don't want to start this game while they're in the potty training process because they've got enough to worry about. So, you want to start this only after you've seen that they have finally gotten it and they're starting to do pretty well on their own.

6.1 How to Use Positive Practice for Accidents

Another useful technique is positive practice for accidents. Dr. Schaefer describes this as what you should do when your child has an accident and wets or soils himself.

This technique involves firmly telling your child what he has done, taking him to the potty where he can clean and change himself (although you will likely need to help) and then having him practice using the potty. Dr. Schaefer recommends going through the usual steps of using the potty at least five times, starting when "the child walks to the toilet, lowers his pants, briefly sits on the toilet (3 to 5 seconds), stands up, raises his pants, washes his hands, and then returns to the place where the accident occurred."

Although you are trying to teach him the consequences of having an accident, this should not take the form of punishment.

6.2 Children Tantrums

Tantrums are going to happen. A tantrum is frustration. That's the child not being able to verbally explain or talk about their emotion. So, the only way they know how to do that is through screaming and pitching a fit. Here's how you handle a tantrum... What you don't want to do is make potty training a battle. It's not a battle between you and the child, but the child is trying to battle you.

The child is trying to be in charge, and you're trying to be in charge at the same time. So, sometimes the way that you handle that is to totally ignore the tantrum. If your child is throwing a tantrum, you can walk away and say, "Mommy is not listening to you.

Mommy will talk to you when you are calmed down," or "Mommy is not listening to you when your voice is louder than Mommy's." So you can turn around and use reverse psychology by turning the tables on your child. Once they have calmed down, you will want to say in a very strong and direct voice, "Mommy did not appreciate that," or "Grandma did not appreciate that," or "Daddy did not appreciate that behavior.

We expect better things. Let's go and try again." So, now you go right back to the basics and you take the child back to the bathroom and say, "We are going to use the bathroom and here's what we expect." If they throw a tantrum again, you walk away.

Mind you, while that tantrum is going on, do not give them any rewards. Do not allow them to play with their toys. They are not allowed to do any of that fun stuff that they normally would want to do because you want to associate that tantrum with a bad behavior that results in loosing something.

So, the most important thing I can tell you is to ignore the tantrum, don't pay attention to it because as the laws of physics say, "For every action, there's an equal and opposite reaction." If you react to that tantrum, they are going to react to you. Once you react, they react. You react again, they react and it's going to escalate even more.

So, the easiest way to squash it is not to put in the energy toward that tantrum. Once the child feels and sees that they're not getting energy out of you, then they realize that they're getting nothing by throwing this tantrum and there's nothing to be gained from it.

6.3 Regression in potty Training

What is a regression? A regression is a child that was potty trained, they were doing well, or they were starting to do well and for whatever reasons, they have done an about-face. Now, they are wetting themselves or they are soiling their diapers with poop. The question is "What really is the regression? What are the cause and the root of that regression?" These are the issues that need to be dealt with. Usually a regression is not so much an issue with potty training, but it's an emotional issue. The child will regress as a way to get attention or as a way of expression.

So, most parents deal with regression by dealing with potty training, but the reality is the best way to deal with a regression is to try to find the underlying root cause. It could be one of many things causing the regression. A new baby being born, you've moved, a friend has moved, a family member might have passed away... Something has happened in that child's life and they don't know how to express it except through regression.

Something that a lot of parents have asked is, "When it comes to potty training, we've got a new baby on the way, should I wait to have the baby or will they regress if I potty train them and then we have the baby?" The best thing to do is to potty train them now.

It is a lot easier to retrain a child that has been trained and has gone through a regression than it is to try to train a child that has never been trained. In addition to that as a parent, if you are having a new baby coming, you do not want to have a new baby and potty training duties at the same time. That's very, very, difficult. What I always tell parents is that they'll only need two to three days to get the child to Stage 3. Stage 4 is what will take you a couple of days from there. Some kids even get to Stage 4 in one day.

But the key is, take the two or three days, get your child to Stage 3, then through consistency, work toward getting them to Stage 4. When the new baby comes, or whatever that activity is—whether it's a vacation or a move—if they do regress, they've already been trained. Getting them back and reversing the regression is going to be a lot easier than if you had never started at all. So what you want to do when your child does regress is you go back to the basics. This includes them being on the toilet every 20 minutes for

3-5 minutes. They will continue to do that until they stop the regressive behavior.

The only time our youngest had a regression, I went on a business trip with Greg. Lorenzo had been fully potty trained for about three months both day and night. Then I went on that business trip with my husband, and Lorenzo went to stay at Grandma's. We only were gone Thursday, Friday, and Saturday and came back on Sunday. When we returned, it was as if this child had never seen a potty chair or had been potty trained in his life. Now I have no idea what happened in those four days. Maybe Grandma had let him do whatever he wanted, I do not know. Or maybe he just said, "You know what? You guys left me, and I'm going to fix you guys." Basically, we took him back to the basics, went back to every 20 minutes with him on the toilet. And within about a day, he was back to normal. But it was a little scary seeing that happen.

6.4 Addressing fear in the kids

What you want to do is separate the difference between a fear of the toilet and potty training. Many of the parents that we have worked with have lumped the two into one category by saying that the fear of the toilet is a potty training problem. The reality is that a fear of the toilet has nothing to do with potty training, and, in most cases, it is a fear of the toilet as we noted earlier. So what you have to do is address that fear by sitting and asking your child. Don't be afraid to do this. Just ask them what they are afraid of.

Sometimes it might not be the potty training, but something else. One of the things that you can do to help your child if there is a fear of the toilet is get yourself a potty chair or potty seat insert. An insert is actually put into the toilet and the child can sit on that toilet instead of the adult seat, which is especially helpful if the child is a little bit smaller.

They are usually colorful and have giraffes on them and dinosaurs. There is also a handle so the child can hold on to the handle and balance themselves. This will help them feel safe and comfortable without the fear of falling into the toilet. Placing a step stool under their feet will also assist them in this area. But, if you find that they have a fear of the toilet, then a potty training chair will be the way to go instead of the insert.

Now the question is this, if there's a fear of the toilet, what is the cause of that fear? Sometimes it can be pain that the child has when they are going to the bathroom. This is especially true with number 2. So the question is, have they ever had diarrhea or have they ever had a diaper that was on too long which caused a skin irritation? They are now associating the toilet and potty with that pain.

It might possibly be constipation. As an adult, constipation can be very painful. So, think about the child. It also might not be actual constipation, but some kids naturally have hard stools and letting that go can be extremely painful for them. If that is the case, you want to make sure that you take a look when your child does use the bathroom more if they are in their diaper. Is their stool harder or is it soft? Was there any illness like the stomach virus or anything that caused them some pain? These are all the things that can cause the child to be not only fearful of the toilet, but can also cause a child to regress. So you want to be careful about this and ask yourself whether any of this has happened.

If you find the child has hard stool, one of the things that you can do is start giving the child more water, less sugar, and less starchy items, which will help them become hydrated. When the body becomes dehydrated, it will start to pull any fluids that it can get wherever it can get it. One of the places that it pulls the fluid from is going to be the stomach and the intestines. And once those fluids are pulled out, the result is hardened stool.

Once that stool becomes hard it's going to be very difficult and very painful for that child to go to the bathroom. So having fluids in the system will help give him or her softer stool. Something else that you can do if there is a fear of the toilet is calling it by a different name. Instead of calling it "potty," you can give it another name that doesn't bear a negative connotation. Something simple might be, "Let's go push."

Another thing that will help you make the experience more enjoyable for the child is to place books by the toilet. You should also have some toys in the bathroom or let them bring some toys with them so that it's a comfortable environment and something that is more fun for them. Again, the key is making it a loving time and not a stressful time. If you can read to them or let them look at picture books, it turns into more of an enjoyable process and a less stressful process.

6.5 Potty training Twins or multiple children

I have many parents with twins or multiples ask if this method can work for them. I also have parents with children at two different ages ask if the children can be potty trained simultaneously. The answer to both of these situations is "YES". You can potty train twins, multiples and two or more children at the same time. It's more demanding on you, and may take a few extra days, but it can be done.

If I, personally, had to choose between potty training multiples simultaneously or doing it one-at-a-time, I would bite the bullet and do them all at the same time; "just be done with it." Having someone to help out is by far the best way. Be sure they read the guide. Discuss with them how you want situations handled. The two of you need to handle things identically. You can go it alone if you need to. Just be mentally prepared for some extra work. Also, the children must be right by your side at all times. If one child needs to use the restroom, ask the other child to come with. The underlying principle for potty training two or more children simultaneously is that you need to treat each child as an individual.

Ideally, each child should have their own potty chair. They should each have their own underclothes and their own favorite treats and favorite drinks. Be sure to not use one's successes against the other child or children. Don't say things like, "See, Johnny can do it. Now you need to too." Just because one child might catch on right away doesn't mean that the other child / children will get it the first day or two. Keep in mind that they are individuals and that they may catch on at different times.

6.6 Help from daycare provider

If your child is in daycare be sure to discuss with your daycare providers your plan a day or two before you start. Explain to them that when your child returns to daycare that they are not to put a pull-up or diaper on the child. They may come back to you and say that if the child has an accident, they will put a diaper on the child.

Gently remind them about the importance of being consistent, about how that would send mixed signals to the child, and could undo all the progress you've worked so hard to achieve, and that you greatly appreciate their support. Maybe even offer a pair of movie tickets. You or your spouse may need to take Friday or Monday off from work to give this method the best possible chance for success. Do not put your child in daycare during the three days. It's just too soon.

Day 4 is the earliest that I recommend returning your child to daycare.

Sometimes you may just have to play it by ear. At the end of day 3, if the whole toilet thing has not "clicked" with your child, you may need to take the next day off from work. The "clicking" or "getting it" needs to occur before the child returns to daycare. If your daycare provider is not on board with you then you might have a set back or two. I've never had my kids in daycare but many of the moms that I've helped potty train have kids in daycare.

There are many wonderful daycare providers out there and they are willing to work with the parents but there are some that want nothing to do with helping the parents out. They want the child in a pull-up or diaper until they leave for school. If your daycare provider is one that isn't willing to support you during this training you might need to spend an extra day or two at home to make sure that there are no more accidents and that the child is confident in his new skill. You may need to be firm with your daycare provider with regards to your "no diaper" position.

If you are concerned about your daycare provider putting a pull-up or diaper back on your child, you might want to try Pods. Pods are little thin strips you place in your little ones underwear. These strips will absorb any accident your child has so he doesn't make a "mess" on the floor. Your child will feel the strips turn to a cold jell like substance and asked to go to the bathroom. The daycare provider can then just replace the strip. Pods can be the solution for those hard to work with daycare providers.

6.7 Travelling and Errands during potty Training

Alright, let's face the fact. You are a busy Mom or busy Dad or a busy Grandparent or a busy potty trainer. But you don't want to be stuck in the house during that potty training process. And yes —for a day or two you might be. But don't let potty training keep you from enjoying life and having fun and doing the things that you got to do.You may have shopping to do and errands to run. You might have a family to take care of. You've got things that you need to do. So here are some tips that will help you have a more successful potty training experience especially when you have things that you need to do.

First of all, you want to get yourself a spill-proof travel potty. If you don't have one, try to get one online travel and get yourself a spill-proof travel potty. Basically, it is a simple little potty chair which has a spill-proof lid. With that, you can keep it in the car so instead of having to be home to go to the bathroom every 20 minutes. You can be in the mall, you can be at the grocery store, you can be out shopping, and your child can still use the potty without the fear of having accidents. When you are travelling or you're going to run errands, what you want to do is just like with the day care scenario, you want to use the bathroom before you leave. You will also want to plan your day and where you will be going so you'll be prepared about whether or not those places have bathrooms.

In other words, if you are going to place A and they have a bathroom and place B, does not have a bathroom, then you want to go to place B first right when you leave the house because your child has just gone. Once we would get to a location like a grocery store or a mall, especially if this is a grocery store or a mall that you've never been to, we would find the bathroom. So now, let's say we are out in the middle of shopping and Lorenzo had to go to the bathroom. It's wasn't a problem.

As soon as he said he had to go to the bathroom or we said, "Lorenzo, do you have to go to the bathroom?" and he said, "Yes," we knew where the bathrooms were. Most parents don't take that one step so what happens is the child says, "I have to go to the bathroom," the parents are in a state of panic to find the bathrooms. So, when we first got to the store, we would find the bathroom and then go to the bathroom. We would then get our most important stuff done first because we knew we just went to the bathroom and had more free time now than we might later. So, the smaller, less important things could wait. Back to the travel potty, these are really great because they will also help you out when you are going to take a long road trip. If you don't have one, you know that stopping frequently is going to be an issue.

When Lorenzo was 2 years and 2 weeks, we had him fully potty trained and we took a trip to Florida. Back then, we were at Code Orange, and the government said it wasn't a good idea to fly. So, we decided to take a bus with three kids from Connecticut to Florida. It was a thirty-hour bus ride with a child that just finished potty training. To tell you it was a challenge is an understatement. Back then, there weren't spill-proof potty chairs so we didn't have one to bring, so we bought a huge 2 litre bottle. Every 20 minutes on the bus, we would hide in the corner or go into to the back and say, "Okay Lorenzo, pee into the bottle," and that's what he did. When he had to go number 2 luckily for us, was during a rest stop. But we didn't let the fact that he had the potty train keep us from doing what we had to do.

Chapter 7

Introduction To ADHD

7.1 What exactly is ADHD?

Occasionally forgetting their schoolwork, daydreaming during class, acting without thought process, or getting impulsive at the dinner table is normal. Yet carelessness, impulsivity, and hyperactivity also are symptoms of awareness deficit hyperactivity syndrome (ADHD), also called antisocial personality disorder or Attach.

ADHD is a prevalent neurological condition typically occurring in early childhood, usually before seven years of age. ADHD makes it hard for kids to hinder their aggressive behavior responses which can involve anything from motion to speech, to attention. We all know kids who cannot sit still, and never seem to pay attention, who do not follow the instructions regardless of how obviously you express them, or who blur out insulting remarks at inconvenient moments. Such kids are often branded as miscreants or blamed for being idle and undisciplined. They may have ADHD however.

Is it ADHD or is it a normal kid behavior?

Differentiating among ADHD as well as normal "kid behavior" could be challenging. unless you spot only a few other symptoms, or even the results occur only in a few circumstances, it's definitely not really ADHD. On the other side, if a kid displays a variety of signs or symptoms of ADHD that are apparent in any scenario — at home, in school, and then at play — it's time to look closely. Life with such a kid with ADHD can be stressful and daunting, however, as a parent you can do a lot to better manage symptoms, resolve everyday struggles, and make the family more relaxed.

ADHD Misconception and Realties

Misconception: Every kid with ADHD is hyperactive.

Reality: Many Kids with ADHD seem overactive, but far too many may not have issues with concentration. Kid with ADHD who've been intentional and not overly energetic may seem spacious and unambitious.

Misconception: Kid with ADHD will never take heed.

Reality: Kids with ADHD often can focus on the actions they appreciate. However, no matter what they've done; whenever the task ahead is dull or repetitive those who have trouble keeping the focus.

Misconception: If they wished, Kid with ADHD might behave better.

Reality: Kids with ADHD might be doing their utmost to be better, but they are still unable to sit even now, stay quiet, or be careful. They may seem disobedient but that doesn't mean they act purposefully.

Misconception: In the end, kids who grew up out of ADHD.

Reality: ADHD also continues on into adulthood so don't wait before your kid overcomes the issue. Therapy will help the kid understand how to control the effects and mitigate them.

Misconception: ADHD is better handled with drugs.

Reality: Medicine is sometimes recommended for bipolar disorder but it may not be your kid's best choice. Effective ADHD treatment also education programs, behavioral therapy, school and home support, workout, and healthy eating.

7.2 What's really ADHD like?

Since many people seem to think about bipolar disorder, those who portrait a kid in perpetual movement out of control, jumping off the doors as well as interrupting everybody around. The reality, however, is far more complicated. A few other kids with ADHD are overactive whereas others sit in silence with miles away from their attention. A few put too much emphasis on an assignment and have difficulty changing it to another. Some are only slightly inattentive but excessively impulsive. A kid with bipolar disorder has the signs and effects based on which traits prominent.

ADHD Diagnosed Kids may be

- Inattentional, but neither excitable nor hyperactive.
- Excitable and reckless, but capable of paying close attention.
- The most prevalent type of ADHD is unobservant, excitable, and impetuous.
- Kids who now have unobservant signs of ADHD are sometimes ignored, even though they're not destructive. The signs of distraction, however, have implications: having in warm water with teachers and parents for just not understanding things; outperforming at school; as well as challenging with the other kids over failing to play by regulations.

ADHD Spotting at Various Ages

Even though we assume very small kids to also be easily forgetful as well as excitable, it is the impetuous behaviors that often speak out during preschool kids with ADHD — the harmful jump, the blurred insult. However, by the age of four as well as five, most kids have managed to learn to pay more attention to everyone else, to stay quiet when commanded, and to not say something which keeps popping into their minds. Therefore, people with ADHD stick out with all three activities by the time they hit school age: impatience, excitable, and implicit.

7.3 ADHD Symptoms and Signs of Inattentiveness

It's not really that kid of ADHD can't even pay interest: whenever they do things that they cherish or hear regarding topics that they're involved in, they don't have difficulty concentrating as well as accomplish work. However, when the job becomes tedious or repetitive, they easily turn in.

Another growing challenge is keeping on line. Kids with ADHD sometimes jump through the project to project without finishing either of these or miss systematic steps that are required. They consider it easier to coordinate the classwork and leisure time than for other people. Kids with ADHD may have difficulty coping while events happen near each other; they typically require a secure, peaceful atmosphere to remain concentrated.

Inattention Symptoms in Kids

• It seems to have a problem keeping centered; it can be easily swayed or frustrated with an assignment before it has been finished.
• Doesn't seem to pay heed when talking to.
• It seems to have trouble concentrating as well as obeying orders; it doesn't really take care of information or make simple errors.
• It seems to have trouble organizing, making plans, and completing plans.
• Loses or sometimes makes mistakes assignments, books, toys, or other things.

7.4 ADHD Symptoms and Signs of Hyperactivity

Impulsivity is by far the most directly impacted by ADHD. Although several kids are usually very busy kids are also running with excitable signs of bipolar disorder. They can attempt to do multiple things one after the other, jumping through one task to another. And if they are compelled to stay quiet, which may be really challenging for kids, the foot will stamp, their knee will twitch or the fingertips can beat.

Hyperactivity Symptoms in Kids

- Winces or wiggles continuously
- Has trouble staying awake even now, trying to play still or soothing
- Keeps moving around as well, frequently runs as well as climb up improperly
- Conversations overstated
- Might have had a fast temper, or "soft trigger"

7.5 ADHD Symptoms and Signs of Impulsiveness

Kids with ADHD impulsive behavior can cause self-control issues. Since they control themselves rather than other kids do, they can disrupt discussions, violate the privacy of other adults, pose trivial class questions, make presumptuous comments, and pose excessively specific questions. Directions such as "Be careful" and "Wait somewhat longer" are double as challenging for ADHD kids to adopt than they really are for many other young people.

Kids with impetuous signs and ADHD symptoms also appear to still be grumpy and have an emotional overreaction. As a consequence, some might start viewing the kid as disrespectful, strange, or vulnerable.

Impulsiveness Symptoms in Kids

- Unthinking behavior. Rather of wasting hours to address a dilemma or blurring solutions in the classroom without asking for the entire issue to be answered or understood
- Intrudes into discussions or playing with other individuals

- Sometimes delays others; only at the wrong moment, picks the dumbest stuff
- Reluctance to hold intense feelings in place, culminating in furious outbursts as well as aggressive behaviors.

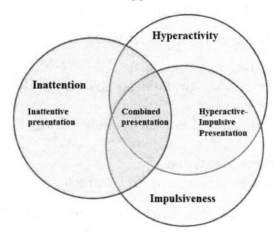

7.6 ADHD Positive Aspects of Kids

ADHD has neither intelligence nor talent. Moreover, kids with bipolar disorder often show the following good attributes: Creativity – kids with ADHD may be extremely inventive and innovative. The kid who sees daytime and has ten separate thoughts at once will become a problem-solver leader, a generator of inspiration, or an imaginative maker. Kids with ADHD may be overwhelmed quickly, but often they note something others don't.

Flexibility – Since adolescents with ADHD are exploring multiple choices at once, they don't get fixed up early on one solution and are much more open to various suggestions.

The excitement and spontaneity-ADHD kids never get bored! They are involved in several different items and have a vivid personality. In brief, they're a lot of fun to work with if they don't exasperate you (and occasionally even if they are).

Energy or even drive – Working or playing hard whenever kids of ADHD are inspired and strive for success. In fact, distracting others from either an assignment that fascinates them can be difficult, particularly if another action is interactive or thumbs-on.

7.7 Is it ADHD, Really?

And even if a kid has a lack of attention, impatience, or even hyperactivity symptoms doesn't really mean if he or she also has ADHD. Some health issues, psychotic conditions, as well as stressful events in life may be causing side effects that seem like ADHD. Until the proper diagnosis of such ADHD could be made, it is essential to see a very mental health issues specialist to discuss several following prospects and to rule out them:

- Having difficulties like literacy, writing, communication ability like language issues.
- Stressful events or emotional trauma (for example a recent move, a loved one 's death, harassment, break up).
- Mental abnormalities including anxiety, bipolar disorder, and depression.
- Psychosocial disorders as well such as disorder of conduct, a reactive disorder of attachment, and as well as oppositional disorder of defiance.
- Health issues include concerns with liver, psychiatric diseases, autism, and sleeping disturbances.

7.8 Supporting an ADHD Kid

Regardless or not the signs of carelessness, hyperactivity, and implicit in kids are related to ADHD, if kept unchecked they will trigger several issues. Kids who cannot concentrate and monitor themselves might also struggle with reading, encounter repeated problems, and find it difficult to get along or make friends with others. These frustration, anger, and hardships could even give rise to low self-esteem, friction, and tension for the entire family.

But care may make a noticeable change in the effects of your infant. Your kid could get on the path to success in all aspects of life, only with the right support. If your kid suffers from ADHD-like signs, don't try to get medical support. Without a prognosis of bipolar disorder, you can treat the symptoms of impulsivity, inattention, and impulsivity in your kid. Choices to start with involve bringing your kid through therapy, adopting a healthy diet and fitness schedule, and improving the home atmosphere through eliminating distractions.

When you have an ADHD diagnosis, then you should consult with the psychiatrist, educator, and school of your kid to develop a customized recovery program that fits their individual needs. Effective childhood treatment for ADHD includes cognitive-behavioral treatment, parent training, and education, social protection, and school assistance. Medicine could also be utilized; even so, treatment of deficit disorder should not be the sole focus of attention.

ADHD Kid Parenting Tips

Whether the kid is overactive, forgetful, or hyperactive, it can require a great deal of effort to just get him and her to hear, complete a job or stay still. The continuous tracking can be boring and irritating. You might feel like your kid runs the show occasionally. Yet there are actions you may take to recover ownership of the circumstance, thus having your kid make the best from his or her talents at the same time.

While antisocial personality dysfunction is not impacted by terrible parenting, positive parenting tactics could go a huge responsibility for correcting behaviors of problems. Kids with ADHD require order, discipline, direct contact, incentives, and behavioral effects. They just need a lot of love, encouragement, and support.

Parents can do many things to decrease the symptoms and signs of ADHD without compromising the energy resources, cheekiness, as well as a sense of optimism that is distinctive throughout every kid.

Take good care of yourself, so that you can look after your kid better. Eat well, workout, get more sleep, focus on reducing stress, and pursue face-to-face help from friends and family, as well as physicians and teachers for your kid.

Create and adhere to structure. Help your kids remain centered and disciplined by observing everyday rituals, streamlining the timetable for your kid and keep your kid occupied with safe activities.

Set expectations that are clear. Simplify the rules of conduct and illustrate what might occur when they are accepted or broken — and obey through with a prize or a consequence each time.

Encourage sleep and exercise. Exercise boosts mental focus and encourages growth in the brain. Importantly, it also contributes to improved sleep for adolescents with ADHD, and in effect will reduce the ADHD symptoms.

Help your kid eat well. Healthy balanced meals or snacks are scheduled every 3 hours to manage ADHD symptoms and reduce spending on stuff and sugary snacks.

Teach kids how to make buddies. Support him or her to become a stronger listener, try to understand expression and sign gestures of men, and communicate with others more easily.

ADHD Kid Schooling Tips

Clearly, ADHD is getting in the manner of learning. If you're actually running all around the school classroom or pass out on whatever you're perceived to have been reading and listening to, you cannot understand things or even get one's work done. Think about what kids need to do in the school environment: sit still. Plainly listen. Lookout. Follow directions. Stay focused. This is the same activities that kids of ADHD have trouble doing not that they're unable, even though their minds won't make them.

But it doesn't mean that perhaps kids of ADHD can't succeed in school. Almost all teachers and parents can do many things to help kids of ADHD adapt in the classroom. It begins by identifying the unique vulnerabilities and capabilities of each infant and comes up with innovative approaches to help the kid concentrate, keep on track, and develop to its maximum potential.

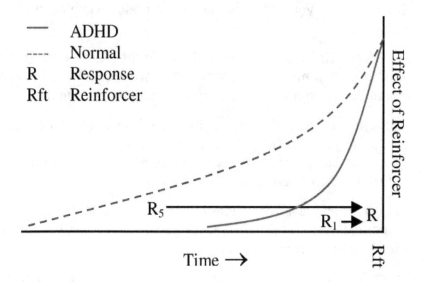

Chapter 8

Adhd Diagnosed Kids Treatments

8.1 Treatment Options for ADHD

Care for hyperactivity deficient concentration deficiency (ADD or ADHD) isn't about taking drugs. There are also other successful therapies that can help adolescents with ADHD enhance care, reduce impulsive behavior, and mitigate hyperactivity. Healthy food, playing and running, developing new coping strategies, and improving cognitive skills all are part of a healthy recovery program that will enhance the success of your kid at school, reinforce interactions with anyone, and alleviate depression and frustration for them and your entire family.

8.2 ADHD Medications

Drugs like Adderall and Ritalin are sometimes recommended for ADHD, but they may not be your kid's only option and they're definitely not only medication.

ADHD medicines can help your kids focus better, or seated still, throughout the short period at least. Yet there is no proof to date that in the long run, they are strengthening student success, marriages, or behavioral problems. And also, in a brief period, medication will not solve all of the problems or eliminate the ADHD symptoms completely.

In fact, there are questions regarding the impact such potent medications can have on the growing brain of an infant. And the side effects such as irritability, appetite loss, and insomnia can be problematic as well.

Everybody reacts to ADHD medicine differently. Some kids are experiencing significant improvement whereas others have next to no relief. The adverse effects often vary from kid to kid and for others, the advantages are much outweighed. It takes time to find the right treatment and dose, as everyone reacts differently.

ADHD medication is more useful when taken with other therapies. If they also take advantage of many other medications that teach healthy coping strategies, your kid may get far more out of their medication.

Medicines with ADHD should always be monitored closely. Drug treatment for ADHD includes more than just taking and forgetting about a pill. The doctor of your kid would need to evaluate adverse effects, check up on how your kid feels, and tweak the doses accordingly. When ADHD medicines are not carefully monitored, they are less effective and riskier.

When you choose to keep your kid on medication, it doesn't mean they 're going to have to stay there forever. While bouncing off is not healthy, even regularly on every medicine, you can easily opt to avoid using drugs to control your kid's ADHD if things don't go well. Unless you want the kid to stop getting treatment please let your doctor know about your schemes and operate with them to slowly tap off the drugs.

8.3 Treatment for ADHD Begins at Home

Being a parent, you do have an enormous impact on the treatment of your kid. Data proves that eating healthily, exercising, and allowing other intelligent daily choices could even help your kid handle ADHD symptoms. Which ensures your kid will continue ADHD therapy today at home. Physical exercise instantly increases the rates of norepinephrine, serotonin, and dopamine in the brain all of which influence concentration and concentrate.

The workout is one of the simplest and most successful approaches to reduce ADHD symptoms. Workout and ADHD drugs such as Adderall and Ritalin function closely in this manner. Yet unlike treatment for Add, rehabilitation requires no medication and is completely risk-free.

In specific, sports that include careful attention to body motions such as dancing, gymnastics, skateboarding, and martial arts are ideal for kids with ADHD. Group sports are a nice idea too. These are held important by the social dimension.

Sleep Importance in Treatment of ADHD

Daily sleep quality will contribute to significant enhancement in ADHD symptoms. Many kids with ADHD possess difficulty getting to fall asleep though. Such sleep disturbances are often induced by stimulant drugs, and the issue can be fixed by raising the dosage or avoiding the drug entirely.

Nevertheless, a large number of kids with ADHD who don't really take stimulants also have sleep problems. The following advice will aid if your kid is one of these.

Create and follow a daily bedtime routine. Switch off all the electronic gadgets (Televisions, laptops, smartphones, games) min one hour before sleeping. Limit nighttime physical activity.

Healthy Diet May Help Reduce Symptoms of ADHD

Research suggests that what you consume and what can create a difference in handling ADHD. Timetable daily snacks or meals not more than 3 hours apart. This should help to maintain blood sugar steady for your infant, reducing irritability and promoting attention and concentrate. At each meal or snack try to include a small amount of protein as well as complex carbs. Such items, although reducing hyperactivity, can make your kid experience more aware.

Test the amounts of iron, magnesium, and zinc on your kid. Such essential minerals are small in many kids with ADHD. Scaling up their rates will help regulate symptoms of ADHD. Growing iron can be hugely beneficial. One research showed effects changed with an iron substitute almost as well as when consuming stimulant drugs.

Adding Omega-Three fatty acids to the diet for your kids. Studies suggest that Omega-3s decrease impulsivity and hyperactivity, and improve focus with ADHD in kids as well as adults. Omega-Three is present in cod, sardines, and trout as well as some enriched eggs and milk. The simplest way to enhance your kid's intake, though, is through additional fish oil.

8.4 ADHD Professional Treatment

As there are several approaches you might support a kid experiencing ADHD at the household, they might want to receive medical assistance along its way. ADHD experts can assist you in developing an effective methodology for your kid. Seeing that ADHD often leads to a variety of therapies and approaches, it is important to contact multiple clinicians. You will want to call your acute care practitioner, your kid's pediatrics, nearby clinics, or hospitals to locate service options for ADHD. Other alternatives for supplier citations involve your insurer, school officials at one's kid's school, or a counseling service for local parents.

Psychiatrists for Kids and Adolescent

- Diagnosing ADHD & prescribing medicines

Psychologists for Kids and Adolescent

- Diagnosing ADHD & giving speech therapy
- Assist individuals with ADHD to fully explore one 's sensations

Therapists for Cognitive Behavioral

- Establish behavior change programs at work, at school and at home
- Set clear behavioral and performance goals
- Support parents and instructors to maintain incentives and repercussions

Educational Experts

- Teaching strategies to excel in school
- Support kids with school lodging
- Encourage families on aid technologies

8.5 ADHD Behavioral Therapy

Behavioral counseling, commonly acknowledged as behavioral intervention, proved to be a very effective approach for ADHD kids. It is extremely helpful as a kid's treatment who are taking stimulant drugs and can also encourage you to reduce the drug dose.

Behavioral treatment includes improving positive habits through establishing boundaries and outcomes by incentives and affirmation and reducing troublesome behaviors. One intervention, for example, could be that an instructor benefits a kid with ADHD for taking small steps towards raising a hand before speaking in school, even though the kid still blurts a remark. The concept is that appreciating the fight to change promotes a whole new behavior.

ADHD Kids Behavioral Therapy

There seem to be three fundamental rules of every approach of behavior counseling as per the American Academy of Pediatrics:

- Set clear targets. Set clear objectives for the kid, like focusing entirely on some time 's homework or sharing toys with buddies.
- Offer bonuses and aftermath. Provide your kid with a defined incentive (good behavior) while displaying the correct behavior. Offer your kid a result (undesired effect or penalty) whether he or she refuses to reach a goal.
- Keep taking advantage of incentives and repercussions. Consistently utilizing the benefits and ramifications for a longer period will influence the behavior of your kid in a positive manner.

Being parents, with the aid of a behavioral psychologist or by a CBT consultant, you should set up a tailored behavioral intervention plan for your kid that has ADHD. A CBT psychiatrist revolves around realistic solutions to daily issues. This kind of psychiatrist can establish a benefits and risks behavior intervention system for the kid at school and at home, and help you shape the behavior of your kid.

Patience is essential to cognitive behavior therapy, as individuals with ADHD have extremely varying symptoms. Your kid might also start behaving brilliantly one day, and then the next, drop back to the traditional pattern. It may sometimes seem as if the workout is not working. Cognitive-behavioral therapy, though, does enhance ADHD effects over time.

Training of Social Skills

Since kids with ADHD also have difficulties with normal social relationships and cope with poor self-esteem, other forms of therapy that may improve is an instruction in social skills. Social skills teaching is generally operated in a group situation and is brought by a counselor who shows acceptable behavior and then has the kids practice reiterating them. A community of social skills shows kids how to "sense" the responses of others, and how to respond more satisfactorily. The group of social skills should also work to transfer those skills to the actual world. Ask your school counselor or a local medical clinic to relate you to a social skills place near oneself.

8.6 ADHD Kid Treatment Supporting Tips

Kids with ADHD often find it difficult to translate whatever they have learned from one adjusting to another. They might have learned to control irrational outbursts at school, for example, but interrupt others impatiently at home.

Kinder with ADHD needs stability to encourage progressive change throughout all settings. It is critical that parents with kids with ADHD learn to implement methods with behavioral therapy at home. Kids with ADHD are much more able to win when the duties occur in regular patterns and predictable places, so they know exactly and what to do.

Follow on with a routine. To help kids with ADHD grasp and meet expectations, it's good to set a time and place for everything. Set up quick and regular dinner, school, play, and bad habits. Utilize Timers and Clocks. Consider placing house-wide clocks, with a large one in your kid's bedroom. Give time for what one's kid wants to utilize in the morning, such as school assignments or getting prepared. Simplify the timetable for your kids. Avoiding idle time is a smart thing because if there are so many after-school events, a kid with ADHD can become much more overwhelmed and "wound up."

Set up a peaceful place. Ensure that the kid has his / her own quiet, private space. A porch or bedroom will fit well — as long as it's not the same location for a time-out as the kid goes. For successful management, set an example. Arrange the house in an ordered manner. Be sure that your kid understands that something has its location. As much as possible, the role model is neatness and organization.

8.7 Praise Importance

Please remember that kids with ADHD mostly get criticism as you develop a reliable routine and structure. Look out for positive conduct and applaud it. Praise is beneficial for kids with ADHD because they usually get less of it. The smiling face, positive statement, or other praise by you can enhance the attention, concentration, and control of your kid's impulses. Do the utmost to concentrate on providing constructive feedback for good actions and accomplishment of assignments, while offering as little derogatory reactions as possible to improper conduct or bad execution of tasks. Praise your kid for small accomplishments this will lead to bigger hits down the road.

Chapter 9

Causes Of ADHD

Since attention deficit impulsivity disorder (ADHD) signs lack of attention, aggression, and hyperactivity impact a kid's potential to understand and even get together with many others, certain may believe that the behavior of an ADHD kid is triggered by either a lack of knowledge, a dysfunctional home environment, or perhaps too much tv. Evidence currently shows ADHD is primarily a neurological disease. Some external conditions, though, may also play a part. Here we distinguish fact from opinion about ADHD reasons.

Pesticides

Investigation suggests a possible link between pesticides and ADHD. A 2010 research in pediatricians found higher rates of ADHD in kids with higher concentrations of outside organophosphate in the urine, an insecticide utilized on goods. Another study in 2010, had shown that people with a higher concentration of organophosphate in urine were much more probable to have a kid with ADHD

Drinking and Smoking in Pregnancy Period

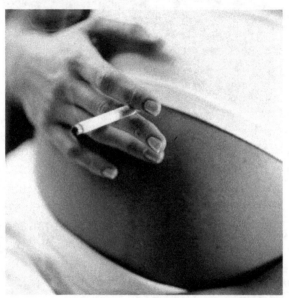

Deadly alcohol and tobacco exposure are believed to perform a role in ADHD. Kids who are prenatally subjected to cigarette smoke are 2.4 times more probable to have ADHD than people who are not, evidence indicates. "Fetuses subjected to alcohol may produce fetal alcohol or fetal alcohol disorder, and the signs you see of ADHD are common with both," said Mark L. Wolraich, MD, director of the Developmental as well as Behavioral Pediatrics division at the Institution of Oklahoma medical sciences complex, Oklahoma town.

Exposure to Lead

Neurotoxic substance lead has been eliminated from several households and classrooms but there are still signs of it everywhere. A 2009 research showed that kids with ADHD appeared to have higher rates of blood-leads than other adolescents. "Lead may be toxic to the development of brain tissue could have maintained impact on the development of exposing kids to such substances at an early age," said Leavitt, who is practicing under Richard Oelberger's supervision. "Still, such exposure is unlikely to account for brain differences advancement in the large majority of ADHD kids and teens."

Food Flavourings

After research, several European states have banned specific additives, which connected impulsivity in small kids to food only with blends of some and sodium preservative benzoic. The FDA said that when utilized "correctly," dietary supplements are safe, but most additives are not required to be evidently labeled on the packaging. Experts believe that a small percentage of kids will benefit from trying to avoid brightly colored foods that are processed and appear to have even more preservatives. "Seek advice with your kid's doctor before you put your kid on a specific diet," Leavitt says. Reducing the utilize of such preservatives may not contribute to excitable behavior; in ADHD many factors play a key role.

Sugar Intake

Mother and father often blame the excitable behavior of a kid for sugar but it is time to stop it. "The overpowering numerous studies have failed to show behavioral changes in kids due to sugar intake," said Dr. Wolraich. An investigation published in the journal of such unusual kid development found that women who thought that sugar was given to their kids assessed the behavior of their kids as being more excitable than moms who were told that a sugar substitute was given to their kids — irrespective as to whether their kids actually ingested real sugar. If you are worried regarding caloric intake or limit sugar, dental cavities, ADHD isn't the cause.

Video Games or TV

So there's no evidence that ADHD is caused by much TV as well as video game time, even if the research has suggested that school-age and college and high school-age learners who spent a lot of time next to a camera had much more attention difficulties than others who did not. The continuous exposure of television and video gaming will, in principle, make it easier for kids to pay focus. And yet experts stress that only screen time didn't comprehend ADHD. There's an affiliation between the (ADHD) and the number of more hour's young kids watch TV as well as play computer games, but much more study is needed to determine whether it's a causal connection or because kids with ADHD are gravitating more towards those actions," said by Dr. Wolraich.

Bad Kid Parenting

Symptoms of ADHD may be associated as disruptive or inappropriate conduct, and it's not unusual to seek to pin a kid's actions on the mother. But there is no significant evidence, as per the statewide counseling center at ADHD, too that authoritative parenting leads to ADHD.

"Although it's clear that authoritative parenting and social conditions can exacerbate ADHD habits, authoritative parenting is not the trigger of ADHD," said by Leavitt, that says family and friends who may have specific behavioral boundaries, using incentive and outcome behavioral strategies, and have a simple range of goals will help minimize symptoms of ADHD. But on the other side, the side effects can be made worse by a difficult living environment as well as parents who fail to admit ADHD as a medical condition.

Injuries of Brain

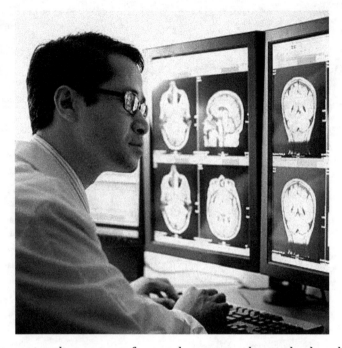

"Head trauma that occurs from a heavy stroke to the head, either neurological disorder, an injury, or illness may trigger inattention issues and impaired control of physical function and tendencies," Leavitt notes. But due to the community mental wellbeing Institute, kids with some forms of brain damage can have signs close to ADHD. But since only a limited percentage of adolescents with ADHD also experienced brain trauma, this is not deemed a significant risk indicator.

Heredity

The research clearly shows that caregivers pass on the ADHD, not the parental method.

"ADHD possesses a very proud legacy," Smith affirms. "It is perhaps one of the greatest inherited psychological conditions." Indeed, a kid is 4 times more likely to seems to have had a close relative who also was given a diagnosis with ADHD, and the results of various twin studies signify that ADHD frequently occurs in families. Continuing work seeks to classify the genes that are responsible more for ADHD. The latest analysis mostly by researchers at the University of Cardiff in Wales reported that kids to ADHD are far more actually likely to have more lacking or overlapped DNA segments.

Overdiagnosis for ADHD

Since there is no definitive check for ADHD, caregivers, physicians and educators are often arguing if ADHD is now over-diagnosed. A few say that physicians are too fast to diagnose behavioral issues in a kid as either ADHD without taking into consideration so many other possible reasons. Researchers at the Colorado state institute have found that kids who are so many inches shorter just like their peers may be accidentally medicated with ADHD when they are in fact only less smart, unlike their fellow students. Even so, as per said by Dr. Wolraich, "many other pieces of evidence are underrecognized with ADHD."

Exposure to Chemicals

Although cigarettes, alcohol, and insecticides can be an issue, observers are also going to look at other toxins. For example, researchers at the Boston school of public safety identified a correlation between the polyfluoroalkyl compound's industrial substances typically utilized in items such as stain-resistant coatings and packaged food — and ADHD. Phthalates-found in items such as gadgets, packaged food, and cosmetics-were also associated with ADHD. The proof, however, as with other causes, just points to a connection and cannot conclude that such chemicals lead to ADHD.

Chapter 10

Adhd Mindfulness Meditation & Hypnotherapy

10.1 What exactly is Mindfulness?

Mindfulness meditation sometimes called "mindful consciousness" or "mindfulness" is a type of cognitive therapy intended to alleviate tension, encourage self-control, and increase concentration. Caution takes several types. This may include relaxation techniques, visualizations, or the disappointingly simplistic act of giving further attention to what you are doing or what is around you.

Most researchers agree that mindfulness could help alleviate the effects of ADHD, such as hyperactivity and inattention, in adults and kids when practiced daily. It may also help relieve everyday tension, along with the more serious depression and anxiety symptoms which sometimes coexist with ADHD.

10.2 Is it Spiritual?

Knowledge is a feature of other faith practices. For starters, Buddhism incorporates a type of meditation on the mindset recognized as Vipassana, whereas some faiths view the act of prayer as a form of therapy.

Yet faith should not automatically be defined as moral or spiritual. It includes paying careful attention to the emotions, feelings, and body experiences in their most simple shape. In other terms, it involves having a better understanding of what occurs to you from minute to minute. Unless you want to, this could be spiritual, but it does have advantages that take place outside any spiritual or religious understandings.

And being mindful works mostly on your brain. It may be utilized as a tool (in accordance with adequate medical treatment) to foster their physical health. For managing chronic pain and reducing blood pressure, stress, and anxiety disorders, carefulness techniques were utilized.

10.3 How will individuals with ADHD be improved by being mindful?

Mindfulness helps you to give attention, which improves the "concentration muscle" over time. This operates by enhancing the capacity of an individual to regulate concentration, self-observe, and establish new attitudes to typically negative interactions. This will even help you more conscious of your emotional condition and you won't respond too impulsively often a major concern for ADHD-persons. Experts have discussed for some while about utilizing mindfulness to resolve Symptoms of ADHD, but the issue has still been how individuals with ADHD will really utilize it, especially if they are hyperactive. However, and new research demonstrates that perhaps the flexibility and versatility of mindfulness allows people with ADHD to fix things for themselves.

10.4 Working of Mindfulness Meditation

Practicing conscientious meditation implies paying more attention to the breath, thoughts, and body sensations. It means remaining in the most straightforward way (ideally standing quiet, where you are less likely to get distracted) and concentrating on the air while it moves in or out. As your mind wanders (and the utterly normal phenomenon even for those without ADHD!), just make an attempt to concentrate on the breathing.

Experts believe that doing this regular exercise for less as 5 mins at a time could even help you become more conscious of how one's attention strolls and give you techniques to regulate it in your everyday life. Even before you realize able to concentrate on one's breath for 5 mins at a time, the duration of your guided meditation increases gradually to enhance your endurance.

You should also exercise good feeding (watching out about what you consume and keeping your concentration on your food while your mind is running around). And you should incorporate deep sleep with certain forms of tension management such as yoga. For example, careful walking is indeed an option; yoga is yet another widely known way of integrating mindfulness into better living. Since you feel as if you need a bit more help, meditation techniques can help cope with a proper mindfulness practice, some of which are freely available online.

You should still practice your awareness. Turning on the "culture of mind-awareness" at every moment in the day, even if just for just a few moments, is excellent preparation that can long-term help the brain. Basically, you 're letting go of your thinking activities and turning your focus to what's occurring in real life in the current moment.

10.5 What if I cannot Concentrate?

It's the essence of the human mind that distracts us. That's why experts stress that distracting yourself doesn't mean you 're "failing," it just implies you 're a human being. Mindfulness consciousness is not about sticking with the air; it is about going back to the wind, even though you get interrupted. That's what improves your concentrating capacity and this concentration on changing the mind is what enables this approach especially beneficial to those with ADHD.

10.6 Who can do Mindfulness Meditation?

Almost everyone, of just about any age, might exercise mindfulness.

10.7 How much it costs?

Mindfulness is free and is practicable anywhere. There are brief courses or "mindfulness retreats," at different prices, but these are not required in order to cultivate a successful practice of mindfulness. For starters, it costs $185 for a six-week program at the MARC (Mindful Awareness Research Center) at the UCLA. Apps for Meditation, such as Zenytime or Calm, might help create more composition, and thus are usually available free of charge or at a minimal charge.

10.8 Researches About Mindfulness

Meditation work has risen significantly over the years. The core characteristics include:

• Decade-old research, published in the medical journal of Applied School Psychology, discovered that after an eight weeks meditation practice program kids with general cognitive deficits reveal significant improvements.

• A tiny, unregulated 2007 research reported in the Journal of Focus Disorders found that "Practice in mindfulness is a viable therapy in a subgroup of adolescents and adults with ADHD, and can enhance behavioral and neurological disabilities."

• A recent study has found that carefulness training for both ADHD parents and kids enhanced adherence with kids, resulting in greater overall happiness with home life for kids and parents.

• In 2007, a UCLA group completed a joint-type study involving twenty-five individuals and eight teenagers, half of whom had ADHD. Subjects made substantial gains in both hyperactivity and inattention, increased their performance on cognitive tests, and recorded becoming "less worked out" by the end of the analysis.

• In 2013 the Journal of Family and Kid Research released a report named "The Importance of Awareness Instruction for Kids with ADHD and Conscientious Discipline for their Parents." This research review "evaluated the efficacy of an 8-week carefulness program for kids aged 8 to 12 with ADHD and concurrent cautious parenting instruction for their parents." Following the 8-week program, they observed a substantial decrease in parent-reported Symptoms of ADHD, and also a decrease in parental tension and over-reaction. The research, however, discovered no progress in Symptoms of ADHD after the instructor-completed the assessment scale of the mindfulness program.

To present, 8 kinds of research have tested the effect and usefulness of carefulness instruction in a therapeutic environment for adolescents and adults with ADHD and have shown positive results in this growing region.

Parents were given proactive leadership instruction in six experiments in conjunction with the kids' mindfulness study. Combining kid care preparation for ADHD for similar diligent parenting instruction appears to be a rational and balanced strategy that approaches both family and adult level ADHD. It would have the additional benefit that kids and parents actively demonstrate mindfulness, helping parents to better grasp what the infant is experiencing and assist them in improving awareness skills.

A new analysis involving eighteen adults with ADHD (Aged between 13 to 18) with their caregivers have utilized the MYmind approach. 4 weeks before the school, on the last and first preparation days and 6 weeks following completion, all teenagers and parents filling out surveys. There were no major improvements in the time before school. Compared to the scores of the guardians, the inattention of kids, handling conflicts, and peer interaction concerns increased dramatically immediately after instruction. In fact, parents viewed themselves as less anxious and more diligent in their upbringing. These outcomes were maintained during the 6-week aftermath, with further reduction in parental stress. Kids and teens didn't disclose any necessary changes after mentoring, but during the 6-week follow-up reported considerably fewer validating issues.

10.9 Training of Mindfulness for ADHD

ADHD is marked by inattention, impulsive, and hyperactive actions and is one of the most prevalent behavioral health issues, with 5 percent of kids currently fitting the diagnosis requirements. Medication is currently the best and prevalent treatment for ADHD. The last thirty years have witnessed a sharp increase in opioid prescriptions for ADHD, with about 70 percent of kids and teenagers currently seeking treatment being ADHD diagnosed in the USA. However, concerns were raised about limitations of ADHD drugs along with their adverse effects, the need for continued utilization to maintain positive impacts, low response to medication, stigma, and unsure long-term efficacy and safety. Therefore, the need for non-pharmacological therapies for ADHD is strong, but the efficacy of those presently accessible, such as nutritional supplements, free supplementation of fatty acids, cognitive therapy, neurofeedback, and therapeutic strategies, is uncertain. As such, there is a need for more approaches addressing central ADHD symptoms.

One revolutionary approach that aims to address key signs for childhood ADHD is safeness preparation. Mindfulness program is based on east meditation practices combined with Western psychological knowledge and aims to raise awareness by deliberately paying close attention at the present time, improving considerate observation, and decreasing automatic thoughts.

10.10 ADHD in Early Years and Mindfulness

At the first glance, ADHD and mindfulness seem to be a contrasting mixture of practicing meditation, and staying still for a prolonged time period may sound like an unlikely feat if one has difficulty holding concentration and wants to be busy. However, taking into consideration some of the main elements of understanding it is evident how it would be helpful to someone ADHD suffering. ADHD diagnosed kids are easily swayed by inner and outer stimulation such as emotions and external noises, particularly during tedious or difficult activities, and sometimes forget to shift their focus to what they're doing. o During carefulness preparation, kids with ADHD diagnosed are encouraged to concentrate their thoughts on an 'attention source' like their pulse or body, to remain mindful of when to how their focus wanders; sometimes they are overwhelmed by the behavior of other kids, listening or daydreaming to a disturbance in other room. The key to the practice of mindfulness is to recognize when someone is sidetracked, to be conscious of distraction, and to draw awareness back to what the focus was. In this way, kids practice their so-called 'attention muscle' which requires endurance and practice, like physical training, but is likely to increase their ability to control and maintain attention. The idea of getting back attention while interrupted is the same when the object of concentration is breath or a condition in daily life that needs attention from an infant, such as classwork, play, activities, or interactions.

ADHD diagnosed kids are often taught during carefulness exercise to evaluate internally and externally stimuli that enter their consciousness, without functioning on them automatically. It's another critical feature of mindful meditation and tries to target disruptive behavior's basic symptoms. For example, kids can show a propensity to be anxious during yoga, come to their senses out of concern over how many kids have been doing, and blur the responses in answer to the instructor's query WHEN it's not one's turn. These behaviors may also go beyond the reach of a kid; but, by concentrating emphasis on the urges that occur, and understanding unconscious trends in their thinking and actions, kids may learn the potential to choose whether to respond rather than responding to triggers immediately. This, in effect, can improve their ability to control their irrational and overactive actions during mediation activity, and also in situations of every day. While this can sound rather vague, through playing video games and utilizing examples like the roadway (the quick way to react irrationally) vs the walking route (the quicker way to respond with more consideration and foresight) we illustrate this more clearly to kids.

10.11 Mindfulness Parenting by Parents

ADHD diagnosed with kid raising could be a difficult and frustrating activity. Parents should have a disciplined atmosphere and they need to be honest, transparent, and peaceful. Since ADHD has an inheritable element, it is reasonable to assume a parent will also suffer from symptoms of ADHD. This may further worsen the mindfulness procedure utilized was just an updated prototype of Youth Mindfulness Learning (MYmind), initially invented by parents and kids at an educational mental medical clinic. The curriculum consists of 8 one and half hour weekly classes, which was performed by their parents in limited groups of five to eight kids in different grades. A total of 20 ADHD diagnosed kids, ranging in age among 6 and 13 years, participated with their parents. Evaluations were conducted one week since the school, immediately after the school and again 8 weeks after. Eleven households were expected to wait for at least 6 weeks until the preparation started to deliver, because families with ADHD may have considerable difficulties with delivering this treatment.

Parenting education programs are sometimes confined to teaching the strategies of parents to deal with the behavioral issues of their kid, and so don't target the psychopathy of the parents themselves. Parents who already have ADHD are far less likely to profit from these programs. During careful parenting preparation, parents are trained to watch their kids in a cool, nonreactive, and respectful way with an impartial and transparent focus which helps them to be more receptive and attentive to difficulties.

And conducted a time-effect monitoring waiting list review. Results revealed no improvements over the waiting list era, but that at the final moment of the waiting list phase, teachers scored their pupils slightly higher for dissent defiant condition. After the training, the parents noted a strong decline in the symptoms of both his\her own and their kid's ADHD; these impacts were retained at the 8-week follow-up evaluation. Directly after school, teachers brought a substantial decrease in the intentional actions of their pupils. Parents also thought of oneself as being more attentive immediately after the behavior and the needs of their kid. Parents are often encouraged to become more mindful of their own pressures and problems, take control of their own time and take control of themselves, and are allowed to develop a nonjudgmental approach towards their own challenges and vulnerabilities. Mindful discipline tar- makes caregivers' own psychopathy, which may be the manifestations of a parent's own ADHD, in the case of caregivers with ADHD diagnosed kids.

10.12 ADHD Kids Mindful Activities

You may have witnessed that mindfulness meditation could even serve to boost focus, calm a beeping brain, or decrease impulsivity or hyperactivity symptoms. And like other parents, you would like to add this optional, non-medical intervention into the recovery program for your kid with ADHD.

The concern, of course, is that several kids do not leap at the chance to try meditating, particularly those with ADHD. Some are still not fully mindful of their thoughts, body stimuli, and breathing to better implement mediation techniques. And parents (who never practice self-awareness) don't really know where to continue, what activities are acceptable or were to help their kids get through barriers.

At any age, however, mindfulness is feasible and successful. The trick is to adapt therapies to maturity and degree of curiosity for your kid, and not assume therapy to be a solution-all for ADHD for your infant. If not, stay optimistic and motivate your kid to utilize awareness throughout the way that is convenient for their ideal self-awareness, construct crucial skills, and find their happiest and gentlest self along its direction.

10.13 Mindfulness Advantages for Kids

New studies have shown repetitively that a daily intake of awareness enhances attention, self-esteem boosts and aids kids in better emotions monitoring. "Research shows that cognitive therapy involving mindfulness meditation can improve brain regions that are accountable for emotional controlling, problem-solving and attention," says In This Moment psychologists and authors. "Evidence is emerging that mindfulness-based cognitive training results in fundamental structural brain changes."

Some researchers have also indicated that kids who regularly exercise awareness are more empathetic and compassionate than peers. For one small sample, stickers were issued to preschoolers and instructed to disperse them to whomever they wanted. The kids primarily gave the stickers to peers before practicing mindfulness; subsequently, they enthusiastically gave the stickers to kids they didn't meet or didn't want.

10.14 Kid's Mind on Mindfulness

The study demonstrates that through performing consciousness cognitive health programming aimed at creating a real-time and caring understanding of our lives instead of being stuck in confusion, on autopilot, everyone will boost focus.

Using this type of therapy to combat (ADD or ADHD) when people learn that focus is trainable. Yet more than concentration is influenced by ADHD and mindfulness. The ADHD and Awareness processes mirror one another. ADHD is marked by problems with executive control, not just concentration, and mindfulness has become an outlet for improving interrelated thinking abilities, all of which apply to cognitive control, not just treatment.

Future guidelines for treatment with ADHD can integrate mindfulness-based strategies. After all, care improves if you prepare attention with carefulness. This alone is a powerful therapeutic strategy that can help anyone, both with and without ADHD. Although nothing reported to date indicates that knowledge alone can transcend ADHD's pathology, cultivating understanding builds a wider range of characteristics, including sensitivity, adaptive thought, and empathy. Of ADHD, mindfulness promotes increased flexibility and capacity to tackle life's difficulties.

10.15 Cognitive Traits Building

For these kinds of factors, carefulness impacted the behavior of family members who dedicate themselves to practice it together. Over the previous quite few decades, the number of journal dedicated to consciousness has risen exponentially, and the studies clearly point to the very same extraordinary fact: We also have the ability to build perceptual traits that progress both overall health. Attention helps everything from anxiety and depression to mood disturbances, even within a week of work.

Evidence suggests that the brain is coping through physical adjustments to the mindfulness exercise. Shrinking of the outer surface of the brain has been identified as an unavoidable part of aging, but one research by Harvard found that there was no loss of long-term intermediaries. Research has found that after an 8-week mindfulness plan, many regions of the brain, particularly areas linked to emotion control, were that. And experiments using both MRI and activity processes in the brain have demonstrated changes that associate with improved cognitive regulation, well-being, and satisfaction.

Whilst also study in kids is not as substantial as that in adolescents, it has usually seen the same advantages as other mental rotation, with enhancements in stress reduction, increased focus, and sharpening of cognitive control. In one UCLA study, kids who lagged in cognitive control behind their peers at the beginning of a mindfulness plan encountered greater gains, unlike their classmates.

Following the practice of mindfulness, kids also may participate in further acts of love. In one test, preschool kids were asked to send stickers to kids in a category that included kids they defined as loving, un-liking, or unknowing. Most were initially issued to mates. The same kids handed out all the badges more evenly between all the groups after taking part in a mindfulness initiative.

Work on awareness and ADHD is already zeroing in. In one study, after a careful program, both kids and teens with ADHD as well as their parents significantly lower levels of stress and fewer symptoms of ADHD. For several elements of focus and cognition, carefulness has been associated with similar improvements to someone with medication. And ADHD-inherent traits, like impulsive behavior and sentimental reactions, respond to the practice of mindfulness, as do certain aspects of cognitive control.

Strain, ambiguity, and being a mother or father, everything falls in line. This stress influences how you work, how you respond to others, and how you prescribe ADHD for your kid. Much like you may profit from understanding the struggles of your kid through the prism of cognitive control, it is important to consider how you might be influenced by your own neurobiology — especially how you handle stress and its impact on the behaviors.

Some tension keeps us focused and safe. Our nervous system is wired when we feel threatened to generate the physiological responses known as the response to stress (or combat-or-flight), preparing us to safeguard ourselves or to flee from danger. Without thinking we leap into action — a good thing to do when we dodge an oncoming car. The bodies push strength away from the digestive tract and into the muscles. Reflexes bring our legs and arms under pressure, and logical thought ceases.

Such responses will save lives while we are at actual risk. The issue is that our reaction to stress isn't implicit. Since something buzzes us, the same biochemical responses pop up, like thoughts: I am late. I'm really poor at that. They just don't like me. The cycle revolves around the body and closes down cognitive abilities, as when we are in severe danger, there's no time to think. The brain then sends out messages that a crisis is looming, but these are not life danger circumstances in most cases; there is no lion going to immediately eat us.

Stress most often begins with a view, possibly outside of our consciousness, something's not as we believe it should be. We only run a little late or think about the to-do list. And there is a strong response to the pain. None of this would ever remove tension absolutely. In reality, a certain level of strain may also inspire us. The bodies are therefore not designed to tolerate overly constant or extreme pain. And because stress weakens both overall health, it affects the people all over you, not just you. It will make it impossible for you to remain on top of the kid's ADHD treatment, and other issues.

The invention of neural plasticity is among the most significant things in the neurology of the last couple of years. The human mind reshapes itself depending on some actions that we perpetuate by reinforcement or just thinking that. Neurological improvement happens as you strive to increase your concentration, or deliberately develop new patterns. You can't eradicate DNA, but you can alter other characteristics by changing the way of living that would otherwise appear entrenched.

You can choose to develop traits that enable you to manage whatever life can offer to your way. It usually starts by giving greater attention to the real-time environment and having greater flexibility among what you are doing and what you want to do next. Leaving aside just a few mins every day for practice of mindfulness will help build up your power.

The latest research studies also have shown that brain plasticity — affects the way the brain works — is likely during existence. There is still space for improvement. You should remain aware of any behaviors to assume otherwise, especially by classifying yourself or your parents and thus defining your living, with feelings like I will still be temperate. My kid is being dispersed all the time. We will never adhere to the fresh schedule.

Let go of hypotheses about where you're with ADHD or attentiveness up presently, and focus instead on your motives.

Commit to developing the characteristics you wish to grow as just a parent and also in your kid. Growth usually comes through with stubbornness.

Variation is Healthy

Once you actually pay attention all improves. You should stop for long enough to see the behavioral and emotional behaviors and the usual response patterns. Inclinations to get ended up losing in the long term or history can be noticed, and you can return to the moment. When it is, you will see it more plainly, and add more ambition to tackle whatever occurs. You can opt to adapt to your situation, instead of responding, so you can allow yourself a break in those occasional times where you struggle to do so. You reconfigure your brain along the way: I'm avoiding dispute again. I need to stop and look through my thoughts again. I am going to try things differently for a change.

The truth is that there has been ADHD in your kid, so you and your relatives live with it. It affects the experience of your kid and your own and hurdles you by disrupting everyday activities, interactions, and the education of your kid. But you could still solve these challenges through realistic and empathetic decision-making, and rebuild a new path after yourself and the kid.

Mindfulness offers you the strength to surmount ADHD and lead a happier existence. You can feel happy or unhappy at any given moment. You will carry on having both negative and positive experiences. Yet if you consider it easier to calm down, handle your tension, and enjoy life to the full, you, your kid, and family can achieve the joy, security, and well-being that you both deserve.

10.16 Other Remedies for ADHD Treatment

ADHD Neuro-feedbacking

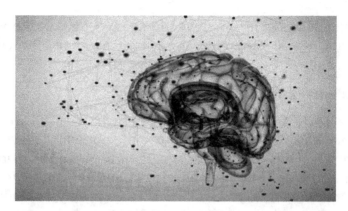

Neuro-feedback is indeed a high-tech manner of treating the effects of ADHD. The participant dons an electrolyte-lined cap after a test and is challenged to perform a specific cognitive function. The goal is to train patients to generate focus-associated brain wave patterns. The sessions are short (thirty min) and pain-free, but onerous. A treatment course can stretch around $5,000. The success of Neuro-feedback in the management of symptoms of ADHD is not definitive, with several trials and reports showing only conflicting or insufficient support for the therapy.

ADHD Mind Training Methods

Mind training for ADHD is becoming increasingly popular and accessible. There are applications for smartphones, pcs, laptops, and much more. Different cognitive stimulation programs, such as concentration, impulsivity, and working memory, assert rising mental processing problems in individuals with ADHD. Some of the applications have interfaces that look and sound like computer games but are programmed to execute particular brain functions.

Neuro-feedback learning generally includes programs that attempt to improve physiological responses by observing brainwave activity and cognitive training that aims to improve particular brain skills such as reading skills and problem solving mainly via games and some other workouts.

ADHD Workouts

Exercising makes the cognitive work of ADHD more safely and effectively. A significant benefit of exercise is an improvement in endorphins, which may boost mood. Workout also enhances the dopamine and norepinephrine levels in the brain, which boosts attention and focus.

Studies have found that moderate short-term exercise, including meditation, has beneficial impacts on concentration, impulsivity, hyperactivity, cognitive performance, and other symptoms of ADHD. Walking 4 times a week for thirty min will also do the trick and skill-based exercises such as ballet and martial arts are extremely good for those ADHD diagnosed individuals.

Zinc, Iron, and Vitamins B6 and C for ADHD Treatment

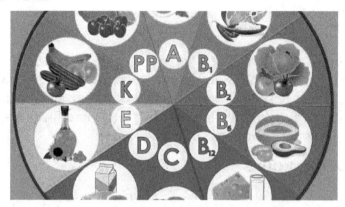

Quite a few ADHD minerals and vitamins are essential to generating and controlling rates of neurotransmission, particularly if one of them is defective in an adult or kid. Vitamin C is a neurotransmission building block whereas vitamin B6 and iron boost the levels of dopamine. Zinc controls dopamine, and when combined with traditional medicine and therapies, can better relieve Symptoms of ADHD in certain kids. One recent study demonstrates that 84 % of kids with ADHD had low ferritin concentrations (a proportion of iron), compared to 17 % of a treatment group. Low concentrations of iron as well as low rates of zinc, and also severe ADHD, but patients must not start using pills without their medical care and guidance.

Proteins for ADHD and ADD

A nutritionally rich ADHD diet is a strong tool for controlling Symptoms of ADHD. Researches also have shown that protein activates alertness-inducing areas of the brain while carbohydrates induce drowsiness. Protein as well protects blood sugar surges which can boost hyperactivity. Fiber enriches foods like vegetables and fruits, legumes and whole grains may help to balance energy rates. A low-fat meal will increase its potency whether you or your kid is using a stimulant drug. Fats could even cause a person to digest the medicine more slowly, thus postponing the efficacy of the drug.

Kids need between twenty-four to thirty grams of protein per day, depending on their age. The adults need between forty-five and seventy grams. Most nutritionists advocate beginning the day with a breakfast consisting of a combination of complicated carbs and protein like whole-wheat toast eggs or whole grain yogurt pancakes.

CBT (Cognitive Behavioral Therapy) for ADHD Treatment

CBT intends to improve unreasonable or unfavorable patterns of thought that meddle with staying on the task or doing things 2 obstacles for people with ADHD. CBT explores the validity of such feelings by allowing the counselor to analyze the facts with an individual with ADHD who feels, "It needs to be ideal or it's not healthy" or "I cannot get it correctly"

Evidence strongly supports the idea that CBT will help people effectively handle their problems relevant to ADHD. For instance, a 2016 adult brain imaging research with ADHD which completed a twelve-session CBT course showed increases in ADHD symptom ratings and positive changes in the same brain regions usually observed in drug treatment trials.

Many in the science world would also want to see more comprehensive work carried out with precisely designed monitors. Experts at MGH (Massachusetts General Hospital) and HMS (Harvard Medical School) stated in their 2010 paper, "The scientific and clinical foundation for CBT strategies in adult ADHD is increasing and indicates that focused, skill-based treatments play a role in successfully addressing this condition.

Fatty Acids of Omega-3 for ADHD Treatment

Fatty Acids of Omega 3 present in fish oil are essential in the functioning of the brain and nerve cells. The body itself cannot produce omega-3, but people will obtain them from diet, vitamins, and supplements. This is particularly important for persons with ADHD, who could have lower nutritional levels. The fish oil comprises two forms of omega-3 fats, DHA and EPA. The best medications have two to three times more EPA compared with DHA.

Although the effects of omega-3 fats are obvious, some reports proof of their function in the management of symptoms of ADHD is still inconclusive. For instance, a 2018 review of research involving kids with ADHD having undergone omega-3 therapy discovered some evidence supporting the role of the mineral in ADHD therapy, whereas a related 2017 review found something else.

Behavioral Meditation for ADHD Treatment

Behavioral treatment for ADHD is a standardized intervention technique aimed at educating kids better strategies to respond by reinforcing desirable habits, like following instructions and removing undesirable acts, such as missing assignments. The APA (American Psychological Association) says occupational counseling will be the first phase of care for kids below six with ADHD. It could also be beneficial for older kids.

10.17 Hypnotherapy for ADHD Treatment

Upon first, ADHD hypnotherapy may seem doubtful but the evidence for this widely underestimated yet effective alternative medication is remarkably optimistic.

An increasing number of ADHD kids and parents with ADHD are now taking into consideration alternate treatment therapies to help them overcome this situation as the scandal over possible excessive-diagnosis of ADHD persists, and the dangers of medicine keep going to be discussed and researched. There are a variety of issues that may be troublesome for them in interacting with either an infant or a person with ADHD, such as focus, organization, education (a job or classes), partnerships, and even more. Patients are sometimes diagnosed with treatments like dextroamphetamine and methylphenidate, which may result in a number of adverse effects like decreased appetite, fatigue, irritability, and depression. So this-size-fits-all solution doesn't resolve the nuances in the preferences of the patient — what works for one person cannot work with another. Parents also are worried about the future-term effects of their kids being administered psychotropic treatments. And, as with so many chronic diseases in babyhood, parents turn to alternative therapies system of treatment, like hypnotherapy.

While hypnotherapy has been correlated with stage performances for too long, the scientific attention it clearly needs is progressively receiving, and it is seen as being efficient for a broad range of issues from smoking to anxiousness and even depression. Nowadays ADHD hypnotherapy is broadly acknowledged as offering positive effects.

Utilizing Hypnosis for ADHD Treatment

Work was carried out utilizing behavioral treatment approaches which produced promising results; in fact, hypnosis was shown to aid people with difficult circumstances of ADHD attention, a concentration which power. Maybe the most alleged involvement brought to ADHD patients by hypnosis is the possibility and revelation that they might improve their situation and be in accordance with the facts.

Hypnosis is quite efficient as a substitute, or parallel, type of treatment for ADHD patients: it assists both kids and adults control their health issues without the medicinal side effects. People with ADHD have a terrific natural multi-task but also highly energetic level capability, which can enable them to succeed if utilized efficiently.

The purpose of utilizing hypnosis in a way would be to allow the individual to do more in their everyday lives. Kids develop into more successful adults whilst adults can utilize their intensity and management skills at doing a job more effectively or do simple homework.

Hypnosis would also create self-esteem for kids and adults alike. This is essential to fulfilling some of the other objectives that they aim to accomplish, as well as better knowing themselves.

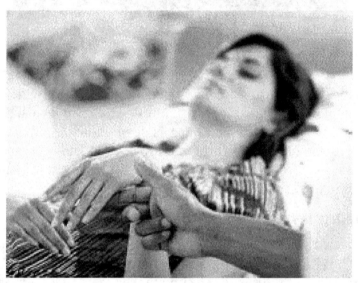

Hypnotherapy Working

Hypnotherapy could benefit ADHD patients using the below methods:

Positive Ideas Planting

By putting patients in a relaxed state, the hypnotherapist may create a heightened concentration state which makes the person highly sensitive to positive stimuli. For starters, if the individual has trouble falling asleep due to disturbances and tiredness, the hypnotherapist will help them calm at will and seek the strength to continue to rest in the evening.

No Adverse Effects of Hypnotherapy

Hypnotherapy may enable patients to manage their conditions without taking medication. In addition to the negative adverse effects, several licensed ADHD drug companies do not resolve the root cause of the disorder: they merely suppress the symptoms. The treatment will therefore always be effective in helping patients proceed as people.

Moving Ahead

Our subconscious performs a significant part-it influences our actions, forms our personality, and stores values, thoughts, and impressions of life. It is also utilized as a place for planting ideas and could be indoctrinated with hypnotherapy in a way as to resolve side effects and impulses. For instance, if an individual is continually scared they would not be able to improve their focused capacity then there will be little improvement. A hypnotherapist, even so, can allow the patient to grow his ability to concentrate and focus over time, eventually approaching a point at which a person is truly pleased, healthful, and self-assured in his abilities.

If it is an adult or a kid, hypnosis may be an effective tool for coping with ADHD challenges and travails. While it's not a replacement for standard treatments, hypnosis could be a valuable tool to support a patient's treatment in order to obtain the best results possible.

In addition to learning disabilities & behavioral issues, particularly ADHD, hypnosis could benefit your kid:

- Learn how to concentrate
- Ignore disruptions
- Research practices improvements
- Boost self-esteem
- Start releasing of traumatic experiences & irrational fears connected with ADHD

- Transform believes in ADHD to being optimistic
- Enhance productivity and remove the fear of failure
- Sleep Improvements
- Reduced anxiety and depression

Reasons for you as well as your kid to take into account ADHD Hypnotherapy

It points out that you can hypnotize adults and kids with ADHD even so.

Indeed, the sluggish brain activity found mainly in adults and kids with ADHD seems to be similar to whatever we discover in someone who is hypnotized, and also in kids up to 12 years old. Interestingly, they are all very hypnotizable kids.

Hypnotherapy can be utilized for ADHD by itself or in combination with other medications, and two could work well together.

For all those worried that individuals aren't even hypnotizable due to ADHD, it must be found that researchers have shown that the utilize of medicines in those who have ADHD can improve the hypnotizable. Hypnotherapy can often be an acceptable choice if you did not pursue medicine at the moment or are afraid of taking it, and it can also help to reduce the number of prescribed drugs and the risk of adverse effects connected with the drug.

ADHD Hypnotherapy is quite safe and has relatively rare adverse effects.

It might be worth considering if hypnotherapy for ADHD may potentially be enough to stop treatment until you or the kid seek medicine. This is highly important for young kids, who have medication might be a final resort, and there can be almost certain to be several kids and adults whose ADHD might be helped by behavior therapy and other methods such as cognitive hypnotherapy or CBT.

ADHD hypnotherapy is a safe choice for anyone in the 20 percent where medicine doesn't function or has serious adverse effects.

Whereas medication appears to work with next to no adverse effects for 80 percent of patients, it leaves 20 percent for those it perhaps doesn't function or for which the adverse effects are just too intense. Hence it is important to find certain alternatives. One may try, or a mix of, mentoring, Neuro-feedback and CBT.

ADHD hypnotherapy is fast, and hence cost-effective.

Hypnotherapy appears to work quickly on average. Mostly somebody would go to a CBT therapist for about 40 sessions to cure depression, with an average of 12 hypnotherapists. Hypnotherapy will slash in half the amount of ADHD neuro-feedback meetings, from as much as 80 to 40, or 30 to 15. Because Neuro-feedback could amount to hundreds of pounds for each session, it still represents a huge time- and money-saving. Likewise, ADHD hypnotherapy may require on average fewer sessions than CBT or mentoring would necessitate.

Operating with a Hypnotherapy consultant for ADHD enhances the likelihood of having ADHD hypnotherapy work against you or the kid.

It is built especially for the kid or person with ADHD, so it operates much more effectively. Meetings are personalized to every person and as per age.

Chapter 11

Home And School-Based Mindfulness Activities For Kids

Living a complete life is part of truly understanding the universe around us and in us. The idea of mindfulness is accustomed and well-practiced for all who practice yoga. However, if we retain to ourselves our mindful methods, we 're not sharing an essential skill to live a good and productive life. And whoever else might benefit greatly from the practice of being mindful? Oh, our kids.

Educating our kids to explore, challenge, and value the universe around them also adds to their early childhood, but also helps to create intellectually curious and thoughtful adults. Tend to be curious and carefree and these characteristics can be very powerful, especially when they are focused and widened. Kids who practice awareness have better emotions and increased self-esteem. Those who usually do better educationally, and have enhanced social skills such as the ability to traverse and settle disputes peacefully. Meditation is also utilized as an important way to combat fear and violence.

Trying to teach our kids' awareness via mindful activities tailored to their desires isn't difficult. Of course, they could be impatient or fail to understand why it is worth being aware, but there's no hurry. Here are some kid care activities that can be carried out with parents, teachers, or caretakers at home or in school.

Beginning with Itself

The easiest approach to inspire a kid to develop a fresh, constructive habit is to make them watch you put it into action. If you have a ritual of contemplation, a journal of thanks, or a ritual of pranayama let them check it. Practice open-mindedness and respond to any queries raised. No need to press so hard – the safest approach to encourage kids to grow at their own speed is always to. If we insist, they do anything, then we would be likely to be swayed or rejected. So, be open to your own work first, and allow them to participate if they wish. You might discover them completing the same after a long time since you least suspect it.

Keeping Things Easy

For young kids to grasp meditation is indeed a big word, thus to put it more simply, consciousness recognition. It is realizing everyone thoughts, feelings, physical reactions, and whatever is occurring today now around us. You wouldn't even need to call it "consciousness." it could be hearing, emotions, realizing, or being conscious. Perhaps utilize this chance to let your kid name it whatever they desire. Gain the ability to choose from, and make them quite meaningful.

Turn it into a Family Matter

By making mindfulness a custom in the family and a subject that everybody addresses freely together. You start making it more like a lifestyle and much less of a hassle or learning experience to be endured by cultivating a society of mindfulness inside of your parents' home. An idea of perfect family activity is to set up a routine of thanks at dinnertime. At the dining table every night, everybody takes turns exchanging whatever he or she is grateful for. Welcome the family to find appreciation together with the bigger, more visible occurrences in the tiny, regular occurrences. Together, making the family training attentiveness would slowly render attentiveness an easy and quick addition to the routine of your kid.

Relax and Squeeze

Once bedtime comes and the kid has difficulty calming, a wonderful practice you should do before sleep is "relax and squeeze" This is a fantastic method to ease the mind and body to make your kid feel relaxed and in sync with the moment. Also, your kid lies down with his eyes closed and tell them to squeeze as firmly as they could to each tissue in one's body. Let them keep the pose for a couple of seconds, then ease and relieve completely. Do the same activity as often times as they can, still encouraging them to sit still and rest for several seconds and make their body relax fully.

Mindfulness Apps Exploration

This is indeed a perfect way to bring together the enjoyable and immersive environment of mobile technology and kids' mindfulness. It can help adults too! Exercising with the assistance of a meditation app together is a good way to set a journey of meditation. 'Headspace for Kids' is a famous kid-specific meditation app with 5 domains, Focus, Calm, Sleep, Wake Up, and Kindness. The activities target 3 age ranges (below 5, 6 to 8, and 9 to 12) which involve sweet noises, visualization, and breathing exercises, many others.

Meditation by Raisins

Multiple families are balancing the job, baseball games, chores, and house cleaning. While we do have a meal it's on the move and in a rush occasionally. But the feeling of taste is a strong anchor to the current moment, and it is essential for kids and grownups to eat consciously. It can appear like a test to introduce careful eating to kids and that is where the 'raisin meditation' could help! Encourage your kid to keep a raisin and wait a couple of instances discovering its size, stench, and shade. Then, welcome them, without biting, to gradually put the raisin into the mouth and try these with their tongue. Warn them to give special consideration to the senses of flavor and touch until they are able to chew and drink the raisin.

Begin Crafting

Crafts have become an excellent activity for kids to be mindful of. Teaching kids to "notice things" is great, but maybe you just need to develop it more attractive to maintain their interest and rile up their creativity. Using a multitude of various, inexpensive crafts practices, you will invoke meditation in a pleasant way. Seek to knit and encourage your kids to learn about the wool 's color and look as well as the needles' sound clicking. Start painting, and talk of the pencil's feel, the paper's scent, and the material 's pre-history as they start their journey from the mountains to your dining table.

Listening Activities

Listening enables us to connect with the present time and is yet another wonderful opportunity for kids to exercise awareness. When kids develop the ability to listen actively, they welcome their minds to keep silent and concentrate on one thing that can be of great help in our extremely induced culture. Try that active exercise of listening. After making a noise (you can also utilize a singing bucket or pot/pan with a spoon), ask the kids to listen intently to the echo and to put their hands up if they cannot hear it.

When they can't detect the buzzing tone anymore, remind them to stay silent and pay careful attention to other noises they make. After a moment, ask the kids to share every noticeable sound. Invite the kids to get input. How were they so when they could sit in quietness and listen? Are they in a place to consider more than they knew? Keep continuing to do that during their day.

Questions to Build Awareness in Kids

Support and encourage the kids to utilize contact to communicate with their sensing and exercise mindfulness. Workouts based on touch sensation help to develop greater awareness. Kids are inspired to study via contact to help build sensory discovery and play. Ask your kids to choose their preferred pet. Invite them to cover their eyes, and spend their time in their grip to feel the item.

After a few moments, ask them to explain how they feel about the piece. Work to expand consciousness by posing questions such as, how does the toy feel when it's moist? or In case I place the toy under the sun, how does it feel? Keep inviting your kid to develop their thoughts and senses.

Breathing Hot Chocolate

This approach ends with your kid putting her hands up while holding a cup of hot cocoa under her nose. Prompt a simple imagination and ask her to visualize first tasting the hot cocoa inhaling intensely via his/her nose and afterward blowing it to chill it off, effortlessly exhaling from her mouth over the air. Have his/her redo this method visualization and breathing through the smelling of her nose, and return via his/her mouth, chilling down for a few minutes. Motivate her not that fast, or not very slow, to let his/her exhalation find his/her own tempo.

Utilizing visuals like this integrating the exercise with an enjoyable feeling of drinking chocolate gives kids a strong correlation and enables them to make an understanding of their respiratory patterns. Slow, steady relaxation is what calms the brain and body down; the imagery leap activates the frontal lobe and allows kids with ADHD to concentrate their distracted mind.

Breathing 4 to 7 to 8 Activity

Breathing is often the only thing that you might do when you are swamped. No special instruments or devices are required simply you, your lungs, and yourself. A few of the techniques people utilize with anxiety, ADHD, or more is the 4 to 7 to 8 relaxation technique, created by Dr. Andrew. Slowly inhale and exhale via nose 4 seconds to perform it, and hold the breath for 7 seconds. Then, exhale 8 times via your mouth. When it comes to performing relaxation exercises, the practice itself is not necessarily the most important component. This strategy is fantastic to start with but if it doesn't match you, you may pass on to another. Whether you are practicing the 7 to 11 version or attempting to relax resonantly, all these relaxation techniques have similar purpose soothing the nerves. Breathing techniques stimulates ramped-up production of oxygen in the body, sending more blood moving via your organ systems. When oxygen and blood flow to the brain rapidly, you will be able to focus better, which could make much difference in reducing ADHD impulsivity.

Whenever you take deep breaths, the Vagus nerve (an integral part of your digestive tract) responds and makes your parasympathetic system come to life. Your digestion and heart rate are controlled by parasympathetic nervous and your anxiety levels. The PNS seems to be what helps relieve your banging heart and wet palms when you encounter a bad panic. Diaphragmatic respiration that utilizes the diaphragm connects the PNS which lets you concentrate, a calm which regulates the impulses. 8-week research on breathing in adults found that there were less tension and a higher degree of concentration among participants. Study subjects also experienced a decline in negative feelings, showing how mindful respiration could also greatly improve one's emotional response. Mixing this workout with other healthy activities could lift your spirits and level of cognitive ability to a world of good.

Coloring Activity for Mindfulness

If you are an adolescent or a teenager, coloring could be a shockingly enjoyable way to lessen volatile feelings and carving out a quiet moment. Art enables you to explore different media, like colored pencils, oil paint, and watercolors. You could even pursue predefined design elements in a sketchbook, or utilize a blank canvas to express your creativity. However, using a book can help you concentrate on keeping inside the lines and usually sharpens the self-control and fine motor skills of an individual.

Because of their complex architectures, mandalas are common designs but any creative intent would do so. Coloring books full of wildlife, elaborate scenes, or popular prints such as paisley and plaid are available. Getting a creative outlet can offer you a room at every given moment to convey what's on your mind, so working with thoughts and feelings in this manner is important to your comprehension of ADHD and yourself.

Numerous people say written work is the ideal way of expressing oneself, but you may find art a better choice. This all relies on which form to properly respond to. Art therapy generally is a commonly accepted aspect of health practice, but while at your own moment it is distinct from painting or coloring. It requires working with an accredited psychiatrist who would also help you investigate how your designs relate to your emotional and cognitive condition.

Maze Walking

Go outside with a chalk stick and create curvy zigzagging paths, a large splash, or perhaps spider web, challenging your kid to trek it, tightrope-like. Using sticky tape on the rug for the same reason, for a raining day operation. There has to be an end-to-end, slow, controlled, focused, heel-to-toe challenge. You would hate him falling into imagined lava at last.

Breath Toggle

One of the cornerstones of awareness is to learn how to take a big, pleasing deep breath and to recognize how great it feels to get them out. This could be done by relaxing still, or by designating a Breath toggle. You and your kid choose a door handle, a special gift, a scrap of paper on walls that reads "breath push" somewhere in the home, and create a law that any time your kid hits that thing, he/she will take a huge, conscious breath. For instance, allowing your kids to touch the door handle every-time you leave the home and take the breath to calm his/her head. This teaches her to avoid worrying and to incorporate peace and concentration in her everyday routine. As a reward, you could even educate a stressed kid on how to find out using the Breath toggle as a self-calming tool.

Playing "I Heed"

It's "I Spy," basically, and with a variety of responses that help your kid to build knowledge. Odds are, as they search, they will still discover stuff that you have never seen previously. Seek to locate an object, note various textures (gentle, rough, itchy, squishy) or forms (triangle, circle, square) in rainbow color.

Yoga for Mindfulness

The ultimate solution for individuals of every generation, although holding the body in one position, Yoga helps you to regulate respiration and emotions. The purpose of Yoga is not to push oneself to stand still, but to exercise becoming conscious of your positioning of the body. One of the very first moves to gaining influence over certain facets of your existence is to gain ownership over your body. And besides, the body is the organ that holds you every day and serves all the tasks you need. You could also help improve the emotional and mental confidence by discovering a revived physiological affiliation. 8-week research of ADHD kids discloses that yoga has good effects on the maintained control and attention of impulses from the subjects.

As part of a post-school program, the kids participated in various forty-mins sessions per week and did not make any other changes in lifestyle. On 2 cognitive tests, the exercising group showed improved response and accuracy times. This research revealed introducing yoga to the everyday activities of kids could make a significant difference, with no need for large upheavals in daily lifestyle. It might seem too easy of a patch, but it could have a big effect. With 8.4 % of kids experiencing ADHD symptoms, for hundreds of kids, several mins of yoga per day can motivate calmer minds.

Knitting Activity

Knitting also demonstrates attention, balance, teamwork, and certain mathematics. This includes sensory feedback with fine motor growth as an additional benefit. Start knitting your fingers or even crocheting when daily knitting becomes too difficult. The constant action is relaxing, the yarn 's sound is calming, and the kids feel happy to make it.

Garden Digging Activity

Adults and kids with ADHD may love being close to nature through compassion for it. A garden could even teach a teen to take care of another life form, and can often help set up a routine too. Routines encourage habits that can make mindfulness a part of everyday life. These are not the only advantages on their own, greenery could have a substantial impact on the growth, health, and focus of the individual. A prospective study of young adults engaging with nature demonstrates that after having experienced natural scenes many developments led mental health. 10 out of 35 researches featured kids with ADHD/ADD, whose diagnoses improved with ease of access and significant exposure to nature.

A various study has shown, on a similar note, that natural habitats can make a person feel pleased, lower their levels of stress, reduce one's blood pressure but far more. Due to its favorable properties, forest wash has also prospered in Japan for years. Whether you are unpersuaded, just catching a few vitamin D is essential to various body functions. if you're not using the greenery for a packed garden. Some locations do have open planting areas where you could just communicate with each other through mutual nature links.

Sparkling Jar Activity

A sparkling jar activity could be a creative means of teaching younger kids with ADHD how feelings work — and how they would regulate them in various environments. Fill the empty container or jar with water, and insert a few sparkle-filled spoons. Shut the lid and start shaking the jar, watching the sparkling swirl and push around. The sparkly mimics how you feel when you are upset, scared, or worried. These emotions are tough to monitor and are most difficult to determine or recognize. You could feel dispersed and powerless like you can't even control your emotions or behavioral outcomes. How that happens so if you eventually calm down to feel OK is really the sparkles settling back down to the bottom of the jar. Even so, you wouldn't have to wait until your body governs to feel at ease. At the moment, you can assume accountability for your practice and development coping training to assist handle your emotions yourself.

Often the feelings of others get the best of them, but they wouldn't want to let them reign over your acts. The risks of negative acts are like the expansion of far-reaching sparkles, cluttered, and difficult to erase. One method of teaching kids about good health regulating emotions is by allowing them to exercise their social skills. learning and Watching is one factor, but doing so in actual environments assists a stick for the lesson. Applaud or encourage them for good behavior, and let them realize that it is wrong to behave negatively. Make them talk, like: What acts can you take for another chance to revise your emotional reactions? How does disagreeable conduct make us feel? Adults and kids can also gain from structuring through managing time; explicitly through the utilize of planners, calendars, and lists. Almost always you may underestimate or overestimate how much time a project required, or you may be struggling with impulsivity or self-doubt when you complete the work, which may promote fear of failure. It can result in positive outcomes and avoid emphatic outbursts or burnout by offering oneself frequent breaks and time limits recording.

Scanning of Body

Scanning of your body will enable you to get a better understanding of the biological being. This appears to take yoga signs, as you would already presume, but you don't need to pose for a picture to do scanning of body. It is also correlated with mindfulness which underlines the idea of allowing stimuli to go and come without being focused hyper on them. It helps you to recognize places of stress or pain within the body and gradually relieve the fear until all of the beings is calm. For individuals who haven't done it, scanning of the body takes somewhat practice but it happens easily after a few pieces of training. A mindfulness meditation template will be of massive help in this if you are attending a school or listening to a video recording.

The presenter will possibly begin by bringing you via the initial steps of intense respiration to relax your nerves. If you're more comfortable, you 're going to start moving your focus to each part of your body — head, hands, back, stomach, etc. Some instructions will show you how to relieve the body stress, and some will remind you to remember it and transfer it to the next section of the body. It could be simpler for novices to just recognize it because you wouldn't have to concern about removing every tiny discomfort. Additionally, acknowledgment is a central mindfulness principle. You could even learn in seeing it as it is rather than lambasting yourself about any physiological nervousness you encounter and later lessen it.

Visual Experience

Whenever the subconscious is overwhelmed it can be an efficient way to settle yourself by taking advantage of the environment. What are you seeing, feeling, hearing, smelling, and tasting right now? Have you ever experienced any perceptions, artifacts, or scents here before? Kids learn to adjust stuff out to get through their day, and for individuals with ADHD, it could happen doubly. Even when you're attempting to have something particular done, your brain may wander in many directions, but perceptual methods utilized in this research can help prevent that from occurring.

Begin by noticing the universe that is right around you, for example. Choose an object for each rainbow color, or identify all green items in a house. The emphasis of the mindful analysis is on taking into the ecosystem as it is without decision or of the topic thoughts.

The STOP technique is a very well-known technique for sensory observation, involving 4 phases:

Stop whatever you are doing for a couple of minutes whether you're feeling nervous, panicky, or frustrated. You might have to step away for a moment physically and put yourself anywhere that is amenable to harmony.

Take some gentle breathing to relax the body, and start to calm down. The mind could be prepared to leave behind every situation but the body still may experience the impact.

Observe what is in your field. Even though your environments aren't quite so intriguing, you still can find anything really small to concentrate on. Perhaps there is a strangely shaped sign upon this wall or a string on your sweatshirt. Do you breathe anything pleasurable or unpleasant, or really anything? Are there really any noises but your heartbeat and breathing?

Proceed after you have observed for several mins, with a revived point of view, you could proceed for the rest of the day.

Some other varieties include SEAT technique and careful walking, yet they still represent the very same key rules. In an instant, checking your perceptual skills which will help you edge yourself and resist being pushed aside by thoughts of racing. By hearing, feeling, or sensing you connect oneself to the moment as you view the environment on several levels.

Chapter 12

Parenting Tips And Guidelines For Parents

12.1 ADHD Kid Raising Guidelines

ADHD is basically a behavioral self-control condition or what some experts consider the cognitive skills necessary for long-term preparation, coordinating, and carrying out complicated human behavior. That is, the "CEO" in the brain, in a kid, who is obligated to be arranging and behavior controlling, assisting the kid plan for the future and pursuing those plans, seems to be doing very poor work. In several cases, the kid doesn't suffer from inadequate knowledge or skill, so it won't help much to show the kid how to do something to correct her problems. Instead, you will find it more effective to mix such learning or knowledge and skills with the following stuff: offer clear directions, reorganize the tasks so it is more motivating and interesting, break that down into narrower allocations with repeated short breaks, reorganize the setting being less disruptive and help to focus the kid's attention about what is essential to do in such a scenario, reroute the actions of the kid towards potential goals against immediate gratification, and offer immediate incentives for completed tasks or rules. In brief, in circumstances that had earlier been an issue for them, we would like to help kids with ADHD "demonstrate what kids know"

Sound easy, right? In theory, it is fairly straightforward. It isn't always simple to execute in practice. Work showed that parents greatly benefit from general concepts that are derived from our acquired knowledge of ADHD. As for turning points of kids with ADHD 's everyday behavior therapy, these concepts have guided parents well during designing intervention strategies for these kids at home and in school.

Note that raising an ADHD diagnosed kid based on theory requires taking a moment before responding to the kid's current abuse. Utilize this pause to focus on the concepts found in this text, pick a kid answer compatible with those values. To maintain the kid rearing rooted in this strategy.

Providing Kid Instant Consequences And Feedbacks

ADHD specialist noticed a long time back, kids with ADHD are far more under the sway of the time than regular kids do. If you are a part of the time, or you're going to have no control over your ADHD kid.

Because as explained, kids with Disabilities will get the desire to find something else when faced with a job they find irritating, uninteresting, or unfulfilling. If you really want them to remain at a task, you will need to organize for constructive comments and implications that occur across the task, which will make the job more enjoyable, and also slight negative effects on off-task shifts. Likewise, when you're trying to change bad emotions, you have to provide speedy benefits and feedback for good behavior and rapid negative effects for acts of violence. Good reactions could be provided in the form of admiration or praises, as long as you explicitly and specifically state what the kid has been positive about that. But don't expect it to always suffice. You can even utilize physical affection forms, but don't overthink it as kids may see it as disingenuous. In certain scenarios, you would need to utilize incentives such as additional allowances, or programs in which the kid wins coupons or points to rights, as the reinforcement would not be enough to inspire the kid to adhere to the assigned mission. However, whichever sort of input you provide, the sooner it can be given quickly, the more successful it can be in altering potential attitudes.

For instance, when a kid with ADHD usually has trouble playing very well with a sibling, a very effective reassurance of group activities would be and when you're on the alert for just about any instances of collaboration, exchanging, and generosity being shown by the kid and then offer instant admiration (and coupons) whenever you detect it. Similarly, after harassing the younger kid the kid will provide prompt and slightly adverse reviews and repercussions. They remind the kid precisely what he gets accomplished wrong (instead of shrieking) and why it's not appropriate; instead, you withdraw a right that the kid has exposure to that day and some won coupons in a coupon scheme.

Providing The Kid With More Regular Response

Kids with ADHD need not only swift and moreover frequent consequences and feedback. And when given rarely, instant effects or suggestions may be useful, but they are most valuable when given regularly. Arguably, going too far this could get your kid annoying and invasive and exhausting for you, but this needs to be done even more than your time, timetable, and energy license especially if you're trying to modify some form of significant misconduct. For example, instead of trying to reward a kid who has significant difficulty completing homework until all homework is actually finished, or shaming the kid for failing to finish for many hours when it would have taken twenty min, inform the kid that she would now gain points to solve each math question, with the points stacking additional to buying a privilege. Again, a fair time limit says, twenty min is set for the whole task, and when the period expires the kid is punished (ends up losing) one point by each unfinished question. And during the work period, you regularly praise the kid for staying on-task and offer words of support to continue working hard at the very same time that you are tallying points.

Almost always parents get quite busy at their own obligations in the residence and bother checking the kid often. Yet another way to remember is to put small posters with smileys on them across the house in places where you often look in the corner of the bedroom mirror, on the top of a kitchen digital clock, and so on. If you see a sticker, focus on what you think the kid is doing at a particular moment as it's only sitting peacefully watching television. You could also set a baking timer or enjoy for different short intervals, or utilize a tool called MotivAider that is draped on a belt or even in a pocket and buzzes at the configured periods.

Utilize Bigger and Strong Aftermath

Kid with ADHD will necessitate more powerful or salient repercussions than other kids to motivate him to do work, respect authority, or behave well. These may include emotional support, advantages, special snack foods or treats, coupons or points, personal gain such as toy cars or goods that can be collected, and even sometimes money.

This would appear to contradict the conventional belief that kids will not be compensated financially so much as these incentives may override rewards such as the enjoyment of reading, the urge to impress parents and mates, the joy of completing a job or new task, or the respect of peers for well playing a game. But these aspects of reassurance or reward are far less likely to influence well-behaving kids with ADHD. Nor do they regularly inspire these kids to continue learning, to suppress their desire to do harmful activities, and to succeed in their jobs. The condition can also be correlated with a natural process deficiency in self-motivation ability, one of the cognitive functions that allow parents to maximize their support, or any certain social or emotional incentives with more important effects than most kids need to maintain commitment in a mission. The essence of your kid's condition means that you would possibly have to employ greater, greater, and even more severe effects to create and sustain healthy attitudes for your infant.

Utilizing Inducement Before Penalty

Whenever a kid disobeys or misbehaves it is normal for parents to revert back to the penalty. That might be good for an ADHD-free kid, who only every now and then behaves badly and therefore gets a small penalty. It's not ideal for an ADHD boy, who is prone to falls much more frequently and may have a lot of negative implications. The study suggests that the majority with ADHD have already been penalized considerably far more than typically developing kids, so it is unlikely that you will start one's behavioral changes strategy with much more penalty. The penalty is not really successful in improving behavior, whether applied individually or in the complete absence of continuous incentives and constructive reviews. It generally leads to frustration as well as hatred in the kid, and ultimately to avoidance by the kid. Sometimes this can also lead to efforts at what doctors call pro-control: one's kid is finding ways to hit back, react, or even get over punishment with over punishment

It 's essential that you prevent this very common slide towards first using a penalty. Recall this maxim often: Successes before Drawbacks. It can help to note that the kid experiences much more adequate rebukes, threats, and exclusion by those who may not recognize the condition of the infant. and they more with you to strengthen their behavior? Very unlikely. Starting the program with opportunities and bonuses would be more apt to show what you want the kid to do, rather than simply how not to.

The principle to utilize the constructive even before drawback is simple: first, make the decision what good behavior you would like to replace with whenever you want to alter the unwanted behavior. It'll also impulsively prompt you to continue following for or teaching such good behavior if you know your kid is uncertain about exactly what you are expecting. If that attitude takes place, you'll be more probable to praise it and praise it.

Only after that new attitude has been consistently rewarded for at least a couple of days to a week must you begin to punish the unwanted opposite behavior. Then again, try to only utilize mild penalty including the loss of entitlement or particular interaction or a short period-out, and maintain the penalties in alignment with the bonuses: just one penalty for every 2 or 3 situations of reward and praise. Penalize continually but preferentially, only for this specific bad attitude to occur. Do not blame your kid for anything that she is performing wrong. Let have a look at an instance of a kid at the dining table who often interrupts, blurts, and intrudes comments.

You speak to the kid about whether you'd like seeing the kiddo more at the table right before next household mealtime: strive not to chat too soon, wait till others are done before communicating, and speak just until chewing food is over. You demonstrate that perhaps the kid could really earn points to abide by those rules. You label marks on a little chat during the meal to making sure that the kid notices something occurring, but at the same time offering a nonverbal signal such as a smile that allows the kid to realize that you understand how much the kid is working to stick to the laws. For a week or two, you disregard rule breaches and only let the kid realize until the next food that violating a law implies losing one point from now on. Note that for every 2 or 3 bonuses you offer, a penalty will be levied not exceeding than one

Bridge And Externalize Time Where Essential

Kids with ADHD are slow in improving their capacity to utilize their own perception of time and potential to control their current behavior. Since they do not have the same capacity as regular kids to feel and utilize energy, they cannot adapt as easily as others to demands that include deadlines and plans for the future. They need an external connection to the authorized time period for an assigned mission. Since they appear to exist in the present or "the now," they are less sensitive to time-related mental details but are more reactive to events that arise around them in the "now." They become more apt to be driven by time as you have constant alerts about time and the time period allocated to a task. For eg, if your kid is given twenty mins to clean up his house, you would need to set a twenty mins cooking timer, put it in the kid's room so it would be noticeable and attract his attention to it. Also, you should utilize the Big Time Counter, a one-foot high clock that you can schedule for a red disk time period. As time goes by, the disk shrinks in size until the time is up when the kid is alerted by a signal. just a recorder where you recorded your voice counting backward for a specified time interval, indicating when each minute has elapsed ('10 minutes until the time is up). Utilize any tool you could to outsource the time interval to provide the kid a more accurate way of passing the time during the period of work.

You will need to pass resources with tasks that involve even longer time spans, such as book reports or science projects given to your kid as homework — that is, split the job into small daily measures so that a small piece of the activity is completed every day. You create little bricks in the bridge by bridging time across the distance between when the job was allocated and when it might be due (a few weeks or even a few months from now). Without these approaches, the kid will probably postpone the work to be done until the very last minute, which often makes a good job unlikely.

Essential Information Externalization At Performance Point

Since functioning memory, or the capacity to hold an eye on the details needed to perform a job, is greatly compromised in ADHD kids, I find it very useful to put essential knowledge in a tangible form at the stage when the research is done. I name this stage when the research is performed the success expression coined by Dr. Sam Goldstein to apply to the crucial position and period for executing an action or function in the natural environment, such as home or education. If the kid has assignments to do at the kitchen counter (for instance, where she'll be supervised all through preparing meals), place a card with crucial aspects and reminders on the table before her, such as "remain on task, do not even space out and seek for assistance if you'd like" or "Read instructions cautiously, do all the tasks, and when finished, go back double and-check all your replies for clarity. If the kid has problems whenever a buddy comes to the home to play, sit her downright well before a friend arrives and evaluate the social norms she requires to follow, such as "toys sharing, regulate your aggression, take turns in gameplay and enquire your buddy about herself and her desires." You also could write it down on a card and check it out with your kid a few times while you're in private. Again, the most valuable knowledge you will make accessible at success stages, the more probable the kid is to understand the knowledge and utilize it to direct her behavior.

Motivation Source Externalization At Performance Point

Kids with ADHD have not only problems utilizing their inner timer and psychological rules and moreover self-inspiration.

Those who are unable to summon up the often-needed inner strength to remain with a task which is otherwise dull, frustrating, effortful, or prolonged. This innate motivation deficiency can be effectively resolved by offering the kid an external inspiration boost as in an encouragement, promotion, or motivator to obey, limit his behavior, and follow laws — whatever is challenging for the kid at that point in the game. As I talked about being a belief-centered parent earlier, Dr. Stephen R. refers to this kind of thing as developing a win/win condition in his 7 highly effective people's habits. This reward could be an opportunity to encourage the kid to get whatever he/she likes after the job is finished (special treats or treatments), to get the privilege he/she loves (extra Screen time or playing on social media or online games devices), or to receive any coupons or points he/she may save for a later benefit.

Problem Solving And Thinking More Physical Or Manual

Kids with Adhd may not appear to be able to exploit or mess around with sensory knowledge as do others once they have to avoid worrying about a circumstance or question. We respond irrationally, without taking proper account of their choices. Furthermore, I believe seeking ways of portraying an issue and its possible approaches in a more realistic manner can be useful. For starters, if your kid wants to compose a brief paper for schooling and doesn't want to be reacting well to this task, have her own a word document to quickly write down all that comes to mind in a quick period. Thus every idea is collected instead of lost to inattention, and the kid could then broaden and play with concepts in a physical form rather than a psychological form. The same could be done through using sticky notes or even sketching tiny images or signs on a blank piece of paper, each representing some idea that needs to stay in mind in order to fix the issue.

This is perhaps the most difficult sort of material to outsource, but it seems to be especially effective with classwork. Because when solving problems of any kind needs to be done, see if you really can think of a certain way of making the issue and the portions of possible medical solutions so your kid could hold them, modify the bits, push them just over, and develop new information pieces arrangements that could help him resolve the issue. This is much about utilizing the shape panel and sheet furniture parts that designers sometimes utilize in furniture shops to help you imagine various space configurations of furniture you 're talking of buying. By keeping things manual and clear, you will help see a problem's choices and what's going to progress for fixing things. The two DNA detectors, Drs. James Crick and Francis Watson, it appears they did exactly that as they wandered about the DNA layout. They placed the numerous pieces suspected of involvement in DNA on paper scraps and then continued shifting them in different configurations playfully before the right structure was obvious somewhat by mistake.

Consistency Struggle

Each time people are using the same skills to manage your kid's behavior. Adding coherence means pressing matters like being stable over time, being consistent but not giving up anytime quickly when you're just beginning a behavioral change scheme, replying in the same manner even though the way to set changes and making sure both parents utilize the same methodologies. Being erratic or capricious in applying the regulations is a growing welcome to fail. And, when the current management approach struggles to produce drastic, positive outcomes, it lacks confidence. Start a change of behavior plan for a minimum of 1–2 weeks until you realize it's not effective. Don't fall victim to the pit that snares other parents: reacting to actions one way at home than in public spaces in a totally different manner. Finally, seek to establish as much as you can a single parental front, despite the inherent variations in modes of parenting.

Stop Yakking! Act Now

Dr. Goldstein, a counselor, and ADHD medical practice specialist expressed it perfectly while urging parents to avoid communicating and using implications: Speak, don't banter! As said at the start of this essay, your kid is not deficient in intellect, ability, rationality, or knowledge, and talking to the kid clearly won't alter the fundamental neurological condition that renders her and unimpeded. Your kid is far more delicate to the implications and responses you utilize, and far less responsive to your rationale than a kid with no ADHD. To respond swiftly and often and your kid will act better for you. Continue communicating and all aggravation, not enforcement, is what you'll receive.

Future Planning For Problematic Cases

I am certain you are acquainted with the situation: you 're in a supermarket and your ADHD kid begins ripping open bags, dragging items off racks, and simply making mayhem amid constant warnings and orders. You become flustered and irritated, unlikely to be able to think fast and accurately, and you're deluded by an answer. The disapproving glares of salesmen and other retailers intensify your dismay and you attempt to skull out from the shop, trying to pull your kid crying behind you.

I am frequently gripped by the ability of parents to anticipate where their kids are likely to be misbehaving when pressed. But I'm shocked how few appear to make effective utilization of the knowledge. Why not use it to wake up again in readiness for these problems? You will spare yourself a lot of distress as you begin to predict problem scenarios, evaluate in advance how best to cope with them, create an action plan before approaching this problem scenario, discuss the strategy with your kid in advance, and only carry through with the strategy if an issue occurs. People can find it impossible to accept that only discussing the program with the infant before reaching a possible environment of difficulties significantly decreases the likelihood that behavioral issues may occur. But it does work!

Follow these steps before trying to do any problem solving:

1st Step: Stop right before you reach the destination of a possible issue, like the home of a shop, cafe, relative's home, or church.

2nd Step: Evaluate 2 or 3 laws for your kid that they sometimes have difficulty upholding in this case. The rules may be "Stay beside me, ask for nothing, just do as I state" for a shop. hardly any long-winded reasons, just a quick comment including its guidelines. Then remind your kid to say the basic rules again.

3rd Step: Establish the offer or reward, for instance, to pick a treat at your shopping counter, or to stop for a delicious treat on the drive home, whether the kid complies with the laws.

4th Step: Describe the penalty that would need to be given, as in a points deduction or a right.

5th Step: Support the strategy when you reach the environment, and try to provide direct and regular input to the kid whilst there.

Unless you have to, quickly discipline your kid for any actions which break the laws.

Keeping A Perspective Disability

On occasions when confronted with a kid with ADHD that is challenging to handle, parents can lose all focus on the current issue. They may get upset, angry, ashamed, or at least irritated when their current management efforts don't work. They also might stick to the kid's level and argue about the problem as another kid might. You must always remember that you're an adult; you are coach, shepherd, and teacher, of this disabled kid. If either of you is about keeping your wisdom about you, it must clearly be you.

In difficult situations, one way to sustain your calm is to seek and retain a personal distance from the issues your kid has. Turn away from the boy, count to Ten, think about some location you would just like to be (the coast), and seek to more logically reassess the circumstance. You could even suppose you all are an outsider so you can see the scenario for what it represents the regularly scheduled attempts of a parent to cope with a kid with behavioral handicaps. If you're doing this, you are able to engage more fairly, fairly, and logically to your kid than when you let your kid's issues upset you and react rashly in kind that 's hard, so you may need to remember your kid's disorder every day maybe even the many times per day, and particularly when you're trying to come to terms with behavioral problems.

Stop Personalizing The Kids' Disorder Or Problems

Do not let your own perception of personal dignity and self-worth get tied up in if you're not "winning" an argument or meeting your kid. Nobody keeps score here. If possible stay cool, have a sense of fun about the issue and seek to obey the other concepts mentioned here as you react to your kid. This may also involve withdrawing oneself from the scenario for a moment by running to another space to collect your wits and recover the power of your emotions. Don't conclude that when a scenario goes horribly wrong you are a bad parent or don't turn out because you wanted. Occasionally, both parents struggle to control their kids and that does not make them poor people. Your ability to get things correct or do something better next time is more essential, which contributes to my last theory.

Forgiveness Practicing

A very significant concept is to exercise grace but also the toughest to follow reliably in real life. It implies 3 things. First, training to let some of them go of your frustration, anger, or dissatisfaction every day after issues have happened and have also been resolved. Start merely 3 mins of meditation termed mindfulness wherein you sit for just an instant, shut your eyes, concentrate on your respiration or pulse rate, free your head of any and all thoughts and let every negative emotion go from your mind. Deduce this temporary break by simply saying "I absolutely adore you and I pardon you" in your head about your kid. You also can start training compassion at the end of the day while your kid is laid to rest or before you leave for the night. Take a minute to glance at the day and pardon your kid for just about any violations. Let go of the frustration, indignation, dissatisfaction, or other directly damaging emotions that occurred that day due to wrongdoing or disturbance of your kid. The boy can't always regulate what he's doing and needs pardon. Don't misinterpret that crucial point. That doesn't mean your kid shouldn't be held responsible for wrongdoings. This implies you need to let go of some resentment towards them.

Secondly, focus on accepting the other who may well have misinterpreted the improper conduct of your kid that day and acting in ways objectionable to you and the kid, or simply ignoring the kid as stupid or ethically defective. You know much better; do not even give in to what your kid feels of others. Take any necessary corrective action and continue advocating for the kid, but just let go of all the pain, frustration, embarrassment, and hatred that such situations may have inflicted on you.

Finally, when handling your kid every day, you will strive to exercise forgiveness of yourself over your own errors. Kids with ADHD are capable of bringing out some of the worst parents, which often leads to parents having felt horrendously guilty about their own mistakes. Without granting yourself permission to repeatedly repeat the same mistakes without side effects, get over the personality-deprecation, embarrassment, despair, anguish, resentment, or rage that surrounds such self-examining acts. Substitute them with such a frank assessment of your productivity as a mother or father that day, classifying areas for improvement, and making a direct dedication to aspire to get it correct the following day. You will find this concept the most difficult to conform to but the most crucial to your kid's art of effective and civilized management with ADHD.

12.2 How Parents Should Take Care of Themselves?

You certainly also know how tough it could be to raise an ADHD infant. These kids need far more oversight and guidance than most kids because they release headlong with all their hazards into adulthood. They may be unreasonable, arrogant, rude, greedy, and aggressive; their incessant speaking, though more benign, is taking a toll. Yet another recent research found that somehow parents of kids with ADHD, particularly those of kindergarten/preschool age, suffer greater levels of anxiety, depression, and self-blame even than parents of kids without ADHD. In addition, another research has found that parents raising kids with ADHD experience the same rates of tension as parents with kids with serious intellectual disorders, such as an intellectual disability or autistic. To make matters worst, most parents also quit socially confined as family members, neighbors, and friends, try to ignore family contact.

This pattern, as I have seen too often, could even bring parents across a downhill trajectory which tends to leave them depleted and tired, demotivated, and in hopelessness. We have little to do about ensuring the medication of their kids so that eventually leaves themselves with little means to take care of the infant either. That's a case, naturally, that doesn't help anybody.

I don't promise to offer you a magic cure for all the ills a family dealing with ADHD afflict. There is an inevitability of some amount of stress. However, it doesn't have to kill you or anybody else inside your house. Therefore, this chapter is for you only: some practical advice and general recommendations to avoid traumatic situations, mitigate the effect of the unthinkable and allow yourself the escape you need

Averting Form Stressful Cases

The first step you need to do is to pinpoint the specific sources of one's stress to lower the number of traumatic situations you have to deal with. Many parents with whom I have worked seem to focus more on their strong emotional responses fatigue than on the references of that stress and anxiety. They actually mistake each other and assume those who need to remove the feelings of anxiety, irritability, depression and despair, fatigue, and migraines, rather than precipitating events. There are, of course, major stressors that cannot be avoided-more for you than for kids' parents without ADHD. For most of these, you will need to succumb to stress control methods such as formal methods of relaxation, yoga, exercise, in extreme cases maybe even medication. But in many cases — although how many would confuse you — you will recognize the first step you need to do is to pinpoint the specific sources of one's stress to lower the number of traumatic situations you have to deal with. Many parents with whom I have worked seem to focus more on their strong emotional responses fatigue than on the references of that stress and anxiety. They actually mistake each other and assume those who need to remove the feelings of anxiety, irritability, depression and despair, fatigue, and migraines, rather than precipitating events. There are, of course, major stressors that cannot be avoided-more for you than for kids' parents without ADHD. For most of these, you will need to succumb to stress control methods such as formal methods of relaxation, yoga, exercise, in extreme cases maybe even medication. But in many cases — although how many would confuse you — you will recognize although stop or at least might the tension trigger and cut it off. Seek the easy ways although stop or at least might the tension trigger and cut it off. Seek the easy way:

Sit down with pencil and paper while you have some calm time and look back about the moments about the past few weeks that you have experienced psychological stress: nausea, frustration, aggression, fear, or anxiety. Then mention the stressors — not how you feel but the things that followed almost every stress revulsion instantly. What was the circumstance that you believe your response to stress may have caused? What did you or somebody else do that triggered the whole bad response? What did the other people do to your Kind? What may have been your girlfriend doing? What issue came up which made you this feeling? During each stressful event, you describe leaving a few empty lines.

Please show the first case near. What might you have executed to avert this occurrence or question, or remove it? Did your answer render matter worse? Would some of the seven precepts of Dr. Covey have managed to help you get rid of the source of stress? Or did anyone of the 14 precepts on raising an ADHD kid help you prevent the circumstance? Do you see how some of these precepts can assist you to remove this source of stress or avoid it next moment approximately? Or can you just plan on avoiding this exhausting organization or an entity entirely? Write down to at least 1 way of coping during each of the mentioned tension happenings.

Currently, concentrate on the one (and at most 2) of such sources of stress and decide to either stop the source of stress in the long - term or to utilize the coping mechanism the next moment the incident occurs, whether it is inevitable. Shut your eyes then take a new, more positive perspective of yourself in this scenario.

Mind the plan by putting tiny reminders around the work and homeroom for yourselves. Going to take every day a few more minutes to start envisioning the application of this current course of action. This method will strengthen your trust that when it endangers to increase again, you could in reality head off the cause of tension.

When you've built up your trust or tried a new strategy, think about moving onto the next or 2 stressful events. Work on just either one or two stressful events at a period until you master or minimize them; after which start moving on to the next or two. Success there comes with incremental measures because you manage only one and maybe even two stressful events at a moment, not from attempting to tackle them all at the same time.

Confronting Certain Stuff

Since tension these days appears to become a part of everyone's existence, several successful means have been arranged no reduce its harmful effects. Any specialist with whom you interact will direct you to sites of further knowledge on the topic, and so can the Web, the community librarian, or a book shop. You could even find videos and audio files that will educate a few of the best existing techniques. The limits of space render it difficult to be in detail here, so just a few brief suggestions follow.

Delay Your Response

Many of us respond to a stressful situation, quickly and hyperactive. Because we are mentally excited angry or anxious we are always physically excited: our heart is racing, we feel hot, and adrenaline is training us for "battle or flight." Sadly, none of this is leading to mental acuity. It is really such impulsive impulses that we normally end up panicking. And the right thing to do, occasionally, is zero. When the only way to postpone your answer is to walk up, either leave the space for a brief period or send your kids up with a relaxed "In a few minutes I'll explore this with you."

When you face a difficult experience with your kids, simply seek to wait to let your mind focus on the scenario and its probabilities. This will not suggest you load your head with thinking like "Oh, what am I going to do? What do I do? "And 'I think I can't do this,' and 'It won't fit, I don't have any ideas and I don't think what to do.' Rather, seek and remain cool and let the mind address the problem. That's the great thing with the human brain: the only way you have to do is not mess with the innate issue - solving skills to support it come up with this concept. Just give it some time.

Excercise Meditation or Relaxation

Some individuals routinely utilize relaxing methods to reduce their average degree of tension. As these technologies can have a significant preventive effect, they will represent you well even when confronted with a forthcoming stress incident which can not be prevented. For instance, say the teacher has called and told that your kid is sent home to start a fight with yet another kid, and the next day you have to meet only with the principal. Anxiety is likely to accumulate as you rethink the potential consequences even before meeting. Exercising methods such as gradual muscle stimulation will hold you out of reach from losing the circumstance. Many books sum up this technique and many others. Mindfulness meditation of the muscle includes breathing techniques and stimulation of each category of muscles, in turn, accompanied by visual visualization of oneself in a comfortable, peaceful environment. Learning is simple but it is most successful when you have some principle, so expect tension and start teaching in advance.

Increase The Concentration

Some other way to prevent out of percentage blow stuff is to expand your attention when you are engaged in a difficult situation. Seek to stop tuning in on the little information and then concentrate on the entire thing from the viewpoint of your own lifespan or that of your family. It can often make you visualize that the traumatic event isn't as essential as you make it, that it could be handled, and even if it's not going well, it's not as big of a problem as you might think. During the school session of our earlier case, you should hear to the nuances of what the administrator is thinking while reflecting on the idea that this is only one school session, that the views shared are not definitive and should not create a disruption of your life or in that of your kids, and it as an administrative parent you 're actually in control of this session and what occurs to your kid.

Start with Ending in Mind Cases

Describe how you'd like circumstance to switch out again for your kid, before and during a difficult situation. Trying to keep your optimistic plans in mind could really reduce the effect of nasty comments, reduce the frequency of your very own responses, and thus ignore escalating the conflict and deteriorating its overall result.

Personal Revival Excercise

The raising of an ADHD kid places enormous demands mostly on mind, body, heart, and spirit. Check out the following recommendations to restock yourself mentally, feel too much in control of the situation, and get better equipped to handle unanticipated traumatic situations. You have seen a number of the first, so it's always likely to have something different. You intend to receive as good medication of yourself because your kid does, and that indicates trying to set aside a specific amount of time.

Take a Holiday

Even walking out is the best way to refresh your resources. Should not fail to do exactly that. Go home, and take care of your kid with your companion/partner. Visit friends, go out to a spa, lmao a good book on the seashore, or do anything that tries to appeal to you in a unique way. This is well throughout the hassle of planning this escape to refresh your mental battery and catch up on your bunk. seek to get back from your companion/partner once and a while as well because there is anyone you expect to provide about your kid — adult marriages ought to be refreshed too.

Search a Social Activity or Hobby

The whole last thing a kid with ADHD wants is a freedom fighter for a parent — one who has made sacrifices all personal delights and leisure time to spend time with the kid. That parent is going to be wearied, fatigued, depressed, and often untainted or grumpy. You commit it to yourselves because your kid to pursue something that can consistently offer a feeling of individual fulfillment and contentment.

Each parent I notice was also an inexperienced winemaker and formed a tiny club of likeminded people who met regularly and make new vintages, study wine production, and take trips to beverage tastings. someone else also entered cricket groups, choral bands, quilting bands, cycling clubs, musical bands, reading groups, or sports leagues. Unofficial get-togethers are also available, like coffee klatches as well as cookout suppers. Also, there are private activities such as woodworking, fly binding, model construction, vintage collection, genealogy study, drawing, knitting, crochet, or knitting, studying.

The number is endless. The argument is that following a personal goal will offer you the same feeling of relaxation as heading on a quick vacation, as much as you enjoy it.

Join Supporting Groups

Probably the last activity you should do whenever you decide to be revitalized is to find a community of individuals that have the similar issues you do, yet holding help group sessions on a daily basis has many benefits. True, community groups are indeed a good source of knowledge and guidance, but they often provide encouragement release, and there, numerous parents ultimately make real friends. A few groups have even looked after the kid's cooperative societies; see whether your local branch supports the person.

Meet With Close Buddies

Renew your positive affiliation with all those that you've been near to it for decades. Many of us, when we're distracted, let these partnerships move away from most of us, but as we all also need "secure escape" Aristotle named real friends. Extricating oneself to a good friend provides immense psychological value; somebody who understands and cares well about you will give not only a leaning shoulder but also a different outlook on your issues.

Shared Parenting Practising

Just because taking a few of these ideas sounds like nourishing yourselves and they think you don't have time to do that, you might need to speak to your companion/partner about reallocating a few of the ADHD parenting burden on your kid. Sometimes an excessive amount of this load tends to fall on the mother, or even if this is not the situation in your residence, you may benefit from deciding to take huge responsibilities for a kid every other day (and, if either one of you operates away from family, every other night). This gives you relatively stable times in which to pursue individual ambitions, and also just providing you time to breathe deeply and have some time off as well.

Try to be Aware of Certain Moments

Most of those world's great spiritual leaders and scholars have recommended us to concentrate our mind at any moment in time on the beautiful nature, joy, peace, and wonder of the world in front of us. Yet in preparing people for forthcoming events we get so wrapped up that we sometimes miss the mystery of this very present time. My work friend doctor Jon Kabat-Zinn authored a novel that I highly suggest, anywhere you go, Where You Are. A key principle of this book seems to be that reflecting only on the moment — its tactile riches and textures, and their variety, both wide and minute — repays our expenditure in time a thousand-fold in renewing our personal strength, mental awareness, and emotional equilibrium and power. The sense of anxiety, time, and immediacy too that parents of kids with ADHD feel every day can be seriously reduced.

As described earlier, such an approach includes halting what you're doing and, opening the eyes, having a central focus for your concentration, like your movement, and then making the other emotions fall out of your head while you focus on this central focus. If any ideas arise into your head, just mention their appearance or then let them move on but don't delay them or participate in them with you in any intellectual discussion. Then open up your eyes or just try and focus on the perceptual knowledge you are going to receive at that time or on your inhaling, what others might consider that moment's texture in interaction, regardless of any opinions, what's just happened, or what might come after that.

Analyze and Change Nerve-racking Thinking

At least mentally, you are, to a large degree, what you believe. You've actually realized that while you're feeling humiliated and acting, say, by throwing your kid's tantrums with ADHD into stores, both these parents seem to have been dealing with the similar misconduct of their kids in a matter of fact, without alert system or discomfort. Ok, you might think, maybe they should be cool because their kids don't behave like that if they go to a shop, whereas yours does.

Needless to say. A renowned psychotherapist, doctor Albert Ellis, came up with a theory many years ago that we evaluate how we could feel about those happenings or people in a particular scenario by what we think about. We fan the fire of our toxic feelings as we speak about grim, disturbing over-critical thinking. But if we recognize these harmful thinking processes and transform them into proactive, optimistic, personality-empowering patterns, the unpleasant emotional responses will potentially be reduced or even removed.

So, you might think when one's kid throws a temper tantrum into a store:

"How does my kid render me so embarrassed? Everyone needs to watch. What do they mean of me? They must think that I am a terrible parent because I cannot properly manage my kid. I knew I needed to stay home. How dare I embarrass the kid like that really? Now I will never come to this location ever. why am I such a pitiable parent or guardian?

In the same circumstance other parents those who've seen acting so calmly may think:

"I will not give in to the effort to extort my boy. He understands the law and I told him that we did not buy any gadgets or candy on just this trip already when we got here. I am the instructor of this boy, and maybe he's got to learn it the hard way I'm not going to be overwhelmed by those tantrums. He calms down after a few minutes. It's saddening that he has to offend himself this way and disturb shopping for other people. I've seen a lot of parent's mentor their kids for such kinds of overreactions. In reality, many kids sometimes act this way through stores. Yet letting him in now would be telling him the big lesson.

By having a good diary with you and recording in it whatever you were actually saying to yourself before an incident that caused a traumatic or emotionally disturbing response took place you will try to recognize negative thinking. Once you have started to recognize your pessimistic or disturbing patterns of thinking, try to replace more constructive, uplifting, constructive patterns and forgive them next time you feel the same chronic stress taking place.

Workout Daily

Alright, we've all noticed this guidance before, but when it comes to stressful life, it would be very important to pay attention to it, so it's worth mentioning again: daily exercise reduces stress, builds endurance, replenishes our self-control energy,

And usually puts us more in a position to satisfy the demands of each day. Seek to mix with another self-renewal task if you don't believe you can find the time: invite a buddy to become a commuting partner, bring together a daily foursome for baseball (and stroll, don't run, the course), or schedule frequent gatherings with close pals (and see the managing time sidebar). But remember, according to the physical therapists, you'll benefit from as little as twenty-thirty minutes of gentle exercise 3 times per week.

Avert Chemical Items

You have heard it all before: tobacco, caffeine as well as nicotine will steal far more from you then they offer back. By now we all recognize the risks of smoking, but the intake of alcohol as well as nicotine seems to be more volume issues. Very clearly, if you want to conserve your resources, balance is necessary. Alcohol is indeed a painkiller; when taken excessively to abundance, it may contribute to weakness, tiredness, poor intensity to agitation, and discharge to obligations. Tobacco and caffeine are also stimulants; in a setting, they may raise heart rate, bp, respiration rate, brain function, muscle pain, drowsiness, and perceived discomfort or nervousness. The very last factor you will need overreact is, I 'm sure you'll comply with that. So, take a few minutes to assess your behaviors and to see if they really represent you properly.

12.3 Managing Time A Survival Key For Parents

Time scheduling clearly doesn't apply to most individuals because it isn't exactly management skills at all. Time cannot be exploited or handled; it just flows along and seems to flow. Time control is self-help, a capability that needs to be learned over time. It requires practice and effort, but its bonuses can be huge especially in ADHD-affected families, where there are so many requirements on parents.

In library resources and bookshops, there are several good reads that can give you complete details on how to effectively manage your time. Most of them start by demonstrating that the first move must be to establish precise, well-defined, realistic long- and short-term goals. While you're doing it, you end up with plans every day, every week, every month — a plan you could even effectively follow, giving you the feeling of satisfaction which you 've achieved what you've set out doing. A kid with ADHD, unorganized and problematic by nature, can leave you feeling as if their life has little order at all, so it is extremely significant to get this sense of achievement.

Time management professionals split the usage of resources into five categories: essential and critical, but not critical, urgent but not significant, neither immediate nor essential (busy work), and idle time. Knowing the difference will help you understand where your task normally lies, and maybe teach you how to adjust the essence of your existing home or work habits to accomplish your goals.

• Essential and immediate. Duties to be performed immediately, and at the very coming years. They always get finished, even though they are immediate and significant. That's not usually the place in which time gets thrown away.

• Crucial however not immediate. It is here where it is easy to differentiate successful parents from unsuccessful ones. There are duties you or others find essential and they're not urgent. You may not get around to completing them the rest of the time. Time schedule will help lift certain specific goals to a more critical level and you can make things possible. Able to take time for self-renewal, exercise, linking with good friends, or your emotional connection with your companion frequently falls into the latter category and will be neglected to the detriment of you in the longer term.

• Highly urgent but not relevant. Very small or insignificant items certain people find urgent for their commitments but those are of just moderate value if you think about it. However, even though they are pressing (immediate), you may be giving closer attention to them than some of your more crucial but less urgent objectives. Returning emails, posts, and text messages on Facebook and replying to queries via the mail may fall in that category since we feel like we have to react to them as rapidly as we could to or as other people ask. However, a large percentage are not significant.

• Working hard. This may include trivial activities such as house chores, answering unwanted phone calls, performing errands, reading snail mail, odd jobs, and the like. Before the essential ones, you can do them since they are quick and deflective or offer you a sense of accomplishment, but they never lead to the actual objectives for oneself or the ADHD kid.

• Missing time. If this is having to watch terrible Television programs or twenty - four - hour news channels, sitting through a bad film, or visiting an unnecessary group meeting, this kind of activity usually leaves you feeling you might have spent all that time and do something else better. Most folks assume this is the reason for their poor time planning, but generally, experts believe, the real reason is to allocate much more time to classifications 3

& 4 just not adequate to the 2nd category. Check out how you're spending your time. This could be true for you?

Look out for the true time wastes of time too: indecision, accusing someone about the loss of energy, chasing success instead of quality, going off track because of irritating distractions, meaningless social media (emails, text messages, tweeting, Social sharing, etc.) and having the tiny snippets of time being spent sitting go unfille.

Conclusion

A lot of kids and adults are suffering from ADHD. Individuals diagnosed with ADHD have trouble holding a focus for extended periods, have trouble keeping goals and strategies in mind, and also have difficulty hindering a before the-potent response. ADHD is largely genetic and so parents of kids with ADHD can also exhibit symptoms of ADHD. Being a parent, you do have an enormous impact on the treatment of your kid. Data proves that eating healthily, exercising, and allowing other intelligent daily choices could even help your kid handle ADHD symptoms. Which ensures your kid will continue ADHD therapy today at home. Physical exercise instantly increases the rates of norepinephrine, serotonin, and dopamine in the brain all of which influence concentration and concentrate. Mindfulness helps you to give attention, which improves the "concentration muscle" over time. This operates by enhancing the capacity of an individual to regulate concentration, self-observe, and establish new attitudes to typically negative interactions. This will even help you more conscious of your emotional condition and you won't respond too impulsively often a major concern for ADHD-persons. Experts have discussed for some while about utilizing mindfulness to resolve Symptoms of ADHD, but the issue has still been how individuals with ADHD will really utilize it, especially if they are hyperactive. However, and new research demonstrates that perhaps the flexibility and versatility of mindfulness allows people with ADHD to fix things for themselves. ADHD and mindfulness seem to be a contrasting mixture of practicing meditation and staying still for a prolonged time period may sound like an unlikely feat if one has difficulty holding concentration and wants to be busy. However, taking into consideration some of the main elements of understanding it is evident how it would be helpful to someone ADHD suffering.

ADHD hypnotherapy may seem doubtful but the evidence for this widely underestimated yet effective alternative medication is remarkably optimistic. Hypnosis is quite efficient as a substitute, or parallel, type of treatment for ADHD patients: it assists both kids and adults control their health issues without the medicinal side effects. People with ADHD have a terrific natural multi-task but also highly energetic level capability, which can enable them to succeed if utilized efficiently. The purpose of utilizing hypnosis in a way would be to allow the individual to do more in their everyday lives. Kids develop into more successful adults whilst adults can utilize their intensity and management skills at doing a job more effectively or do simple homework. Hypnosis would also create self-esteem for kids and adults alike. This is essential to fulfilling some of the other objectives that they aim to accomplish, as well as better knowing themselves.

An aspect that any ADHD patient truly wants is somebody who loves enough to want to accept them, to embrace them dearly, and to encourage them to reboot their daily lives with new routines and refreshing experiences for others might be parents or dear ones.

Part 2

"Bedtime Stories"

Introduction

Tell me one story. How many times have they told you to do this? When you're a mom, mother, grandparent, uncle, aunt, babysitter, child-care worker, or someone else still has interaction with babies, I'm sure you haven't missed this regular plea for childhood. Yet have you ever asked what children want when they apply? Are they just looking for entertainment? Do they want to fly into a dream world? Would they like the connection between storyteller and listener of the intimate relationship that exists? Are they trying to connect with a character that can represent what they want to be? Are they looking for explanations of how they will act in practice, explain or cope?

Here there is a basic principle: Children love stories — for several purposes. If we need evidence, just listen to them say, "Please tell me a story." Look at the rows and rows of children's stories books which fill our bookstores and libraries. Look at the stories that come to life in popular children's movies, or the tales of strife, war, and triumph that appear to be the focus of too many video games. This is our appetite for stories we never stop wanting to hear them, even though the form of the questions can change somewhat—"Can I get a new book? "And" Can we borrow a DVD? "The focus of this book is on the pragmatics of sharing tales, discovering metaphor solutions, and structuring your own psychological myths, rather than reiterating the basic metaphor therapy studies. Since both the art and science of metaphor therapy are relevant, at the end of the novel, I have included a comprehensive reference section that will enable interested readers to further explore the essence of metaphors as a language medium, their usefulness study, and the variety of their therapeutic uses. It can also help you discover more educational story content in a range of ways, from children's books to traditional folktales to Web pages. This book has compiled stories for kids of all ages. From fables to inspirational an adventurous stories, all have been beautifully presented.

Chapter 1

The Introduction To Bedtime Stories

A bedtime story is a popular storytelling method, where a child is informed at bedtime to encourage the child for sleep. The bedtime story has long been regarded as "a definite entity in many families" Reading bedtime stories provides multiple benefits for both parents and children. A bedtime story's set sequence before sleeping will boost the growth of the child's brain, language comprehension, and critical thought skills. The connection between the storyteller and listener establishes an emotional link between the parent and the infant. Because of a child's "power of imitative impulse," the adult and the tales they say serve as a role model for the infant to obey. Bedtime stories are often valuable for showing the infant moral values such as compassion, selflessness, and self-control, since most children are known to be "naturally compassionate because they have encountered or can understand others' emotions" Therefore, bedtime stories may be used to explore deeper topics such since death and bigotry. As the bedtime stories grow in scope, the infant can "grow in their understanding of other people's lives and emotions"

1.2 The History of Bedtime stories

Nap-time tale is a popular storytelling method, where a child is informed at nap-time to be encouraged for sleep. Nap-time stories provide many advantages, especially for family / elders and kids. A bedtime story's set ritual just before sleep has a calming impact, and an individual's soothing voice telling a tale makes it harder for the infant to fall asleep. The interpersonal dimension establishes a link among the narrator as well as the audience. Bedtime stories may could be narrated from a journal, or the storyteller may create them. The stories are generally not very long with happily climax. A common type of reading at bedtime utilizes longer books, but breaks them up, therefore they build plot twists. Kids look forward to tales in bedtime, so they will have a set schedule in place. There aren't real "beginnings" to how nap-time tales began as storytelling has been a piece of heritage of world in general as civilization began. The notion of contemporary bedtime tale arose out of traditional storytelling though. Family and fellows would labor hard throughout the day before the industrial revolution; the parents as well as the babies. People will sit round the bonfire at the sunset to chat and share tales of gossip. After the novel, all parents and kids will sleep in the evening together. The tales would include controversy, emotional pain or exploration which parents and children will hear to. With the rise of capitalism, at different hours and in different spaces, parents and children started to go to bed. Schedules were developed for Bedtime. Another main predictor was the transition from verbal story-telling to a book reading. Since the Digital Revolution, the publishers of books were intensely aggressive in seeking to market as much as possible of the finest material. Stories like in Peter Pan were beautiful, joyous and colored. The publishing firms started transitioning to the three-to-six year old age range after WW1. The tale had started to become quite easy. Today most reported bedtime stories with a rather mild vocabulary are from one-to-five min. long. The kids would know the tales the parents would tell in the past which were really bleak and gruesome. Brothers Grimm's were some of the best known legends. And as civilization expanded, the tales changed to make us lighter and happier. Bedtime stories appear to wind up with a sort of morale. Older bedtime books were very detailed and violent, so the lessons were often detailed and violent. A famous illustration is the Sandman, which would spray sand in children's eyes at night while they were sleeping. Bedtime tales will also incorporate other values for children while they're adults. Early on Disney was really well recognized along with Snow White & Sleeping Beauty to represent a pure woman who likes to sweep. Disney's page is distinct from the Brothers Grimm page.

1.2 bedtime stories are very important for you growing son

Children would often ready for sleep, climb into their beds and wait for their parents to read a book until they fall asleep. The classic stories of the fairytale, imaginative books with cartoon drawings and more were piled up high next to their bed waiting to be read every night.

Just like the narrator confronting a dilemma in these novels, bedtime stories face their own problem: they're dying. A recent study showed that a third of parents rarely read their kids a story at night and that 4 percent of kids don't own a single book. Furthermore, a survey in the UK in 2010 showed that 55.7 per cent of primary school teachers taught children who had never read a story.

As the stories about bedtime are diminishing, so are the benefits that the children get from them. It has been proven that reading to an infant before bedtime improves academic achievement. As reading is introduced into the daily life of a child, as they get older, they will have an internal motivation to read. Research has found that children who read for fun are more likely than those who rarely pick up a book to do better in math and English.

Reading is essential to helping children grow as writers. Pie Corbett, a literature specialist and former head teacher at the high school, said: Any teacher still thinks the greatest authors, the most professional authors, are learners. It not only provides the language to youngsters, it also builds their imaginations.

Most parents said lack of time and uncertainty prohibit them from reading to their children every night. Some also said that their kids prefer the books over TV, gadgets and computer games. Yet parents need to note that this time it's all about enjoying time together with their child and developing together.

Bedtime tales are not just for educational benefit. Much of the time, tales are beautifully constructed with a lesson on emotional existence which is subconsciously instilled. These teachings are applied to teenagers and adults including the following from some of my favorite childhood books:

Where the Wild Things Are Mauric Sendak: there are monsters all around us in the universe, yet you can take care of any circumstance in which you are, conquer the monsters and return to a safe location.

The Sharing Vine, Shel Silverstein: We are all growing old but together we grow strong. We will be appreciative of where we come from and when we end up.

For so many merits of Nap-time stories it is our responsibility to make time for our family. There are too many options to discover stories these days-bookstores have wide parts for youngsters, libraries are always free and filled of content, and e-books and online tales are now open to everyone due to technology.

So consider what you did during your childhood the next time your kid gets ready for bed (a study says 91 percent of parents read bedtime stories as an infant)). Choose a book from the bedside table, and read your child to sleep.

1.3 The secrets of ideal bedtime story

Many parents have combined the literature greats with Hollywood blockbusters trends to build bedtime tales to inform their youngsters. But the formula for the ultimate tale of bedtime has now been first revealed.

• **Bedtime phenomenon: scientist creates books that bring children that sleep in minutes:** Protagonists should involve the dragon, with magician & the sprite, said the families that took part in the poll, which would preferably revolve around a magical palace.

217

Children said they welcomed a fleeting moment of suspense in which the hero is confronted before eventually triumphing over the dark powers.

According to almost all those surveyed with most kids shunning love tales in favor of fiction a happy ending is important.

- Why incarcerated dads use bedtime stories to communicate with their children The study also showed that one in ten parents fear that their capacity to say stories is not up to scratch. About half of the children surveyed felt that when the storyteller used various vocals for every role player, tales were most amusing.

A fifth of teenagers said they were anticipating the plot to turn well for all.

Researchers consider August and September to be the most painful time of the year for parents to let their kids go off to sleep. Parents say during the summer break, they tried to bring the kids settled into a bedtime schedule. The lengthy summer season days often provided parents with a task.

Story-telling expert Alex Charalambous said: "When **your baby plans to just go back into school since the holidays are over**, a consistent nap time plan including reading the story is a wonderful thought to set up. The simplicity of a traditional tale pulls children in, as the evidence indicates, and the positive outcome allows for a good night's sleep.

"The story box is perfect means of sharing a novel. Story boxes could be a box of shoe & painted as a background, woodland or a scene on the seaside. For your characters you might use finger marionette and roles who are trapped on lollysticks. This helps you to give the story a lot of room whatever direction you want. "Dermot King, Butlin's managing director who commissioned the research, addedWe have been working to account for the under-fives in each possible way, while ensuring that families may spend more time around the kids despite additional stress. "To insure that nap-time is an experience like the remaining part of the day, we're renting out these creative story boxes at the beach, offering parents the opportunity to truly involve their kids at nap-time, & make sure they're sleeping off in anticipation for another day-long action."

1.4 How to read a bedtime story

Research shows that when dads read the stories of bedtime, their children perform better at school. Bedtime stories promote the growth of expression and vocabulary, which make children appreciate acquiring reading skills. If nothing else, a snooze-time story aids in establishing healthy sleep habits. Then, time to tell some tall stories.

Get into the characters: Bedtime stories can be told in a comfortable environment-so let's continue by shutting off the television. And introduce some dramatization to the tales, whenever appropriate. Seek to interpret in various languages, or do any of the acts the protagonists of the novel do. Anything that makes this tale more interesting would make it more enjoyable story-time.

Have a daily read: If your child only learns to speak, read the same story on a regular basis. It would help them grow their vocabulary and strengthen their memory. The first time a kid listens to a tale they won't catch it all — but hearing it over and over again makes them get familiar with vocabulary and develop rhythms of expression.

Stop making the story-time into a learning activity by utilizing it to check the reading abilities of your infant. Instead, only ask specific questions about the stories and help them create a link with the tale and their everyday lives. For instance: "What will you do?" or "Any some other black cats?" Book a Boys' Night In it's much more necessary for fathers to consciously inspire their sons to learn. Boys still think of reading as a 'girly' activity to do — which might understand why lads fare too poorly in literacy testing — but once young boys see their primary role model loving reading, it would always inspire them. In reality, the Mr. Men stories don't always have to be that. Reeling off your favorite line or two from a newspaper article, novel, comic book, or football match day system can help them create a connection between reading and playing.

Find age level: At the library, spend some quality time with your family. Look for age-oriented novels, and stories you loved as a kid. Let those even select books— even if they want one that is too complicated for them but them like the images. Encourage them to look about to discover tales that they want. In school children who have favorite books seem to perform well when they are small.

1.5 The Merits of bed-time stories

Bed-time stories are considered to promote relationships between parents and children and to ready kids to asleep. Although researchers have lately added certain forces to this nocturnal activity. They claim that when you along with your kid sail to the place of the Wildness with Max or study green eggs and Sam, you are literally stimulating the growth of your kid's cognitive abilities.

"Neural evidence suggests that children grow a lot more than we ever considered feasible while parents and care takers communicate orally with them — this involves narrating to them," as said by G. Reid Lyon, director of the NICS and Human Development's infant growth and behavior division in Bethesda. Those improvements vary from enhanced reasoning abilities to reduced stress rates. But maybe the greatest advantage found recently is the scheme bed-time stories will rewire the minds of children to sharpen their language mastery.

"This is a strong evidence of a cognitive disparity between children those which are read daily, & children who haven't," says Dr. Lyon. The positive thing is that differences will not be lasting. Scientists have shown in NICHD research that visual photographs of children's brains deemed weak readers reveal no involvement in verbal-processing regions. Though subsequently the study spent 8 weeks recitation to the bad readers for one to two hours a day and working out certain learning activities, their mind function had shifted to resemble as of the successful students.

This is how the retraction happens: as you read to your kid the traditional bedtime tale of Margaret Wise Brown Goodnight Moon, exaggerate oo vocal in the moon and draw the locution hush, you activate associations in the portion of her mind which processes linguistic vocals (auditory cortex). There are forty four of such sounds in English, named phonemes, which vary from ee- ss. The more times an infant hears certain signals, the easier it learns to perceive it. After that when she is a baby learning to understand English, she'll be capable of discern the distinction between, perhaps, the words big and doll more quickly. As a school grader acquire to recite, on the screen, she would be more likely to sound foreign words out.

"You will first learn the parts to tear down unfamiliar terms into bits," Dr. Lyon says. "For example, when children hear the term cat, they typically listen it wrap up like one voice (cat) in lieu of 3 (c.a.t),"so he speaks. "But when told to tell cat less with c, they can more readily realize about words that are made of single vocal, thereby eliminating the cuh sound to render at." Reciting rhymes to children is a mean to develop this ability.

Creating an Inner Vocabulary Parents should use story-time as a starting stone for communication to improve the language abilities of a child even further, narrates Lise Eliot, Ph.d AP of neuroscience at Chicago Medical Facility & writer of what's going on in there? How the mind & brain grows during Life's starting 5 Years. For e.g., if a mother points to the baseball cap of Curious

221

George and tells her boy, "Do you have a cap such like this?" she gives him practice in proper language use.

Dr. Eliot, though, warns parent not to constantly fix speech errors created by their infant. "My own kid still thinks he's, like 'That's the hat for him,'" she notes. "So I'm not thinking, 'No, you can tell his hat,' as you do not want to deter him. Instead, I'm only teaching the appropriate expression by accurately repeating his phrase: 'Yeah! It's his hat!'" Over time, communicating with a kid can broaden the language much further than only talking to her would. That's how books will expose children to concepts & things — like kangaroos or porridge — which are not part of their immediate world and often not piece of their everyday communication. Watch out for tales that include especially vivid or vibrant vocabulary, such as the working of Caldecott winner William Steig, He also drops into his books four-star terms like scatter brained and languid.

"One More Moment!" This statement is commonly considered as straightforward attempt by a kid to postpone bedtime. Yet what children & guardians may not realize is that regular reading of a book will assist a kid improve his or her reasoning capabilities.

The initial moment kids read a novel, they don't remember it all, narrates Virginia Walter, Ph.Ds. an assistant professor at the, Los Angeles' University of California. graduate school of education and communication sciences. However when they listen that over and over again, they tend to recognize trends and loops, knowing if single page asks, " bear brown, what you watch?" the forthcoming page would inform the answer of brown bear: "I watch a blue bird staring me." They will even start to anticipate what's going to occur next depending on their previous experience ("Ooo, the wolf wish to break down the house!"). Afterwards, such topics in pattern detection, series comprehension, and forecasting results will benefit kids in many fields, ranging science and math to music and literature. Reciting loudly does not have to end until children can read alone; in addition, that is where they improve literacy skills in reading, says Dr. Walter. To work, inquires a kid how she feels is going to happen after that, or whether she will finish a tale otherwise.

Experts say parents uphold the practice even in adolescence. You'll start to introduce her to latest terms and add and her repertoire by picking books that are just over a teen's ability level. Moreover, reading aloud will offer a forum for discussions with the children. "Talking about difficult problem outside of the background of your daily existence is a much better," states Dr. Walter. "If the problem pops about even in private life, one might ask, 'Recall we spoke about what?'" She recommends reading Katherine's iconic Bridge towards Terabithia for talking to teens about death; similarly, the small Home on the Prairie books gives families the chance to address prejudice.

Soothing Snuggles: The interactions of an infant to books must be fun to help impart the educational advantages of literacy, narrates Peter Gorski, M.D "You desire him to conjugate reciting with fun and emotional warmth, above all else," he says.

The Moment children are relaxed and secure they will also lessen their anxiety levels by reading aloud. The moment a kid is undergoing some pressure — like being teased or beginning a new school — his brain tries to shield him by releasing the hormones cortisol that stimulates the body's reaction to "fight/flight." Cortisol may in turn help children withstand everyday tension in limited numbers. Although it may inhibit learning in greater numbers.

Although no experimental experiments have been done about how bedtime books impact children with elevated cortisol rates, neuro-scientists believe it is rational that reading a popular book when snuggling next to a parent will relax an infant, thus reducing the cortisol levels to help him focus better, Snuggle up in a cozy spot with your boy, with his favorite covers & animals stuffed alongside to enhance the calming nature of the story-time at your home.

"Calm down & enjoy your boy," says Dr Gorski. "Just imagine about the near time you're spent together can do with your cortisol rates

Global Institute of Infant Welfare & Human Growth Director of Child Development & Behavior Division Reid Lyon narrates: "Neural evidence indicates that when parents and caregivers communicate orally with infants — like narrating for them — children understand even better than we ever thought possible." For years to come, you can continue the essential type of stimulation. MomJunction asks you where you can start reading your kid's books, what sort of stories you can hear, story-telling rewards and a few infant bedtime tales. Introduction of the infant into the realm of tales is never too early. Doctors suggest you start reading them from a very early age for baby stories to boost her imagination. In fact, while you are still pregnant you can make a habit of reading aloud, as babies recognize the voice of their mother in the womb.

It is a good habit to set aside time to read the stories every day. The perfect hours are bedtime, and naptime. Getting your baby read a portion of the night time routine will help settle down and realize that it's time to sleep. Set time between 6.30pm and 8.30pm, anywhere. Might cause your little one exhausted every time after that.

Bedtime stories are a perfect way to boost your kid and you connect. She'll love to look at the colorful pictures and listen to the fairy tales in real good time. Numerous other advantages (1) are listed here:

1. Develops comprehension: Story reading helps build oral speech skills, listening skills, memory and language processing skills for your infant. It is a safe opportunity from a very early age to strengthen her language and multiple sentence structures.

Over maturity and age your kid can learn to interact in the same manner as you by body language, communication techniques, listening and learning.

By the time they reach one (2), babies will have learned all the sounds needed to talk their native language. The more you learn, the more phrases the less becomes revealed.

2. Social and emotional development: drawings and stories go hand in hand, so your kid will come up with ideas regarding assorted objects, plants, birds, etc. You'll hear her using new words for thought, experiencing and sharing her emotions.

3. Cognitive abilities: Long before your baby starts speaking, she absorbs information about the language by listening to the stories that you are reading. This will certainly reap benefits as your child starts their schooling.

Babies can learn to turn pages around for about ten months and listen to new sounds. As your little one continues to grow she'd learn from left to right the art of reading. Through listening to bedtime stories, children, who are around a year old, will improve their problem-solving skills.

4. Improves attention: Involving your baby in bedtime stories is a perfect way to help her grow acquainted with the practice of reading. It's a very good and safe habit too. By reading to her every night, you will develop their concentration skills.

5. Relieves anxiety: Calming her mind and body is a safe way to go to bed. Particularly though she is over-stimulated, the reading of stories will help her get interested in a whole new environment and release her from all the anxieties.

6. Improve your knowledge: As your baby ages, she may start searching for and taking inspiration from other people. Reading time is the best moment to affect the little kid, and to show them lessons about life. Which can enhance her personality and expertise.

7. Is a ritual: It becomes a practice and part of her life when you make story-reading the norm of your little one. Gradually reading is a treat, and when she grows up you don't have to remind her to learn it. The reading can open the door to writing later in life.

1.6. Tips for Parents

•   You must not make your baby and yourself hearing stories monotonous. Keep it so fascinating that she looks forward every day to this type of relationship with you.

•   Using various feelings and vocal noises when reading the tale helps the kid to learn socially and emotionally.

•   Let your baby look and answer questions while you listen, in order to encourage emotional learning and thought skills.

•   Let her imitate noises, recognize pictures and study vocabulary.

•   Print it out of exhilaration, excitement and closeness. It allows them to connect themselves with children.

•   While reading, cuddling helps your baby feel connected, protected and wet.

•   Sing rhymes, and make amusing noises like wildlife.

•   Don't think about hearing the same tale over and over again. Love babies, and learn from repetition.

•   Switch off triggers such as Cable, or radio.

•   You will strengthen associations in the portion of your baby's brain that understands language sounds by exaggerating the 'oo' sound in the sky, and utilizing phrases like hush. The portion is known as the auditory cortex.

•   Know the contact with your kid is the secret to getting the best of the story-reading on bed-time.

1.7 Stories that you should read to your kids

Any easy narrative with fun drawings should fit for children. They'll affect your baby's overall growth. For children, choose basic short stories relevant to their present stage of existence, such as how a boy found his missing pet or how a girl discovered how to use the potty seat.

Stories with the right images will show assorted dolls, creatures, birds and more to your little one. Stories with minor information like the variation in color, form and scale will allow her to differentiate between the choices available. But try them out.

Young babies cannot recognise the images, but because their vision is still improving, they get drawn to various shapes and contrasting colours. Add stories with a message in it, and your kid can understand certain values for the lessons of her lifetime.

1. Good Night, Patsy Scarry's Little Bear; illustrated by Richard Scarry: Once there was a little bear that loved his dad too much! Both also appreciated the company of each other. Since the father came home they played together every hour. The father bear recounted to the little one a tale of bedtime during supper. The father will hold the little one on his back after the bedtime tale, and send him to bed. The baby bear had concealed someplace one day. The father went on to playfully hunt for the infant, asking, "Where might Little Bear be? "The father looked high and low-above the china cabinet, outside in the woodbox, under the stove to locate him. Father had not been able to locate the little child. Finally, as they went by a mirror the little bear showed itself. The little bear walks to bed (believing he had fooled his father).

2. **Good Night, Gorilla by Peggy Rathmann:**
There was a zoo full of species such as lion, wolf, bear, horse, mouse, cat, rhino and more. The zookeeper makes nocturnal runs at night and heads back to his house. The zookeeper completed his rounds that day, and was making his way home. A mischievous gorilla then snatched his keys and went after him. It liberated all the other animals one after the other from their cages. The

zookeeper was pursued and they went into his room. The keeper's wife got the mean creatures found. She will lead them back to their rooms. All the animals returned to their homes.

3. Margaret Wise Brown's Escaped Rabbit, illustrated by Clement Hurd: There had been a young rabbit there. She felt depressed one day, and tried to run away from her mother and become a wall. The mother was more afraid as she cherished to the heart the little rabbit. She promised the little one she would accompany her anywhere she was heading. The Mother's unconditional affection made the young bunny feel healthy and happy. She went to bed happily, holding her beloved mother!!

4. Guess How Much I Love You by Sam McBratney and Anita Jeram: A little bunny is adorable and always likes his mum! One day he decided to show just how amazing his affection for his mother is. The parent bunny and the little bunny are exchanging comments of growing affectionate language. As the match comes to a end, all relax into night.

5. A Sung Na Book of Sleep: As the night is dim and the moon shines brilliantly, everybody goes to sleep. Except a vigilant owl!

One owl was up on a starry night observing all the other creatures settling down for the night. It has seen some animals standing up sleeping and some lying on the move! She had some nights there, happily. Some become dead entirely. Every animal has its own resting spot!

6. Margaret Wise Brown and Clement Hurd Goodnight Moon: There was a tiny rabbit who often acted kindly and talked respectfully. Everybody around had enjoyed it. The bunny says "goodnight" to all around "goodnight room" every night, before going to bed. Healthy evening Sky. The cow running over the moon Goodnight. Goodnight, and the gold balloon...' The little rabbit, like the sky, the comb, the broom, the bowl of mush and the cow jumping over the roof, says goodnight to the rhyming items in his house. And lastly, go to work.

7. Rest At Last by Jill Murphy: It's late in the night, so they both find their way to bed tiredly. You are now able to fall asleep. But why do Mr. Bear not fall asleep? It's because the baby bear is still busy with planes. And mommy bear is snoring now .. Snoring! Mr Bear asks if he really gets some quiet!

8. Llama, Llama, Red Pajama, by Anna Dewdney: This is a bedtime for Baby Llama. Yet the little guy isn't yet able to go to bed with his mother. He asks where she's gone, and likes to think until she comes back. Momma reassures that she is "still near, even though she is not here now." This calming tone allows the little one to slip into a peaceful sleep.

9. Nick Sharratt Timothy Pope's Shark: In the Park continues staring through his mirror, now and again. He stared through the telescope into the water, and saw a shark in the bay. But how could it happen? Sure, the finding might only be the fur of a cat or uncle!

10. Julia Donaldson's Monkey Puzzle: Once split a little monkey from his mother. He loved his mum, and tried to locate her. He'd asked a butterfly for support. Support him the nice butterfly decided. Yet butterfly didn't realize if it felt like the mum monkey. Through when the butterfly attempted to suit the mother of the monkey it struggled. During through mismatch the butterfly's silliness made us laugh.

For babies a bedtime tale brings them to an imaginative place, where fun never seems to stop. Telling tales and conversing with babies can be treated as seriously as feeding them. Allow bedtime story- telling your kid one of the best moments. Only don't hesitate making it into a routine!

Chapter 2

The Risky Ventures Of Zorian – An Adventurous Bedtime Story For Kids

There once lived a widowed nobleman and his only child, a daughter called Zapata, in an ancient & crippling home by the delirious ocean shore. Given their high birth, living in poverty, so hapless that the plains & forests of their small realm had been auctioned one by one to purchase essential goods for surviving. He knew that Zapata will be lonely and a miserable condition practically as when he will pass away, he brought her up as not as a girl but as boy, she was not aware of riding the horse instead ride it as an expert so magnificently, outclass her dad in his one of the favorite fencing competition., and even swim like a mermaiden & the good disposition Zapata got it genetically from her mom. Zapata never felt odd or different while she was being brought up different other kids.

By the end of the evening of October, when the violent air stream from the ocean rocked their petty old home to its very base and set the tattered draperies on the walls, Zapata's dad passed away. He left behind a golden florin, a subunit of copper, & only crippling home. The sum of money was adequate for Zapata to spend almost a week or two, Zapata will be on her own when this little amount on money will be gone, what would she do? The father of girl had asked her to visit the King & request him for his guardianship; but the Castle or Palace of the Monarch was very far away from her home, and Zapata flinched from lending his hand in front of someone or the distant road.

The courageous girl eventually decided to pave her footings to survive in this world. She got all the guilder of gold and moved to a small town which was nearby, and purchased an attire. After that she went on to dress her hair up so should looked like a guy, dressed like a boy, wearing clothes she just bought she started moving towards the main bazar of the area to look for any position

At that time it was a usual practice that if a person is a looking for a job as domestic worker he may go near the fountain in that market and the people who were in need of a worker also went to get one there.

No one was present waiting on the owner's side of the spout as Zapata came into the bazar, but contrary to this, preparing for the 1st owner who would come, there was a small number of loud and brazen lairds and bellhops. Zapata, or Zorian, as she called herself now, strode proudly over & entered this party, pounding her heart fast with the excitement of the fantastic venture.

Then a knight-errant-errant, riding on a horse and luring the other cart by Baulk wobbled across the square's gravel stones, and moved towards the spout, shouting to the bellhops to come to him. However, despite the summons of the horseman, the bellhops ignored him and nobody was moved. Curious to learn the reason for this contempt, Zorian asked a nearby bellhop and she was enlightened that the knight-errant was nothing but Enchanter, and that no bellhop or laird should represent him the reason his palace was plagued by trolls, demons, and every kind of frightening spirits. Today, Zorian wasn't a funk, or beggar, as the quotation goes, can't be selector. And, much to the bellhops' amazement, Zorian went over to the Knight, who was apoplectic with tension & longing and told him that he is ready to work for him. The Knight-errant bade Zorian mount the horse that he held; and frisked in the background chatters of the hooting of the bellhops, lairds and masters.

They rode all day long, until the sun was about to set and Zorian found himself on the edge of an uncivilized, abandoned moor. In the ballistic trajectory of the sky, under the light sunlight, there has not been a leaf, not just a home, not even a shepherd's shack to been seen, but the huge desolate wasteland that rolls up and falls to the very edge of space. The sun sank lower and lower; cold grew, & a blue smoke fell. Came Sunset, a dark, green dusk.

Suddenly, Zorian beheld the magical dwelling from a moor hillock down. A huge submerged swamp confronted him, which was starting at the base of the mountain and going interlaced, until its parent side was lost in the darkness catching up. The air stream fussed the brushes at the top, and the fading sunset was gleaming still on the horizon broad bog had captured none of its shine, and lied Packed of turquoise-coiled fog, delicate quagmires, and obscure black islands. A hideous cry of weeping, out cried by some moor witch, echoed across the mist, freezing the gore in the veins of Zorian; so to a response of the shout, hundreds of will-o'-the-wisps emerged, darting and spinning. A great black rock up rose stood exactly in center of this awful marsh, the fortress was standing on this giant solid rock, its walls and battlements set against the blazing light of the moon. Ghostly lights flickered in the glass, now white, now dark. At the edge of the swamp, the Enchanter reigned his horse and wept until the prancing conjuror-fires rushed from both parts of the wet land to him. After a while a path was discovered leading through the marsh to the palace, an enchanting path that which was disappeared in the back of the horses like smoke disappears in the winter breeze. The ghost-fires followed the Enchanter to the first door of his castle; then, rising rapidly high up into the clouds, they fled in all sides like astonished fowls.

The doors opened up by themselves, mysterious and horrible beings left, and shiny, whirling fire globes fled through the courtyard of the castle hissing. As soon as they were entering the palace, the Knight-errand moved himself and starred on Zorian with his blazing pupils.

"Boy," he said, "let nothing you listen or watch scare you. Be told you can't be affected by any force or spirit. In the universe a single ghost is more powerful than me, who has more strength then me and that is terror itself. Be courageous, keep your heart's doors fixed and closed in front of this terror; be loyal, and you will never have reason to remorse for being here. "And Zorian, who was courageous by definition, felt bad of permitting the demon terror to strike at his heart's door, and vowed not to slip his valor ever, whatever could happen. And the lad held faithful to this determination throughout the passage of time he remained at the Enchanter's side. Firstly, for being confident, he needed to fight to overcome his distrust of any of the baggards; so the time tickled away and no demons or baggards again tried to bother him, he became habitual of their appearance & finished by giving no further heed to all than to the might dark clouds that flew croaking across the quagmire. The small bellhop was so obedient and brave that when a year was finished, the Enchanter asked him to stay another year again, offering him lavish bonuses if he lived. Nonetheless, after the 2nd year was finished, Zorian had a desire to witness the normal lands again, and convinced the Enchanter he needed to go.

"Alright," replied the master, who admired the courageous bellhop's bravery, you're a courageous and trustworthy lad. Here's a gold bag for your pay, and here's three presents to honor your bravery and goodwill. "He opened a barrel of copper and carried out a tiny glittery fowl with spread pinions hung from a fine glittery cord, a golden ring, and a ruby sphere decorated with a white band. "This small fowl," the Enchanter added, "will shield you against the curses of any magician or demon whose strength is not greater than my power, and would start singing when you go into secret dangerous situation; this passe-partout will unlock any gate throughout the might lands; and if you get distracted form your path, you just have to place this barrel on the table, and it will start rolling itself and safely take you home. Remember, if you're ever in dangerous trouble, contact me, and I'll come and rescue you. "And Zorian was obliged by the Enchanter and brought his presents back to the world. Yet he was so sweet and generous that he quickly gave away all the golden coins he had received to the poor, then he was forcefully sent to look for some other situation. He joined the emperor and his wife of the Twelve Towers service at long last.

This royal family, famed both for their kindness and goodness in Fairyland as well as for their riches & grandeur, but they only had a son, Prince Wezel. He was famous for his valor and bravery that no other warrior earned such fame. He busted the green cavern dragon out of the realm of his father; he was in combat with 3 evil witches side by side, and killed all of them; he had given an awful spell to the diamond palace that was imposed over it.

When Zorian joined the Monarch & Queen's service, these wonderful guardians were sent their son on a tour to his brother, the ruler of the plan, and Zorian was commanded to follow the nobles, warriors and troops their convivial company, who were set to make the voyage. Prince Wezel was advised to visit to his uncle's, in the hope that he might fall for the ward of his uncle, the lovely Princess Rosamond, according to the company's gossip.

So, however, it was many days the company was in travel on the road for a few days, Prince Wezel, who looked after as closely as a decent captain looks over his men, was conscious of Zorian's courage, trustworthiness and humble appearance, the small bellhop and asked him to be his private laird. Oh, Oops! He was no longer advanced than Zorian's little post, though outwardly remaining a post, was the running away girl Zapata at heart. Though she struggled against her own heart as much as she might, all in vain, as she realized that she had fallen in love with this beautiful prince Wezel. She nevertheless happened to sign or indication of her love to escape her the Wezel thought of her only a small bellhop, and if she was going to utter it may be to unearth the secret she had kept for a quite a period of time so effectively.

One day, as the caravan was passing by a lovely country, Zorian, so we still have to keep naming Zapata, followed closely behind his prince, Prince Wezel saw a beautiful ruby-red flower something like a ruby plant, glittering by the side of the lane. The exact instance, as if it were real, the little glittery fowl Zorian worn in his neck sang a few simple notes. "What a beautiful flora!" The Prince said. "I want to take it." And when Zorian spurred ahead of him, he almost came off the horse to collect the flower, Zorian came forward tossing magical flower to it into a trench. "Oh, how naughty you are bellhop!" all the knights and women screamed. The business was traveling a few kilometers on, when the Prince immediately got his eye on a stunning knife with jewels lying on the road. Exactly the same instance the little glittery fowl was singing a few simple alarm notes.

"What a knife! "The Prince shouted, I want this.' And he was about to uninstall & take the knife, when Zorian stepped in, grabbed the weapon, and hurled it into a ditch.

"Oh, what a non-sense thing! "Troops and women screamed.

The business was moving constantly for a couple miles further now, and the Prince again seen a lovely enchanted forest on the roadside. In the bushes, fowls of many shades sang, spouts were sparkling and played in the sunshine and the sweetest of music was being played. The glittery fowl sung harder and much louder exactly the same time.

"How stunning place is this! "Prince screamed. "Let's go inside and explore its beauty." So Zorian dashed to the Prince's side, imploring him not to enter, claiming the place was magical, and any danger may come upon him.

All the officers and their wives, maybe a little annoyed of a bellhop would know better than they did, chuckled at little Zorian, and even Wezel grinned at him, saying, "That's just fun, little Zorian," and squeezed through the gate of the garden. Nothing happened about a little while or so, & the first person who went in ridiculed the Zorian; until the whole company had reached the place, there came a scare sound of thunder, and all but the Wezel and Zorian, who were covered by the magic of the Enchanter, were transformed as rocks. The rumble of echoes had barley quit to roll when two terrifying demons with the heads of lions charged across that place toward them, grabbed the Wezel and took him along with them. Zorian lingered in the garden alone. Night was coming soon.

Now, a witch was the owner of the magical forest, who had a daughter so hideous that only the strong spells of her mother could not make her attractive. However, despite her ugliness, the daughter of the witch thought herself reasonably stunning, and she often imported her mother to invite the princes of the castle that she found deserving of her hand. So the old witch offered lovely dances and parties to which all of the neighborhood's worthy young kings and princes were invited, but as soon as the witch's daughter emerged on her hideous face with a horrid smirk, the young men were sure to make their excuses and ride away.

Lastly, the old witch, who had just had a severe reprimand from her daughter for not punishing the Prince of Hendriya after that Prince had refused to ask her for a dance, could no longer bear the scolding of her daughter and vowed to trap the first prince. The latter came past her yard, and compel him to embrace her hideous daughter, willy nilly. In her pit, poor Wezel had entered, and the witch had thrown him into a dark cellar, trying to turn him to her will by frightening him. The hideous daughter had suddenly looked through the prison's keyhole and, at first glance, fallen in love with Wezel.

The witch was only deciding what to do next when her lion-headed servants told her that one of the company had defied her spell and walked around the yard. So the witch put on her invisibility cloak, and going down to the garden, found poor Zorian wandering under the trees disconsolately. Instantly she witnessed tiny glittery fowl that had saved him from her magic. Being terrified of the beauty and still powerless to do any harm to the little boy while the fowl was in his hands, she resolved to rid herself of Zorian by taking her palace, gardens, and everything else around the globe. So, she muttered a spell, and everything was gone.

The next morning when Zorian woke up and found the castle was gone, his heart sunk. He did not despair, however, but took the little scarlet ball that his lord, the Enchanter, had given him out of his pocket, placed it on the table, and bade it lead him back to the Enchanted Forest.

At Zorian's own pace, the little ball suddenly started rolling ahead; at night, it glowed with a scarlet light. Next day, month after month, the scarlet ball went on; it led Zorian across hill and down dale, through the land of the people who had only one hand, through the area of the dwarfs, and through the valley of the singing trees, never halting until it reached the witch's garden entrance.

A year had gone by, meanwhile, and the witch had done everything she could to persuade Prince Wezel to embrace her hideous daughter during that year. She had attempted to frighten him first, then attempted to win him by offering him splendid fetes, then tried to intimidate him again, but because the Prince was not to be terrified or cajoled, she came to the end of her wits. She told the Prince that if he didn't agree to marry her daughter the very next day, she'd turn him into a hare and put her dogs on him. The Prince did not react to her awful warning, and the witch stepped on and planned for the greatest of marriages. Zorian arrived in the garden that evening.

As it was late, and the moon, a quarter full, had vanished behind a curtain of clouds, Zorian arrived unseen at the door of Wezel's prison, for the witch had locked him up so tightly that she hadn't taken the time to locate a guard. Oh, Sorry! The poor Prince laid at the top of a high tower, and twenty different doors stood between him and the ground, each unlocked by a different key.

237

Yet Zorian was not to be daunted, and taking the key that the Enchanter had given him from his bosom, he unlocked one door after another before he entered the Prince's inhabited cell.

The unfortunate Prince laid bound on a straw bed, struggling to read a book by single candlelight. He became despondent, as he had agreed not to marry the ugly witch maiden but to let himself be ripped in half. You would be sure he'd been delighted to see Zorian.

"Dear Zorian," the miserable Prince said, "if I had just obeyed your counsel, everything would have been fine." And he begged Zorian to tell him where he had been all year long. So Zorian described his exploits to the Prince.

Now the chains the Prince wore were cruelly riveting around him, and because there was no lock on them, there was no use in the magic ring. Nevertheless, Wezel tried to work them off at length; but in doing so, he hurt his foot and discovered to his dismay that he was still able to walk along. Gradually the warm air and the movement of leaves started to foretell the dawn's arrival. Eventually, just as the dawn-star has begun to fade, Wezel and Zorian rushed through the twenty doors from the jail and raced to the highway.

But when the wicked witch learned Wezel's flight, they had driven just a few miles, and, dreadfully enraged, ordered her dragon car to be ready so she could go after him. So the car rolled out, and the witch leaped into it and climbed into heaven. Hearing the dragons' hissing and screaming in the air, Zorian and Wezel attempted to hide under some trees; but the witch spotted them immediately and pronounced a spell to turn them into hares. Even while the witch's hate was swift, Zapata's woman's heart was faster, and she sacrificed herself for the man she loved, she flung the chain and the golden fowl over the head of the Prince. She had transformed a moment later into a little gray hare crouching at the foot of Wezel. At the same time, the wicked witch, who had entered her castle, let loose her pack of fearsome hunting dogs, who soon picked up the hare's trail and came in full cry running toward her. The unfortunate Prince picked up the hare and hobbled on as soon as he could, ignoring the awful agony it caused him, but the dogs raced a hundred times faster than he did. The pack came closer and closer, their red tongues clinging out of their black throats. Through a good chance, even when the pack leader was not more than fifty feet away, Zapata had enough intelligence to recall the vow given to her by the Enchanter and to call upon him. Immediately a solid glass wall rose from the ground behind Zapata and the Prince, as high as a castle tower, and the pack, hurrying on, found themselves pulled by their prey. Snarling and screaming, they hurled themselves against a pillar of magic; but in vain.

The Enchanter himself stood before them in another moment, and brushing the hair with his hand, returned Zapata to its human form. Nevertheless, she still wore Zorian's clothes, and the Prince always thought of her as a child.

Suddenly a shadow appeared behind them on the table, and everyone looked up and saw the evil witch and her hideous friend, riding out in the dragon car to celebrate the gruesome death of Wezel. The Enchanter caused the dragon car to vanish suddenly, and the witch and her daughter plunged into a pond tumbling through the air and became disgusting little fish. Then the Enchanter took Wezel and Zorian back to the castle of the witch, where the tables were set, and the meal was served to celebrate Wezel's wedding and the daughter of the witch. Last, of all, he rescued the business of Wezel from the spell of the witch.

Now, one of the ladies, when she learned how the witch had attempted to pairWezelwith her aunt, and when she saw the wedding arrangements, told the Prince that it was a shame that Princess Rosamond was not at home so that after all there would be a wedding there.

239

"A wedding? No, "Wezel said," not until I met a wife who proved to be genuine and loyal as a little Zorian." "She's already here, "the Enchanter said. And Zorian touched his sword. There was a burst of flame suddenly, and out of it, Zorian no longer emerged, but herself, Zapata. Her hair had grown again long, and she was clad in the most magnificent gowns by the Enchanter. No lovelier girl was ever to be seen on earth. Maybe you're confident the Prince walked in, took her by the side, and claimed her for his bride. Shortly Wezel's mother, who had been invited by the Enchanter, came, and after all, there was a marriage. The Enchanter returned to his castle on the Black Rock when the merrymaking was over, while Wezel and Zapata returned to their own country, and lived there happily to a right old age.

Chapter 3

Bedtime Fairy Tales For Kids

An instance of a folk genre that takes the shape of a short story is a fairy tale, fairytale, wonder tale, magic tale, or Märchen. Usually, these tales involve creatures such as dwarfs, dragons, angels, fairies, giants, gnomes, goblins, griffins, mermaids, singing birds, trolls, unicorns or witches and generally spells or enchantments.

3.1. A most Different Voyage

Through personal experience, any Copenhagen resident understands how well the doorway to Roddick's Clinic feels; but because it is likely that those who are not Ottawa residents can also review this little piece, we must give a quick overview of that at all.

The comprehensive tower is isolated from the sidewalk by a very high fence, so far away were the heavy metal walls, in all honesty, it has been said, some really slim fellows had once pushed itself into a night to go out and make his small checks to the area. Most challenging area of body to handle on these instances was, obviously, the head; there, like it is the instance in history, fast-headed men get across better. So much for the intro, then.

One of its young people, whom head may be seen like the densest in a sense of physical just, had the watches that evening. It started the rain and burst into streams; yet, in view of such two barriers, the young person was forced to be out, if only for a couple of minutes; and to inform the doorkeeper that, he felt, was very pointless, if he might escape via the railings with an arm. Inside, the galoshes, that the warden had overlooked, lie down; he seldom imagined for a moments that they had been Great deal of money's; and they gave him good customer care in the cold; so he placed all. The problem now was that he could push itself via the grating, just as he had never yet done it. Well, He was standing here now.

"I'd gotten my head open to Paradise!" he stated unwillingly; then immediately passed over it, quickly and painlessly, because this was quite large and heavy. But maybe they had to get across the remaining physical body!

"Ah! I'm too stout," he grumbled loud, repaired as if in a voice figured the brain was the worst aspect of the question-oh! Oh! I can't even push myself in!" He tried to take back his under-hasty hands, but he just couldn't. There was space enough even for his heart but that's it. His first impression was of rage; his second was that his patience had sunk to null. He had been got in very hard and terrible condition by the Fortune Shoes; and, alas, it has never happened with him to desire itself home. In even heavier streams the wicket-black clouds spilled off their innards; no man had to be found in the road. To meet the bell is what he would not want; he had no use in screaming out for help; however, how embarrassed he would have been found trapped in a pit, like an outsmarted fox! How does he pull itself around! He knew plainly that being an inmate before midnight, or although even late throughout the dawn, was his irreversible fate; otherwise the smith had to be removed from reality to put away the stalls; thus all this wouldn't be achieved so easily as he might conceive regarding it. The entire Charity Academy, on the other side, is in action; all the fresh stalls, without their not so courtier-as hot of seafarers, could pursue those because of interest, and it would welcome him with such a wild "hoorah!" as he was sitting in his public square: there is a crowd, a growling, or reveling, and heckling, 10 fold less out of the lines about Jewish people several years before-" O, my blood is piling up to it.

Yet you don't have to accept the relationship is now over; it's getting too worst.

Night gone, as well as the next day; still no one came to get the Socks.

At the King Street small theatre, "Tragic Readings" had been provided in the night. The building was packed with suffocation; and a new poetry by Wells was amongst other parts to recite. C. Anders, entitled, My Aunt's goggles; the details were almost as follows: "The certain individual having an aunt, which spoke with special talent in card-telling, but who was continually assaulted by people that wish to get a glimpse in to the futures. Nevertheless, she remained full of magic regarding her craft, in which a specific set of magical glasses were doing her invaluable service. The hospital's young person, who seems to have overlooked his aventure of the previous night, has been among the crowd. He has on the footwear; for whatever legal holder has yet existed to assert them; so he felt they are just the answer for him, plus it was just so very dusty outside.

With much humility he lauded the beginnings of the verse: he also considered the concept unique & successful. And that the conclusion of it, as the Rhine is very negligible, showed the author's lack of imagination in his opinion; he was beyond extra ordinary, etc. This was a perfect chance to have done something insightful.

In the meantime, he was fascinated because of the idea, he must like to own that kind of duo of goggles for himself; otherwise, just by wearing them circumspectly, he could be able so that can see into the minds of men, which, he felt, would be much more fascinating than just seeing what will occur in coming year; for that we would all know at the right time, but never the other." can now," he said to himself, "fancy the entire row of ladies and gentlemen seated on the first row there; if one can only look into their hearts, yes that might be a revelation, kind of bazar. I would consider for particularly a big milliner's shop in that lady yonder, so oddly dressed; the shop is bare, but it wants to clean surface all along. But among them, there would be some fine, stately shops too. Ah, Sorry! "He sighed," he said, "I am aware of the fact that which one of everything is beautiful; but there's still a tittative young shopkeeper who's the one thing in the shop that's wrong. All will be wonderfully placed out, & we would say, 'Come in, gentlemen, come inside, this is where you can find anything you really want.' Oh! I wish I might go in to Heaven and take a ride straight into the cores which are here! "& look, you see! That was the signal to the boots of Fortune; the every man was shrunk & a very peculiar voyage from the hands of the spectators' front row began now. The very first spirit where he passed was that of a center-aged woman, yet he immediately saw himself in the space of the "Organization for the Healing of the Twisted and Disfigured," whereby sculptures of malformed legs are shown on the gable in bare truth.. And there was one distinction, the deposits were collected at the patient's arrival in the institution; though they were confined in the heart & protected since the voice people went along. We were, including casts of non-male mates whose most carefully maintained physical or cognitive dysfunctions are here. He glided into another female heart with the writhing of an idea; although it looked like a huge, holy fane to him. The white innocent dove flickered on the altar. How gladly he would have sunk on his feet; though he need to go to the adjacent soul; although he was hearing the echoes of the organs, and he was feeling like he has become much more stronger and healthier; he thought it was not appropriate to move in the adjacent place that was revealed by a poor haymow with a ill bed-ridden mother. Yet the bright sun of God shone from the window which was open; beautiful flowers bowed on the roof from the boxes which are made of wood, and 2 birds which are sky blue in color sung rejoicing, as the ill mother implored her devout daughter for God's greatest blessings. He now crawled into a butcher's shop on feets & hands; there was nothing but meat on either leg, both upside down. It was the core of a most sophisticated wealthy man, who is sure to find his name in the database. Now, he was in this good gentleman's wife's head. This was an ancient, dilapidated, mouldering twig. The portrait of the husband was treated like a wind vane, associated with the doors in some manner or another, and then they closed & open themselves as the stern old husband turned round.

There upon he stumbled into a sleeping accommodation made up completely of glass, just as at Rosenberg Castle; yet the lenses are exacerbated astonishingly. On the ground, in the center of the room, the person's trivial "self" stood, like just a Dalai-Lama, very surprised in his own superiority. He instead dreamed that he had reached a syringe-case full of spiky bolts of all sizes. "This is an old maid's head, sure," he said. He still did not understood it was the soul of a soldier. It was the heart of a young soldier; a man with talent and emotion, as people have said. Now he came out from the last soul in a row in the greatest perplexity; he was finding it difficult to properly gather his thoughts, and fancied that his very vivid manifestation came along with him. "Well done heavens!" He sighed. "Surely I have a turn of mind to lunacy — it's terribly warm here; and Blood in my arteries is hot, so the brain is smoking as fire. "But now he recalled the evening before, when his brain had been jammed between the hospital's iron railings. "No way! Is this how it is," he said. "I will do it in time: a shower could be best for me under these circumstances. I wish I'd still be on the upper side. In these Russian (vapor) pools, the individual stretches to the side or form, and as he gets used to the sun, he goes up to the roof, where the vapor is, of course, warmest. In this way he slowly ascends to the top. And so he lay in the vapor-bath on the top bank; still in his boots and galoshes with whole garments over him, however the hot droplets comes down burning from the top onto his nose.

"HI!" "He screamed and climbed down. Through him, the bathing attendant vociferated a big shout of astonishment as he beheld a man clad in the water. However, the other one maintained enough existence of sense to communicate to him, "'this is a call & I earned it! "Although the 1st thing he wanted as soon as he gets back

245

would be to put a big tumescence on his rib cage and take his insanity away. He was suffering from chest pain and blood extravasation back the next morning; and besides the horror, which all he had learned from Fortune's Shoes.

In the meantime, he became fascinated by the notion-he will like to own a set of glasses himself; otherwise, maybe by wearing them assertively, he will be allowed to look into the minds of the people, that, he felt, would be even more fascinating than seeing what will occur the year after; for it we would all learn at the right moment, but not the other.

I may still, he said to itself, decor the entire section of sir or madam seated at the front of the line; if one would only see in the souls-yes, it would be a revelation-a kind of souk. Within this lady thar, so oddly clothed, I will have to find for sure a big milliner's shop; in this one that store is bare, just she needs to wash it well plenty. That was the signal to the Boots of Fortune; the entire person diminished along and a very peculiar trip across the cores of the spectators' first line started now. The very first heart through which he passed is that of a woman of the middle ages, yet he soon liked itself in the space of the "Establishment for the remedy of the bent and disfigured," whereby sculptures of deformed legs are shown on the wall in bare nature. So there was a distinction, the casting are obtained at the patient's arrival in the organization; but now they were held in the core and protected as the sound engineers went along. They are, including sets of women friends who quite diligently maintained physical or mental deformations are here.

He slid into a woman heart with both the wasp-like writhing of an idea; yet this seems to him as a huge, sacred fane. The white innocent dove flapped over the crucifix. How happily he should have fallen on his toes; yet he must go to the new soul; but he always noticed the peeling sounds of the heart, but he indeed just seemed to be a younger and stronger man; he felt ashamed to step in the adjacent temple that was unveiled by a weak garret with such a sick bed-ridden mother. Yet the bright sun of God shone via the air vent; lovely flowers bowed from either the wood bloom-boxes on the wall, or two moon-blue birds joyfully sang, as the ill mother urged her holy daughter with the greatest grace of God almighty.

He then crawled into a butchers shop with hands and feet; there was nothing but meat at only on either leg, both above and below. This was the core of a far more decent wealthy man, who is sure to find his name in the Database.

Suddenly, he was in this respectable chap's wife's core. This was an old, decrepit, rotting twig. The image of the husband is used as a climate-cock, associated with the windows in some manner or another, and then they raised and shut themselves as the strict old husband turned around.

Hereupon he stumbled into a bedroom entirely composed of reflections, like the one at Rosenberg Fortress; but here the lenses enhanced to an extraordinary extent. On the ground, in the center of the room, the individual's trivial "self" stood, like just a Dalai-Lama, very surprised at his own superiority. He instead dreamed that he had reached a needle-case full of pointy needles of all sizes.

"It's an aged maid's head, sure," he said. Still he was wrong. This was the spirit of a young soldier; a man with talent and passion, as people stated.

He then emerged of the last core in the line in the highest bewilderment; he was also unable to place his head clear, and liked that his too wild imagination had flee with him.

He grinned: "Dear lord!" "Surely I possess a tendency of insanity - 'this is incredibly warm here; my adrenaline is boiling in my bloodstream and my brain is smoking like a flame.' And then he recalled the significant incident of the night before, how his brain had been stuck among the hospital's iron railings. "No way this is how it is," he added. "I ought to do it in time: in these conditions a

Russian bath will do me well. I just wished I'd really be on the higher bank. So he laid in the mist bath on the higher bank; still with both his garments on, with his shoes and rain boots, as the warm drops scalded from either the roof on his chest.

"Hoolloa!" he yelled and leaped. On its side, the bathing assistant emitted a loud scream of amazement as he glimpsed a person clad in the water.

The other one however, maintained a decent frame of thought to say to him, "'This was a bet, and I earned it!' But the only move he accomplished as soon as he went back was to place a big rash onto his chest and take his insanity back out.

He used to have a swollen chest as well as a bruised spine a next afternoon; and except the scare, it was all he had learned from Fate's Boots.

3.2. The Pig man

Once upon a time there was a poor Prince, who had a kingdom. His empire was very small, but still large enough to get married; so he decided to get married. To the Emperor's daughter it was definitely very sweet of him to say, "Will you have me? "But he did so; for his name was known far and wide; and a hundred princesses replied," Yes! "And" thank you so much. "We'll see what this princess has written. Hear!

It happened that where the father of the Prince laid buried, a rose tree grew up — a most lovely rose tree that blossomed once in every five years, and even then bore just one bloom, but it was a rose! It smelled so good, that he who inhaled his scent forgot all worries and sorrows. Moreover, the Prince had a nightingale, who could sing in such a way that it appeared as though all the sweet songs were living in her little throat. So the Princess was to have the rose and the nightingale; and accordingly they were set in large silver caskets, and sent to her. The ruler had them carried into a large hall where the Princess played with the court ladies at

"Visiting;" and when she saw the caskets with the presents, she clapped her hands with joy. "Ah, if only a little pussy-cat! "She said, but the rose tree came to view with its lovely rose. "Wow, how beautiful it is!" All the ladies of the court said. "It's more than pretty," the Emperor said, "it's really cute! "Yet it was kissed by the Queen, and almost able to weep. "Fie, Baby!" She said. "It's totally not made, it's normal!" Before we get into a poor mood, let's see what's in the other casket," the Emperor said. So the nightingale came out and sang so delightfully that no one could say something ill-humored about her at all. "Fantastic!" Charming! "The ladies screamed, as they all chatted with French, each worse than his friend.

"How much the bird reminds me of the musical box belonging to our blessed Empress," an old knight asked me. "Oh heck! The same voices, the same execution." "Yes! Hey! Yea! "The Emperor said, and wept in remembrance like a child." I'm still hoping this isn't a real bird," the Princess said. "Yes, it's a real bird," the ones who brought it said. "Well then let the bird go," the princess said; and she declined to see the prince in a meaningful way. He was not to be discouraged, however; he daubed his face over black and brown; pulled his hat over his head, and knocked at the entrance.

"Good day to the Emperor my Lord!" He said. "Will I get a job at the Palace?" Why, yes," the Emperor replied. "I want someone to look after the goats, because we have a lot of

And the Prince was named "Imperial Pig man." He had a filthy little room next to the pigsty, and he was sitting there all day and working. He had made a fairly little kitchen-pot by the evening.

Small bells hung all around it; and when the kettle boiled, these bells tinkled in the most charming way, playing the old song, "Ach! Dear Augustine, Everything's gone, gone, gone! "Yeah!" * * Honorable Augustine!

The whole thing is gone, gone, gone! "But what was even more interesting, whoever stuck his finger in the kitchen pot's smoke, instantly smelled all the dishes that cooked on every stove in the city — this was something very different from the rose, you know.

Now it happened that the Princess marched that way; and when she heard the tune, she stood still and seemed pleased, for she could play "Lieber Augustine;" it was the only piece she knew; and she played it with one finger. "Why is this my piece," the Princess said. "Fair enough, the pig man must have been well trained! Go in and ask him for the instrument's size. "Then one of the court-ladies would run in, but first she drew on wooden slippers. "What are you going to take for the kitchen-pot? "The lady said.

"I'll get ten Princess kisses," the pig man said.

"Hell, hell! "The lady said.

"I can't exchange anything for less," the pig man rejoined.

"He's a brutal fellow! "And the princess replied, and went on; but when she had gone a little way, the twinkling of the bells was so lovely." Dear Augustine, Everything's gone, gone, gone! "Keep tight," the princess said. "Tell him if he's going to get ten kisses from my court girls." "Sorry, sorry! "The pig man said. "Die Princess's ten kisses, or I keep myself the kitchen-pot." "Neither will it be! "The Princess said. "But all of you stand before me so that no one can see us." And the court-daughters stood before her and spread out their clothes — the pig man had ten kisses, and the princess — the kitchen pot. That was adorable! The pot boiled the entire evening, and the whole day after.

They knew perfectly well what had been cooking throughout the city at every fire, from the chamberlain's to the cobbler's; the court-ladies danced and clapped hands.

"We know who's got chili, and who's got dinner rolls, who's got cutlets, and who's got bacon. How inspiring! "Yes, but keep my secret, for I am the daughter of an Emperor."

The Prince's pig man — that is, the Prince, since no one realized he was anything than an unfortunate pig man, could not let a day pass without operating on anything; he eventually designed a rattle that, when it was swung round, played all the waltzes and jig tunes that have ever been heard since the world was created.

"Oh, that's fantastic! "As she walked by, the Princess said. "I have never seen any more pretty compositions! Go in and ask him for the instrument's price; but he won't have kisses anymore! "He'll get a hundred Princess kisses! "The lady who was to inquire said.

"I don't think he is right with his senses! "The Princess said, and went ahead, then she paused again, after she had gone a little way. "Art must be promoted," she said, "I am the daughter of the Emperor. Say him that he should have ten kisses from me, like he did yesterday, and will take the others from the court ladies." "Oh-but we shouldn't like that at all! "They said. "What are you talking about? "Princess asked.

"If I should touch him, you should certainly. Know you owe me something.' And the ladies had to go back to him. "A hundred Princess kisses," he said, "or else let everyone have their own! "Hold on ring! "She said; and as the kissing went on, all the ladies gathered behind her. "What might be the explanation for the pigsty near to such a crowd? "The Emperor, who came to the balcony just then, said, wiped his lips, and put on his spectacles. "They are trial ladies; I ought to go down and see what they're all like! "Then, at the bottom, he picked up his slippers because he had slipped on them.

He walked very quickly until he reached the court yard, & the women were so enthralled numbering the kisses that they should all go on equally, that they could not consider the King. The emperor sprang up on his toes. "What's it all? "Once he realized that actually what is happening, he said, and with his slipper he turned the Princess's mouth, took the eighty-sixth kiss. "Watch out! "The Emperor said, because he was excessively angry; and the princess and the pig man were driven out of town. The Princess was now crying and shaking, the pig man scolding as the rain pouring down. "Woe to me! I am unhappy man! "The Princess said. "Like I have just dated the beautiful **Prince! Oh! How unlucky I am!" And hence the pig man marched next to a bush, cleaned off his skin the black and brown pigment, took off his filthy garments and stepped out in his princely vestments; he appeared so majestic that the goddess also couldn't resist kowtowing to him I have come to scorn you," he stated. "You wouldn't have an noble Prince! You couldn't reward the flower as well as the merlin, but you were happy to kiss the swineherd for trumpery games. You're done properly." Instead he went right back in his own tiny realm and closed the house door in her face. Now she would say, everything is gone, gone, gone!"**

3.3. The Emperor's new clothes:

There was a ruler many years back, who liked new clothing so much, that he wasted all his time dressing up. In the least, he didn't bother himself for his men; neither he want to go to either the theater or the hunt, save for the chances he was then given to show off his new clothing. The Monarch had a new suit for every other hour or two of the day; just as for any other monarch or queen, one is used to hearing, "He is having a seat in cabinet, "it was always like him, "The Queen is having a seat in his closet."

Years gone by happily in the great city that became his capital; visitors appeared at the court every day. Once, 2 scoundrels were there in the court, introducing themselves as craftsmen. They gave away that they have the gut to weave beautiful design the most exquisite colorful items and intricate designs, from which the clothes created would have this characteristic of getting the person invisible to anyone that was not fit for the job and office he kept, or which was exceedingly plain in character.

"It truly must be stunning clothing! "The Emperor thought. "If I had this kind of dress, I could figure out at once what people are not suitable for their jobs in my domains, and even discern between the wise and the stupid! This material needs to be spun for me right away. "And he forced the two weavers to earn huge amounts of money so that they could continue their job un- interruptedly. Thus the two supposed craftsmen started 2 looms & worked quite busily, while they did little at all in fact. They demanded one of the expensive and rare silk and the genuine thread of gold; placed them in their own haversack; and then resumed their supposed crafting on the hollow looms till it started to get dark. "I'd like to see how craftsmen are going with my new dress weaving," the Emperor said to own self later spending some moments; however, he was very humiliated when he recalled that an ordinary man, and person not fit for his job, would not be able to witness the fabrication. He felt, of course, that there is no need for him to get worried about himself; but he would like to send someone else to offer him information about the and their work until he became disturbed in the matter.

All the citizens of the city had learned that the cloth was to possess the wonderful property; and they were all eager to know that how sharp, or how, unlearned their neighbors could be. "I will be sending my very old Cabinet minister to the craftsmen," the Emperor eventually said taking some moments, "he will better understand about the fabric; because he is an intelligent person, and he was the most suitable choice for the office then all." Finally

253

the minister went to witness the craftsmen or weavers in the place where they were working with all their force, in the looms which were empty. "What could the significance be? "The minister said, widely opening his eyes' can't find the smallest piece thread on looms." But he didn't share his feelings openly. The impostors asked the minister quite politely to be so great to come nearer to their hand-looms; & after that they inquired him if he was satisfied with the arrangement, and if colors were perfect or not; while referring to the barren looms. The old minister searched and tried, for a very good cause, but he was unable to see thread on looms, nothing was present there. "So, then! "He wondered repeatedly. "I am a simpleton isn't it right? I never thought about myself that way; even if I am a simpleton, nobody will know it now. Is it true, that if I was not fit for my Job? Sorry, not to say that much. I'm never going to admit that I couldn't see the things. "Said one of the claiming to still function."You don't know if you like the stuff." "Yeah, it's fantastic! "The old minister replied, staring through his eyes at the loom. "These colors & the pattern, and the colors, yeah, I'll let know the king immediately how lovely I think they are." "We'll be very grateful to you," the cons replied, & then they called the various colors and explained the patterns of the supposed things. The poor minister heard keenly to what they are saying, because he had to tell the story again to the king & then the weavers begged for more gold & silk, stating that in order to complete the work they would need more of it. However, they packed all they were given into their kit-bags; & they proceeded to work at their hollow looms concentrating with evident zeal as before. So the Emperor sent another court officer to look how the craftsmen going on, & to see if the cloth might be ready soon. For this gentleman it was exactly the same as with the statesman, he inspected the working on both sides yet was unable to see anything except the hollow frames. "We think you did not liked the working as the minister did when he visited here? "The cons of the 2nd ambassador of the Emperor asked; at that moment, they made the same motions as earlier they did, and they spoke about the patterns and colors not there. "Of course I'm not dumb! "And the messenger thought. "It should be, I ain't ready for my fine, productive office! That's very odd; indeed, nobody's going to talk of it . "And then he admired the things he couldn't see and said he was so pleased by colors and shapes. "Off course, O our Lord," he said to his emperor as he came back, "the fabric prepared by the weavers is exceedingly marvelous." The entire city was buzzing about the glorious fabric that the Emperor had commissioned on his own expenditure to be woven. And so, when it was being manufactured in the loom, the Emperor himself wanted to see the expensive fraud. He had company of small number of court officials, The minister and the other member of court were also with the monarch who already had appreciated the working on project he went to visit the cons who, started much more efficiently as they were informed that the king is soon visiting them to see their hard work, even though they did not move the machine and a single thread. "Isn't the job absolutely superb?"The crown's two officers said, already reported. "If only your Majesty would be able to look at it! What a wonderful concept! What amazing color

! They started pointing and directing at the empty looms so that piece of art could be witnessed by others. "Who is that?" The Emperor said to itself. "I couldn't see it! It is a awful thing really!He started thinking if he was simpleton or incompetent to be a king? It will be the most imaginable thing — Oh! The fabric is lovely, "he said, loudly. "This attracted my absolute support." And he grinned most wonderfully, & gazed deeply on the hollow machines; for he did not suggest that he is unable to notice of what his 2 officers of his court had so much admired. His entire retinue labored their eyes now, wishing to find anything present on the machines, thus they were seeing the same the others were able to see; yet they all exclaimed, "Ooh, what a wonderful masterpiece!"then he suggested to use this splendid and mind-blowing stuff for upcoming meeting . "Splendid! Made of beauty!

Fantastic! "Both sides resounded; and both were uncommonly homosexual. The Emperor expressed in content; and rewarded the cons with the riband of knighthood order to be carried in their buttonholes, and the title of "Great Craftsmen." The criminals sat all night until the moment the ceremony was going to occur, & burned seventeen torches, thus, everybody could see how impatient craftsmen are to finish the Emperor dress. They tried to take off fabric from the webs; they cutter the air by their sharp knives; yet they started sew with help of needles while having no yarn. "Oh! "At last, they screamed. "The new robes of the Emperor are set! "Then the king arrived inforn of the weavers with all the great men of his court; and the imposters brought up their hands, as if by keeping up something, stating, 'these are the pants of your Majesty! Here's the fire! Here's the manteau! The whole suit is so comfortable and light in weight anyone may imagine that, when wrapped in it, this, indeed, is the great quality of this wonderful thread. "But this was real that nobody was being able to see anything, beautiful make, all the courtiers said. If the Lord majesty happily remove the dress you are wearing, we want you to try the new dress we made, " Thus the kind removed his dress, and the imposters tried to posed to fit the King in his wonderful new dress; the King moved round, side by side, before the glass-looking. "How beautiful my Lord is looking, & how precisely they are match in his new garments! "Everyone screamed. "What a makeover! What sorts of shades! These are royal garments too! "The canopy to be carried in the Court over your Majesty is pending," the head of the ceremony stated. "I'm very happy," the Emperor replied. "My new dress match right?"He asked to turn side and round again in front of the glass that shines, so that he could appear to inspect his lovely suit. The bedchamber lords, anybody to bear the train of his Majesty, looked like they were raising the bottom of mantle on the ground; and refused to carry anything; for they must not reveal something like ease or not fitting for their Jobs.

And now the King marched down the streets of his capital shaded by the canopy, in the middle of the procession; & every citizens found nearby, and many at the door, screamed, "Ah! So magnificent are the latest robes of our King! What a splendid ride to the mantle there; and how graciously the scarf falls! "In brief, no one should encourage him to wear such much-admired clothes; for he would have proclaimed himself not fit for job or a simpleton. Of course, not any of the different suits of the Emperor has ever made such an impact as these unseen individuals. "Rather the King has absolutely none on it! A small kid said. "Earn the voice of truth!" His father exclaimed; and whispered from one to the other the point he kid has made. "But he has absolutely nothing on!" All the people have finally yelled aloud. The King was vexed, because he realized the citizens were right; so now he felt the procession would have to proceed! And the bedchamber lords suffered more suffering than ever before, trying to tie up a bus, though in fact there was no bus to catch.

3.4. The Fir tree

A good little Fir Tree stands out in the park. The position he had was a really nice one: the sun shone on him: there was plenty of that as for fresh air, and a lot of big-sized comrades, pines as well as firs grew around him. Yet the little Fir deserved to be a grown-up tree too badly.

He didn't worry of the warm sun and the fresh air; he didn't care for the little cottage kids who played about in the woods in search of wild-strawberries and prattled. The kids always came along with a whole pitcher full of berries, or a long line of them threaded on a stick, and sat down by the young man, saying, "Ah, how beautiful he is! What a cute little tree! "But the Tree couldn't stand to hear this.

He had shot up a good deal at the end of a year and after another year he was another long bit taller; for with fir trees you can still tell how many years they are from the shoots.

"Yeah, yeah! Were I just a tree as big as the others,' he sighed. "I would then be able to stretch my roots, and look into the big world from the tops! The birds would then create nests among my branches: and when there was a wind, I was able to bend with as much stability as the others! "Neither the sun-beams, nor the birds, nor the red clouds that flew over him morning and evening, brought any joy to the little Boy.

As the snow fell on the ground glittering in winter, a hare will always hop along and leap straight over the little Tree. Yeah, that made him so irritable! But there were two winters past, and the Tree was so big in the third that the hare was compelled to go around it. "Growing and rising, growing older and becoming tall," the Tree thought—"that is the most wonderful thing in the world after all! "The wood-cutters also came in the fall and felled some of the largest branches. This happened every year; and the young Fir Tree, which had now risen to a rather comely height, trembled at the sight; for with noise and cracking the majestic huge trees dropped to the ground, the limbs were lopped off, and the trees appeared tall and bare; they could hardly be recognised; and then they were loaded in carts, and the horses pulled them out of the forest.

Where were they headed? What was it that made them?

When the swallows and storks came in Spring, the Tree told them, "Don't you know where they were taken? You didn't get to see them anywhere? "The swallows knew nothing about it; but the Stork looked musing, shook his head, and said, 'Yes; I believe I know; I encountered many ships as I flew here from Egypt; there were splendid masts on the ships, and I went on to say that they smelled too much of fir. Can I applaud you, for most majestically they raised themselves up on top! "Yeah, I was as old as I could float around the sea! Yet in fact how does the sea look? And what is it? "It will take a long time to describe that," the Stork replied, and he walked off with those words.

258

"Rejoice in growing up! "The Sunbeams said. "Rejoice in your vigorous growth, and in the fresh life which moves within you! "And the Wind kissed the Fir, and the Dew wept over him with tears; but the Fir did not understand.

As Christmas arrived, very small trees were cut down: trees that were were not quite as large or of the same age as this Fir Tree, that could never rest, but would still be down. Such young trees kept their leaves, and they were still the best looking; they were put on carts, and the horses pulled them out of the jungle.

"Where do they want to go? "The Fir asked. "They aren't taller than I; there was one that was much shorter; so why did they keep any of their branches? How are they being brought in? "We know that! We do know! "Sparrows chirped. "We opened the windows in the city below! We wonder they're taking where! They are awaited by the greatest splendor and the greatest magnificence one might imagine. We looked through the windows and saw them in the middle of the warm house, adorned with the most beautiful stuff, gold apples, gingerbread, toys and several hundred lights! "What, what? "The Fir Tree pleaded, shaking at each bough. "What now? Then what happens? "We haven't seen anything else: it was absolutely amazing." "I'd love to ask if I'd be meant for such a wonderful future," the Tree screamed with happiness. "It is easier yet than jumping the water! Such a loneliness I am waiting for! Is Christmas going yet! I'm tall now and my roots are growing like the others that were taken away last year! Ah, ah! I was on the cart yet still! Were I with all the splendor and magnificence in that warm bed! Yes; so something greater, something bigger, will certainly follow, or else will they ornament me in this way? Even still, something larger still needs to follow — but what? Yeah, how long I have, how much I have to endure! I don't even know what the matter is with me! ""Rejoice with us!" "Wind and Sunlight said. "Rejoice in a new generation of your own! "But the Tree was not at all happy; it rose and rose, was green both in winter and in summer.

259

People who saw him said, "What a beautiful tree! "And He was one of the first to be chopped down after Christmas. The ax cut deep into the pith; the Tree fell with a sigh to the earth; he felt a pang — that was like a swoon; he couldn't think about joy, but he was sad to be removed from his family, from the spot where he had risen up. He knew well that no longer could he see his poor old friends, the little bushes and flowers surrounding him; maybe not even the birds!

The exit was not satisfying at all. Just when he was dumped in a court yard with the other trees did the Tree come to himself and heard a man say, "This one is perfect! We don't want the rest. "So two servants arrived with a rich livery and carried the Fir Tree to a large and elegant drawing room. Portraits were displayed on the walls, and two large Chinese vases with lions appeared on the coverings by the white porcelain stove.

There were also big easy-chairs, silk sofas, big tables full of photo-books and toys worth hundreds and hundreds of crowns — at least the kids said so. And the Fir Tree was trapped upright in a cask packed with sand; but no one could see that it was a cask, for all around it was draped green fabric, and it sat on a big gaily-colored carpet. Ah, ah! How the Tree rumbled! What would have happened? It was painted by the cooks, and the young women. Small nets cut out of colored paper hung on one branch, and each net was filled with sugarplums; and golden apples and walnuts were hanging among the other boughs, looking as if they had grown up there, and little blue and white tapers were placed between the leaves. Dolls that searched the entire universe like men — the Tree never had seen it before — were seen among the leaves, and a large star of gold tinsel was set at the very top. It was very sumptuous — beyond superb description.

"What a night! "None of them said. "Oh that'll shine tonight! "Ah, god! "The Tree figured. "If the night was not here! If only the tapers lightened! Even then, I wonder what's going to happen! Maybe the other forest trees will come over and look at me! Maybe the sparrows will smash the window-panes! I wonder if I'm going to take root here, and stand lined with ornaments in winter and summer! "He knew a lot about this — but he was so restless that he got a pain in his back for sheer desperation, and that with trees is the same as a headache with humans.

Now the candles were lighting up — what brightness! What magnificence! In every bough the Tree trembled such that one of the tapers set fire to the foliage. It famously blazed out.

"Let's help! Help!Help! "Old ladies screamed, and they put out the fire easily.

The Tree didn't even dare to tremble now. What a mess it stood in! He was so nervous that he would loose some of his splendor that in the middle of light and sunlight he was very bewildered; when unexpectedly both folding doors opened and a group of kids jumped in as if they were disturbing the Forest. The older people silently followed; the little ones remained very still. But it was just for a moment; then they screamed that they re-echoed the entire place with their rejoicing; they jumped around the House, and took off one gift after the other.

"By what do they mean? "The Tree figured. "Whatever happens now! "And the lights burnt down to the very roots, and they were taken out one after the other when they burnt out, and so the children had permission to loot the Forest. So with such brutality they crashed upon it that all the limbs cracked; if it hadn't been tightly rooted in the ground, it would surely have tumbled down.

The kids played around with their pretty playthings; no one looked at the Tree except the old lady, who peeped between the branches; but it was just to see if a fig or an apple left had been overlooked.

"What a novel! A story to tell! "The kids were moaning, drawing a little fat guy to the tree. He stood under it and said, "We're in the shade now, and the Tree will listen too. But I'll tell you only one

261

story. Now what are you going to have; that was Ivedy-Avedy, or Humpy-Dumpy, who tumbled downstairs, and still returned to the throne and married the princess after all? "Ivedy-Avedy," others screamed; "Humpy-Dumpy," some screamed. There was such a crying and bawling — the Fir Tree was quiet alone, and he said to himself, "Shall I not bawl like the rest? Am I to do anything? "For he was a corporation, and he had done what he was meant to do.

And the man spoke of Humpy-Dumpy who tumbled down, who nevertheless rose to the throne, and eventually married the queen. And the kids clapped their hands, and wept. "Oh, just keep driving!

Do go ahead! "They wanted to know about Ivedy-Avedy too, but just about Humpy-Dumpy the little man told them. The Fir Tree remained very still and lost in thought; the wooded birds had never mentioned the like of that. "Humpy-Dumpy dropped downstairs and still the princess married him! Ja, hey! That's the way the universe is! "The Fir Tree felt, and believed everything, because the man who told the story looked so amazing. "Ok, fine! Who knows, maybe I, too, could fall downstairs and get a princess as a mom! "So he looked forward to the morning with excitement, as he wanted to be filled with decorations, playthings, vegetables, so tinsel again.

"I'm not going to be shivering tomorrow! "The Fir Tree thinking. "I'll love all my splendor to the max! I will hear Humpy-Dumpy's tale again tomorrow, and maybe Ivedy-Avedy's tale too. "And the Tree remained still and in deep contemplation throughout the night.

The servant and the housemaid arrived in the morning.

"Now the splendor will start over again," the Fir thought. But they pulled him out of the house, and climbed the stairs into the loft: there they left him in a dark corner where no daylight could reach.

"What did you mean by this? "The Tree figured. "What am I going to do? What am I meant to hear now I wonder? "Then he rested in reverie against the wall lost. He never had ample time for his reflections; for days and nights passed by, and no one showed up; so when anyone actually did, it was only to bring those nice trunks out of the way in a corner. The Tree remained much unseen there; it looked as if he had been totally overlooked.

"'This is natural season now! "The Tree figured. "The ground is rough and heavy with snow; men can't plant me now, so I was put in shelter here before spring! How considerate it is! After all, how kind man she is! If it wasn't always so cold here, and so dreadfully lonely! Not a hare, though! And it was so nice out in the field, when the snow was on the ground and the hare sprung by; yes — even when he leapt over me; but then I didn't like it! It is really terribly lonely here! "Squeak out! Squeak out! "A little mouse said, peeping out of his hole at the same moment. And then came another little one. They snuffed and rustled among the trees around the Fir Tree.

"It's dreadfully cold," the mouse said. "But for that, it would be delightful here, old Fir, wouldn't it? " "I am by no means old," said the Fir Tree. "Most of them are considerably older than I am." "Where are you from," the Mice asked; "and what do you do? " They were so extremely curious. "Tell us about the most beautiful spot on the earth. You've never been in there? Were you never in the larder, where cheeses lie on the shelves, and hams hang from above; where one dances about on tallow candles: that place where one enters lean, and comes out again fat and portly? " "I know no such place," said the Tree. "But I know the wood, where the sun shines and where the little birds sing." And then he told all about his youth; and the little Mice had never heard the like before; and they listened and said, "Well, to be sure! How much you have seen! How happy you must have been! "

"And I! "The Fir Tree said, thinking about what he wanted to do for himself. "Yeah, in fact those were fun days." And then, as he

263

was decked out with cookies and candles, he told of Christmas-eve. "Oh," said the little Mice, "how blessed you are, old Fir Tree! "I am not ancient by any stretch," he said. "This winter I've come from the woods; I'm in my prime, and I'm only pretty small for my generation." "What wonderful stories you say," the Mice said: and the next night they came with four other little Mice to hear what the Tree said: the more he told, the better he recalled himself; and it seemed as though those days were very good. "So they could still come — they might still come! Humpy-Dumpy has dropped off, and he has a bride! "And at the moment of a lovely little Birch Tree rising in the park, he thought: to the Fir, it will be a charming queen.

"Who are the Humpy-Dumpty's? "The Mice asked. So then the Fir Tree told the whole fairy tale, for he could recall the single word thereof; and the little Mice leapt up to the very top of the Tree with joy. Two more Mice came the next night, and two Rats again on Sunday; but they said the stories weren't fascinating, which vexed the little Mice; and they, too, began to think of them not as funny. "Knew you just one story? "The Rats asked. "Just that one," the Tree answered. "On my best evening I read it; but I didn't realize how pleased I was then." "It's a dumb tale! You don't know one of candles with bacon and tallow? Can't you remember any tales about bigger ones? "No" the Tree replied.

"Alright then," the Rats said; and they went off. The little Mice even stayed away at last; and the Tree sighed: "After all, as the sleek little Mice sat around me and listened to what I told them, it was very fun. That, too, is over now. So when I'm taken out again I will take good time to enjoy myself. "But what was it to be? Why, a quantity of people came in one morning and went to work in the loft. The trunks were pushed, the tree was ripped out and put down on the floor — rather rough, it is true — but a man dragged him up to the steps, where the sun was shining. "We'll launch a happy life again now," the Tree thought. He felt the first sunbeam, the fresh air — and now he was out in the courtyard. Everything moved so hard, there was so much going on around him, the Tree forgot to look at himself. The court adjoined a garden and it was in flowers; the roses hanging over the balustrade so young and odorous, the lindens were in bloom, the Swallows flew by and shouted, "Quirre-vit! My husband has just arrived! "But they didn't want a Fir Tree."I'm going to truly love life now," he said exultingly, spreading out his branches; then, alas, they've all been dried up and gray! He lay in a field, between weeds and nettles. The tinsel's golden star was always on top of the tree, sparkling in the sunlight. Two of the merry kids were playing in the court yard who had danced around the Fir Tree at Christmas and were so delighted at his sight. One of the youngest ran and ransacked the golden star. "Now look what the disgusting old Christmas tree actually holds! "Trampling on the trees, he said, so that all of them broke beneath his foot. And the Tree beheld all the beauty of the roses, and the freshness of the garden; he beheld himself, and wished he had stayed in the loft in his dark corner; he thought of his first youth in the forest, of the merry Christmas-eve, and of the little Mice who had listened to Humpty-Dumpty's tale with such enjoyment. "'Tis over-it's not yet! "The poor tree said. "Had I ever been glad I had cause to do so! Yet 'tis past now,' tis past now! "And the boy of the gardener cut the tree into small pieces; a whole heap was lying there. Behind the big brewing copper the wood flamed splendidly and it sighed so deeply! Every single sigh was like a weapon. The boys played in court, and the youngest wore the gold star that the Tree had on the best night of his life on his breast. It was done now, though — the Tree's gone, the plot finished. All, all was over — any tale would eventually finish.

3.5. The Snow Queen:

First story:

There was once a evil sprite there, but he was the most mischievous of all sprites. One day he was in a very good mood, for he had made a mirror with the ability to make everything that was nice and lovely to look bad and evil when reflected in it; but that which was nice for nothing and seemed hideous was magnified and enhanced in ugliness. The most stunning scenery looked like boiling lettuce in this mirror, and the strongest men were terrified or seemed to stand on their heads; their features became so blurred that they could not be recognized; and if someone had a mole, you could be sure that it would be magnified and scattered over both the nose and the ears.

"This is fantastic pleasure! "The sprite said. If a positive idea went through the head of a man, then the mirror showed a smile, and the sprite grinned heartily at his clever discovery. All the little sprites who went to his school — for he had a sprite school — told each other that a miracle had happened; and that it would only be fair to see how the future truly looked like now, as they figured. They raced about with the mirror; and at last there was not a blurred land or human in the mirror that was not reflected. Then they thought they'd go up to heaven, and make a laugh there. The higher the mirror went, the more sadly it grinned: they could hardly keep it steady. They went higher and higher again, more and more to the stars, until suddenly the mirror shook with smiles so horribly that it shot out of their hands and dropped to the ground, where it was broken in a hundred million bits and more. And now it acted even more evil than before; for some of these bits were scarcely as big as a grain of sand, and they spread about in the wide world, and as they came across the heads of the men, they remained there; and then they were something perverted, or they had just an eye for that which was bad. It was because the very smallest bit had the same strength the whole mirror had. These people have got a splinter in their neck, and it caused a shudder, as their neck was like a block of stone. Many of the shattered bits were so large they were used for windowpanes that one could not see one's friends though. Some bits were set in spectacles; and it was a sad affair as people put on their glasses to see properly and well. Then the evil sprite grinned until he nearly screamed, because his imagination was tickled by all of this. The delicate splinters were already floating in the air: so now we're going to know what's next.

Second story:

A little boy and a little girl:

In a big area, where there are so many houses and so many inhabitants, that there is no roof left for anyone to have a little garden; and where, on this basis, most people are compelled to be content with flowers in pots; there lived two little ones, who had a garden that was a little larger than a flower pot. They were not brother and sister; but as if they were, they cared for one another. Their parents lived the reverse. They occupied two garrisons; and where one house's roof crossed that of the other, and the gutter extended down the extreme end of it, there was a narrow doorway to each house: one just had to jump over the gutter to get from one doorway to the other.

There were big wooden boxes in which the children's parents planted vegetables for the garden, and little rosetrees besides: in each box there was a rose, and they grew splendidly. Now they thought about placing the boxes across the gutter so they almost reached from one window to the other, and looked like two walls of flowers. The peas' tendrils hung over the boxes; and the rose trees shot up long branches, twined around the windows, and then twisted one to another: it was almost like a triumphant arch of foliage and flowers. The boxes were very high, and the kids knew they shouldn't be creeping over them; so they often got permission to get to each other out of the windows and sit among the roses on their little stools, where they could play with delight. This joy had come to an end in winter. Perhaps the windows were frozen over; but then they heated copper farthings on the burner, and put the hot farthings on the window frame, and then they had a capital peep-hole, very beautifully rounded; and a soft, polite eye was peeping out of each — it was the little boy and the little girl looking out. His name was Kay, Gerda his hers.

267

They could get to each other in the summer in one jump; but in the winter they were forced to go down the long stairs first, and then up the long stairs again: and there was quite a snowstorm outside.

"The white bees are swarming," Kay's old grandmother said.

"Do white bees choose a queen? "The little boy asked; for he understood that there was always one of the honeybees.

"Yes," the grandmother said, "she flies in the thickest clouds, where the swarm lives. She's the biggest of them all; and she can never keep silent on earth, but heads off into the dark clouds again.

She flies over the streets of the city many a winter night, and peeps in at the windows; and then they froze in such a beautiful way that they appear like roses." "Yeah, I saw it, "both the kids said; and then they realized it was real.

"Will the Snow Queen come inside? "The little girl said.

"Let her just walk in! "The little boy said. "I should have put her on the fire then, and she would have melted." And then his grandmother patted his head and told him other stories.

Little Kay was at home in the evening, half undressed, crawling up the window on the chair and peeping out of the little door. A few snow-flakes had fallen, and one, the biggest of them all, remained lying on the bottom of a flower pot. The snowflake became bigger and bigger; until at last it was like a young girl, wrapped in the finest white gauze, consisting of a million little star-shaped flakes. She was so exquisite and fragile, yet of ice, of bright, shining ice; and she lived; her eyes stared fixedly, like two stars; yet in them there was neither peace nor rest. She nodded to the window, and winked at her hand. The little boy was terrified and leapt out of the chair; it looked to him that a huge bird soared by the window at the same time. There was a harsh frost the next day — and then the spring came; the sun shone, the green leaves emerged, the swallows constructed their nests, the windows were opened, and the little kids sat in their lovely garden again, high up on the leads at the top of the property.

The roses flowered in unparalleled elegance that year. The little girl had heard a hymn in which there was something about roses; and so she thought about her own flowers; and she sung the verse to the little boy, who then sang it with her: "The rose in the valley blossomed so beautiful, and angels went down there to meet the children."

And the kids held each other by the side, kissed the flowers, gazed up at the bright sky, and talked as if they were really seeing angels. What perfect summer-days! How lovely it is to be out in the open, next to the fresh rose-bushes, who look like they will never finish blooming!

Kay and Gerda stared at the picture book full of beasts and birds; and it was then — the clock in the tower of the church was just struck five times — that Kay exclaimed, "Ah! I experience such a strong heart pain; and now something's getting in my eye! "The little girl was holding her arms around her waist. He checked his eyes; little was to be done now.

"I know it's out now," he said; but it wasn't. It was just one of those bits of glass that had gotten into his eye from the magic mirror; and poor Kay got another one right in his face. Soon, it will feel like frost. It didn't hurt much but it was there.

"Do you weep over what? "He asked. "You feel very hideous! There's nothing for me on this issue. Ah, "he said in a moment," the rose is cankered! Oh look, the one is pretty crooked! These roses are really ugly, after all! They are exactly like the box in which they are rooted! "And then with his foot he gave the box a quick kick and picked up all the roses.

269

"What is it you are doing? "The little girl cried; and when he saw her terror, he picked up another rose, stepped through the room, and rushed away from the beloved little Gerda.

He then wondered when she took her picture-book, "What horrid beasts do you have there? "And if his grandma wanted to tell them stories, he would always interrupt her; besides, if he could afford it, he would stand behind her, put on her spectacles and mimic her manner of speaking; he would copy all her habits, and then everyone would laugh at him. Eventually, he was able to mimic everyone's gait and manner on the street. Anything that was odd and irritating about them — that Kay learned how to imitate: and all the people said at these moments, "The boy is actually very clever! "But it was the glass that he had in his eye; the glass that sticked in his heart that made him taunt even little Gerda, whose whole soul was devoted to him.

His games were very different now from what they used to be, they were so quite experienced.

When the snowflakes were swirling around one winter's day, he stretched his blue coat's skirts and captured the snow as it came.

"See this glass clear, Gerda," he said. And every flake seemed bigger and appeared as a glorious tree, or a stunning star; look at it was splendid!

"Look how wise! "And Kay said. "This is much more fun than real flowers! They are as reliable as possible; there is no flaw with them, except they have exploded! "It wasn't long after when, when one day Kay came with big gloves on, and his little sledge on his back, bawling straight into Gerda's ears," I've got permission to go out to the square where the others are playing; "and he was off in a moment.

Some of the boys in the marketplace used to tie their sledges to the carts when they went by, and then they were pulled along and had a nice run. It was so very money! Just when they were at the very height of their pleasure, a big sledge went by: it was painted very white, and everybody in it was bundled up in a rough white fur cape, with a rough white fur cap on his head. The sledge rolled twice across the square, and Kay tied as hard as he could on his sledge, and he pulled away with it. On they went faster and faster onto the next street; and the person who was driving turned to Kay, and nodded to him in a polite way, as if they knew one another. The guy smiled at him every time he would untie his sledge, and then Kay sat quietly; and so on they went until they came beyond the town gates. Then the snow began to rain so thickly that the little boy couldn't see the length of an arm before him, but he continued on: then he abruptly let go of the rope he carried in his hand to get free from the sledge, but it was of little use; the little car he pushed on with the wind's speed. He then screamed as hard as he could, but no one heard him; the snow was falling and the sledge was going forward, and often it gave a jump as if they were driving through hedges and ditches. He was very afraid, and attempted to recite the Lord's Prayer; but what he could do, he could only recall the table of multiplication.

The snow-flakes grew bigger and larger, until they looked just like great white fowls at last. Suddenly on one side they flew; the huge sledge stopped and the guy who was driving fell. It was a lady; there was snow on her cloak and hat. She was tall, slim in figure, and of a gleaming whiteness. She was King of the Snow. "We've gone fast," she said; "but it's cold frozen. Come under my bearskin. "And she placed him next to her in the sledge, wrapped the fur around him, and he looked as if falling in a snow-wreath. "Did you still feel cold? "She asked, and she kissed his forehead. Oh! This was colder than ice; this reached his very core, which was still like a frozen lump; it felt to him as though he was going to die — but for a moment, it was very nice to him, so he didn't mind the cold surrounding him. "My dumbbell! Then don't miss my sled! "He thought about it for the first time. This was tied there to one of the white chickens, who flew behind the broad sledge along with it on his back. Kay was kissed once more by the Snow Queen, and then he remembered little Gerda, grandma, and everything that he had forgotten at home.

"You won't get any more kisses now," she said, "or else I'd have to kiss you to death! "Kay looked down upon her. She was very pretty; a better, or a more stunning woman he couldn't imagine himself; and she no longer emerged from ice as before when she stood outside the window and winked at him; she was fine in his mind, he didn't doubt her at all, and he told her that he could measure in his head and with percentages, even; that he knew the amount of square miles there was in the distance Then it seemed to him that what he learned wasn't enough, so he looked up in the vast open space above him, so flew with him on it; flew high above the black clouds, as the wind moaned and whispered as if singing an old melody. They soared over forests and fields, over oceans and other lands; and the icy wind swept swiftly underneath them, the wolves hurled, the snow crackled; over them soared huge crying crows, but the moon, very big and brilliant, shone higher; and it was on it that Kay gazed through the long winter night; while he slept at the foot of the Snow Queen by day.

3.6. The real princess

Once upon a time there was a Prince hoping to marry a Princess; but then she must be a true Princess. In hopes of meeting such a woman, he traveled across the world; but there was still something wrong.

Princesses he noticed in abundance; but it was difficult for him to determine if they were true princesses, for now one thing, now another, about the ladies seemed to him not quite right. He eventually returned much cast down to his palace because he wished too badly for his wife to have a true princess. A terrible tempest emerged one evening, it thundered and lightened, and in torrents the rain poured down from the sky: it was as black as the ground. A loud banging at the door was heard all at once and the old King, the father of the Duke, went out himself to open it. It had been a Princess standing outside the house. She was in a sad condition with the rain and the wind; the water trickled down from her hair, and her clothes clung to her body. She claimed she was a true Queen. "Oh, my goodness! We'll see that soon! "The old Queen-mother thought; but she didn't say a thing about what she was going to do; instead she went softly into the bedroom, stripped off all the bed-clothes, and put three little peas on the pillow. She then laid twenty mattresses over the three peas and overlaid the mattresses with twenty feather beds. The Princess was to spend the night on this bunk.

She was asked the following morning if she had fallen asleep. "Wow, very poor indeed! "She replied. "I've barely closed my eyes for the entire night. I don't know what was in my room, but there was something heavy beneath me, and I'm black and bruised all over. It has done me so much good! "Then it became clear that the lady must be a true queen, because through the twenty mattresses and twenty feather beds she had been able to feel the three little peas. Anything but a real Princess may have had such a fragile feeling? The Prince made her his wife accordingly; now he's sure he'd find a true Princess. Nevertheless, the three peas were put in the mystery cabinet, where they are now to be found, until they are misplaced. Wasn't this genuinely delicate lady?

Chapter 4

Bedtime Fables For Kids

A fable is an imaginary story and is intended to convey a moral lesson. In a fable, protagonists are typically animals whose words and actions represent human conduct. A type of folk literature, one of the progymnasmata is the fable too. Some of the best known fables are those credited to Aesop, a sixth-century BC woman who resided in Greece.

<u>Variance on the Fabrication of the Fox & the Grapes:</u> ""A hungry fox noticed several spikes of plum dark grape dangling off a trellised tree. She attempted using all the tactics to reach at them, yet she wearied out in vain, because she couldn't not touch them. Eventually, she walked away, covering her frustration then saying: 'the grapes are rotten, but not plum as I thought.' "MORAL: Do not revile anything outside your control." MORAL: Do not revile anything beyond your reach."

"'Alas,' the fox said, displaying a super conscious smile, 'I've learned about it previously. In 12th century, a regular fox of normal nature should have expended his time and power in the futile effort to hit distant ferment grapes. However, praise to my familiarization of vine growing, I've found at once that much tallness & width of the creeper, the flow on the sap by the increased amount of varicose vegetables; 'this is fox's old story, and the grapes. Have you ever seen the Fox story and the berries, sir? One day, the fox was. "Oh, indeed,' Murphy said, who, as fond of nonsense like he had been, couldn't bear fox & the grapes for the fresh." They're nasty,' the fox said.

"'Yes,' Murphy said, 'the story of the capital.' "Oh, the fables are so good!" Wiggins said.

"Everything the rubbish!'The contradictor stated diminutive. 'Drivel, all drivel; ludicrous material of speaking aves & beasts! As though someone should accept these things.' "I do—-for single one,' Murphy stated.' (Lover Samuel, Convenient Andy: A Story of Irish Living, 1907)

4.1. The wolf and the dog

A gaunt Wolf was almost dead from starvation when he encountered a passing House-dog. 'Ah, Uncle,' the Dog answered. 'I understand how it could be; you'll soon have your distracted life ruined. How do not you work like I am doing, and have your food supplied to you regularly? 'I wouldn't protest,' said the Wolf, 'if I could just get a spot.' 'I'll quickly organize it for you,' said the Dog; 'come to my owner with me and you'll share my job.' So the Wolf and the Dog went to the city together. The Wolf found on the way there that the fur on some portion of the Dog's choker was falling down very badly, and he asked him if it had happened.

4.2. The Bear That Set Alone

"There once lived a brown bear in the forests in West that could handle it or leave it go. He might visit to a bar there they palm off mead, a sweet drink made in honey, and only have 2 drinks. So he would bring some money into the bar and tell, 'Look bears will get what,' then he would go home. Ultimately he was a prominent teetotaler and an influential instructor on temperance. He'd warn anyone that arrived at his home about the horrible consequences of alcohol and he'd joke how healthy and good he'd been after he forgo skimming the things. To show that, he will balance on head & hands and spin the house's cartwheels, push down the umbrella frame, turn off the lights of bridge, & smash his elbows on walls. Instead, exhausted from his balanced workout, he will get laid on the concrete, and move for bed. His better half was in great pain, and his kids were in great terror.

"Moral: you could just as easily collapse flat on your face and lean backwards too much."

4.3. The man and the wood

One day a man came into a forest with an axis in his side, asking all the trees to give him a little branch he needed for a special reason. The Trees were kind-natured and offered him one branch of their own. How the Man did, then put it in the head of the pole, and then got to work chopping tree after tree. The Trees then saw how stupid they had been in supplying their opponent with the ability to kill themselves.

'Ah, this is nothing,' the Dog said. 'That's just the place the choker is put on at night to keep me chained; it gaffes a little, but one gets familiar very soon.' That's it? 'The Wolf said. 'So, Master Dog, farewell to you.' Starving free is better than being fat captives.

4.4. The wolf and the lamb

For quite some period a Wolf sat lapping on a mountain at a spring while, gazing around, what would he see anyway a Lamb barely starting to sip back a little bit. 'There's my dinner,' he said, 'if just I could seek an reason to take it.' He instead yelled to the Lamb, 'How could you muddle the waters I drinks from? 'No, no, no,' said

276

Lambkin; 'if the water is dirty up there, I can't be the source of it, because it's flowing over through you to me.' 'Well then,' said the Wolf, 'why would you label me terrible titles each year? 'That can't be,' said the Lamb; 'I'm just 6 months old.' 'I don't know,' snapped the Wolf; 'if it wasn't you, it was your father;' so for this he rushed over the weak little Lamb and.'' Yet she has screamed since she died. "Any excuse would be representing a tyrant."

4.5. The dog & his shadow

It happens a Dog caught a slice of meat & took it to his house in its mouth to enjoy it in comfort. Then on his way home, he have to pass a frontier lying over a flowing marsh. He glanced down as he walked, and found his own reflection reflecting on the water below. Assuming it was a special dog with a particular slice of beef, he decided to get one too. And he took a glance on the water at the eye, but when he turned his mouth open the slice of meat slipped out, fell in the sea & was not sighted again.

Beware lest by grabbing the shadow the meat will be lost by you.

4.6. The Lion's share

The Lion, along with the Duck, the Jackal, and the Wolf once went a-hunt. They hunted and hunted until they caught a Stag at last, and they then lost their lives. Next came the issue of whether to break up the waste.

'Quarter me this Stag,' the Lion roared; so it was skinned by the other creatures, and split into four sections. Then the Lion stood before the carcass and imposed judgment: the first quarter is for me in my capacity as King of Beasts; the second quarter is mine as an arbiter; another quarter falls to me in the chase for my part; and as for the fourth quarter, well, as for that, I would like to see which of you will try to put a hand on it.' 'Humph,' the Fox grumbled as he walked away.

4.7. The Wolf and the crane

An animal he had slaughtered had been gorged by a wolf until unexpectedly a little bone in the meat caught in his mouth, and he did not chew it. Soon he experienced intense pressure in his chest, and jumped up and down, groaning and trying something to relieve the discomfort. He was trying to persuade everyone that he encountered to cut the tooth. 'I'd give something,' he replied, 'if you'd let it out.' The Crane eventually decided to offer, and asked the Wolf to lay on his side and spread his jaws as wide as he could. Then the Crane placed its long neck down the throat of the Bear, and loosened the bone with its beak, before it actually pulled it out. 'Were you gracious enough to give me the incentive you promised? 'Crane said. The Wolf smiled and revealed his teeth, saying: 'Be happy. You put your head into the jaws of a Fox, then comfortably pulled it out again; this would be enough praise for you.' Respect then envy should not go together.

4.8. The man & the snake

Through chance, a Compatriot's son came across the mouth of a Serpent, which twisted and stabbed him to death. The father in anger had his pole, then chopped off half of his tail by chasing the Serpent. Then the vengeance snake began stinging some of the cattle's of Farmer and causing serious damage to him. Ok, the farmer felt it better to patch with snake, and took honey & food to his lair's head, and asked him: 'Let's forgive & forget; possibly you were correct to threaten my kid & take vengeance on my livestock, but I was correct to want and vengeance him; currently that we're both happy, why shouldn't we can be friends? 'Nope,' replied the snake; 'spare your presents; you cannot overlook the demise of your friend, neither I the loss of my tail.'

4.9. The cock and the pearl

Once upon a time, a crow was strutting up and down among the hens in the farmyard, until he unexpectedly spied something sparkling among the straw. "Oh! Hey, yeah! 'Quoth, 'that's for me,' and it quickly sprung from under the grass. What turned out to be just a Gem that had been misplaced in the yard at any chance? 'You may be a joy to people who value you,' quotes Master Egg, 'but I would rather have a single barley-corn for me than a peck of pearls.' Precious objects are for all who can value them.

4.10. The City Mouse and the Village Mouse

You have to learn that once in a while a Town rodent goes on a country trip at his uncle's place. He was not sophisticated, this uncle, though he liked his friend in the town and he accepted him heartily. What he had to sell were beans and eggs, cheese and potatoes, but he gave them safe. At this country fare, the Town rodent really turned his lengthy nose up & stated: 'I don't imagine, Cousin, In which way you get going with such bad food like this, though certainly you can't imagine good in the world; come & I will help you learn how to eat. A week when you are in town, you're going to ask how you've ever been able to tolerate a country existence.' the 2 mice left & returned mid night at the city Mouse home. 'When the long journey ends, you'll like some refreshment,' the friendly Town Mouse said, and brought his friend to a very big dining hall. They noticed the remnants of a delicious Food at that place and immediately the 2 mice started eating cakes and jellies & all the stuff which was sweet. All of a sudden they heard howling & barking. 'Country mouse' said. 'What is it? 'It's only the house dogs,' the other responded. 'Ah! 'Country mouse' said. 'On my dinner I don't love this music.' At that instance the door opened, two big watch dogs came in, & the 2 mice had to scam and run off. 'Well done, Cousin,' the country rodent said, 'What! Soon? Soon? 'And the other told.

'Indeed,' he replied; 'More, pleasant beans & bacon despite cookies, and fear wine.

4.11. The giddy Lion

A Lion was reach the end of its life, so laid sick and tired in his cave's window, struggling to breathe. The animals gathered alongside him & inched closer as he grew increasingly vulnerable. They said to themselves before they saw him on edge of death: "Now's the time to claim off old rivalries." Therefore the Badger came then aimed its horns toward him; after that a Bull booted him by his antlers; and the Lion lay powerless before them: so the Donkey, knowing very protected of risk, stepped up and turned his butt to the Lion, kicked his feet in his head. "This is a twofold burial," the Lion muttered. Insult the fading glory just through cowards.

4.12. The crow & the Fox

A Fox one day saw a Crow was flying away in his beak with a cheese's piece and settle down on a tree branch. 'For me it's like I'm a Fox,' Master Reynard said, and he started walking up to the tree's foot. 'Good morning, Lady Crow,' he said.

'How good you feel today: how vivid your feathers are; how luminous your eye is feel confident to have your tone will overshadow that of most birds, even as your appearance is doing; allow me hearing only one melody of you, so I can welcome you as the Goddess of Birds. "The Crow turned her head or tried to catch the finest, however the instant she opened her mouth, the cheese fragment collapsed to the ground, just to be captured by Master Fox. 'That's going to do,' he said. 'I just needed that. I will send you a bit of wisdom about the time to come in return for your milk. 'Do not like flatterers.'

4.13. The Ass and the Lapdog

One day, a Farmer came to the stables to see his burden beasts: his favorite Ass was among them, who was often well treated and always carrying his owner. His Lapdog, who jumped and licked his face and frisked just as pleased as possible, came with the Farmer.

The Farmer felt in his pocket, gave some dainty food to the Lapdog, and sat down while he gave his orders to his servants. The Lapdog hopped into the lap of his owner, and laid dreaming there while the Farmer rubbed his paws. Seeing that, the Ass broke free from his halter and started to imitate the Lapdog. The Farmer was unable to keep his hands from laughter, so the Butt went up to him and tried to crawl onto his lap by placing his paws on the Farmer's back. The Farmer's servants charged with sticks and pitchforks and quickly told the Ass that no comment is sloppy jesting.

4.14. The Miller Mouse & Jack the Lion

Once a Lion rested, a very little Rat started running up and down over him; this quickly stoked up that Lion, who put his huge hand on the rat and extended his wide jaws to consume him. "God forgive, O Lord," the little Rodent pleaded, "chastise me this chance, I'll not overlook it: who cares, but I might be capable of helping you any of these days?" The Lion was really startled at the Worm's suggestion that he should make him raise his hand but let him go. The week after the Lion was trapped in a net, and thus the attackers whom wished to take him to the Emperor safe chained him to a tree as they took the place of the cart to take him on. Only then the little rodent walked through, and she saw the terrible state the Lion is in, she goes up with him and quickly nibbled through the ropes that tied the King of the Animals. "Wasn't I correct?" Mickey asked. "Little buddies can appear to be better partners and a sympathy can go a fair way."

4.15. The wolf and the kid

A Kid was perched on top of a building, and a Wolf walked beneath him looking down. He suddenly started reviling his opponent and assaulting him. 'Murderer and rapist,' he screamed, 'why are you here in the houses of decent folks? How dare you make an appearance where they learn your filthy deeds? 'Curse back, my young mate,' the Wolf said.

'Being brave from a safe distance' is simple.

4.16. The Swallow and the Other Birds

This occurred in a field where a Swallow and several other birds were hopping around picking up their food a Countryman was seeding several hemp seeds. 'Watch out for that man,' the Swallow quotes. 'Why is he doing what? 'And the others told. 'That's hemp seed he's sowing; be sure to pick up one of the pods, or else you'll apologize.' The birds paid little attention to the words of the Swallow, so by so large the hemp grew up and was formed into ropes, so all of the birds who had hated the guidance of the Swallow were trapped in nets formed of that same hemp. 'What am I asking you? 'Swallow said. Doom the seed of evil or it will flourish to your doom.

4.17. The frogs desiring a king

The Frogs existed as happily as they could in a marshy area that was only right for them; they splashed around worrying for no one and no one was bothering them. Yet some of them felt that was unfair, they were meant to have a king and a good constitution, and they agreed to submit Jove a petition to give them what they needed. 'Mighty Jove,' they yelled, 'give us a king who will reign over us and hold us in control.' Jove chuckled at their croaking, and dropped a massive Log down into the marsh, which sprung down to the swamp.

The Frogs were terrified of the commotion in their midst from their nests, and all fled to the bank to look at the hideous monster; but after a moment, seeing that it did not rise, one or two of the boldest of them went out toward the Log, and even tried to approach it; but it did not move. Then the biggest hero of the Frogs leapt onto the Log and started to dance up and down on it, and so all the Frogs came and did the same thing; so for a while the Frogs went on their business every day without having the slightest note of their new King Log lying between them. But that didn't match them, so they sent Jove another petition and said to him, 'We want a real king; one who will truly rule over us.' So this made Jove furious, so he sent a huge Stork among them, who soon set to work to consume them all. The Frogs then repented, because it was too late.

No regulation is better than cruel regulation.

4.18. The Hares and the Frogs

The Hares were being hunted so often by the other beasts that they did not know where to go. They had backed off as soon as they heard a single object chasing them. One day they noticed a group of wild horses stamping about, and in such a panic all the hares were scuttling hard at a stream, ready to kill themselves rather than exist in such a perpetual state of terror. But just as they got close to the lake's shore, a troop of Frogs frightened off in effect by the Hares' arrival, and jumped into the sea. 'Truly,' one of the Hares said, 'things aren't as horrible as they seem to be: 'There is still somebody worse off than you.'

4.19. The woodman and the serpent

A Woodman was trampling home from his job one wintry day when he spotted something lying black on the ground.

As he got near he realized that everything but dead was a Hydra. But as he ran home he picked it up and put it in his bosom to warm up. He set the Serpent down on the hearth before the flames as soon as he got indoors. The kids watched it, and eventually saw it coming back to life. Then one of them stooped to pet her back, but the Serpent lifted his head and stuck out his fangs and was about to bite the girl to death. And the Woodman grabbed his arm, and sliced the Serpent in two in one stroke.

'Ah,' he said, 'No indebtedness from the evil.'

4.20. The Mountains in Labour

One day the countrymen found that the mountains were in labour; smoke poured from their summits, the ground quaked at their feet, trees were falling and large rocks were tumbling. They felt confident something terrible might happen. They all gathered in one location to see what a horrible idea this could be. They were hoping and waiting but nothing was arriving. Then there was a much more powerful earthquake, and a large crack in the side of the mountains emerged. They both dropped to their knees, hoping. Inevitably, and finally, a teeny, tiny mouse peaked out of the distance her little head and bristles and came rushing down towards them, and ever since they had said: 'Much uproar, no consequence.'

4.21. The bald man and the fly

Once upon a time there was a Bald Guy who stood up on a sunny summer day after work. A Fly came up and kept circling around his bald pate, and sometimes stinging him. The Man was looking for a hit to his little rival, but axe palm then fell on his head; the Fly again tormented him, but this time the Man was smarter and said: 'You can only hurt yourself if you find disgusting friends.'

4.22 The fox and the stork

The Fox and the Stork had been on friendly terms at one point and appeared to be really close friends. So the Fox welcomed the Stork to have dinner, and placed nothing in a rather shallow dish before her for a joke except some broth. It the Fox might quickly suck up, but the Stork might only wet in it the end of her long cap, and leave the meal as hungry as she ended. 'Sorry,' the Fox said, 'the broth is not of your taste.' 'Pray not of apologize,' the Stork added. 'I hope you'll come back to this stay and dine with me early.' So a day was scheduled for the Fox to meet the Stork; but when they sat at the table, all they had for their dinner was stored in a very long-necked container with a small mouth through which the Fox couldn't put his snout, and all he could do was lick the exterior of the bottle.

'I'm not going to apologize for dinner,' the Stork said: 'One terrible turn needs another terrible turn.'

4.23. The fox and the mask

A Fox had fallen into a theatre's store-room through certain way. Then he noticed a man looming over him and began to be really scared; then looking closely he realized it was just a mask that performers used to place on their head. 'Ah,' the Fox said, 'you look really fine; it's a shame you've got no brains.' Outside exhibit is a bad match for inner merit.

4.24. The fox and the ox

'Oh Dad,' a little Frog said to the big one sitting next to a pond, 'I've seen such a awful creature! It was as high as a mountain, with horns on its head and a long neck, and it had hoofs split into two.' 'Tush, boy, tush,' the old Frog said, 'that was just the Ox of Farmer White. It's not that wide either; maybe he's a little taller than I am, but I could easily render myself as broad; you just see.' So he blew himself out, blew himself out, and blew himself out. 'Was he taller than that? 'And he inquired.

'Oh, so much bigger than that,' the young Frog said.

The old man blew himself out again, and told the young man if the Ox was as large as that.

The response was: 'Better, dad, bigger.'

4.25. The hart and the hunter

The Hart once drunk from a stream, so enjoyed the solid character he had crafted therein. 'Oh,' he said, 'where you sees these glorious horns, a cervid like that! I wish I could carry quite a beautiful crown with somewhat appropriate legs; it's a disappointment they're too slim or thin.' At the instant an Archer stepped across and fired a whistling arrow at him.

Far sped the Hart, and quickly he became nearly out of reach of the Attacker with the strength of his speedy limbs; but not knowing where he had been heading, he went under some bushes with roots rising low whereby his horns became entangled, so the Attacker had time to deal.

'Sorrow to me! Forgive me, apologies! 'The Hart shouted: 'We still dislike offer to us whatever is of higher importance.'

So the Frog took a deep breath and breathed and pumped, and swelled and swelled. And then he said: 'I'm sure the Ox isn't as heavy as He's bursting at this point.

The boastful and excessively self-regarding attitude will contribute to self-destruction.

4.26. Androcles

Once a slave called Androcles betrayed his owner and ran into the jungle. When he walked around, he stumbled across a sleeping Cat, crying and grumbling. Firstly he started to run, but realizing that he was not chased by the Lion, he turned around & moved towards him. As he approached, the lion took out his foot, which was all bruised and wounded, and Androcles noticed an enormous prick in it caused all the suffering. He took the spike out and tied the lion's foot, which was quickly able to get up and kiss Androcles' hand like a puppy. The lion therefore brought Androcles to his den, and used to carry him meal each day to survive from. Although after short period of time both the Androcles & the Lion were caught, and the detainee was condemned to be hurled at the Lion, Lion had been held for many days without food. The Emperor was present to witness the event, along with all his party, & Androcles had been lead into the center of the field. Soon the Lion was freed from his lair, and charged toward his prey, roaring and bounding. But as soon as he got close to Androcles, he remembered his buddy and fawned at him, kissing his paws like a happy puppy. Amazed at this, the Emperor called Androcles, who asked him the entire thing. Afterwards the detainee was forgiven and released, and the Lion was freed to go into his native forest.

Great fullness is the expression of virtuous hearts.

4.27. The jay and the peacock

A Jay venturing through a yard where Peacocks used to play, discovered a collection of feathers that had come out of the Peacocks when they molted. He bound both of them to his legs, strutting down among the peacocks. They quickly noticed the thief as he came near them, and striding toward him pecked at him and plucked his stolen plumes down. And the Jay couldn't do anything than head back to the other Jays, who had seen his actions from a distance; but they were almost as irritated with him, stating to him: 'Not just good feathers make great birds.'

4.28. The Bat, the Birds and the Beasts

A great fight between the Birds and the Beasts just about to break off. The Bat debated whom to pursue once the 2 groups were gathered around. The Birds who crossed his ledge retorted: "Come with all of us;" though he said: "I am indeed a Beast." Then, several Beasts that crossed below him googled and said: "Join with us;" though he said: "I am still a Bird." Fortunately, during the last minute there has been calm, as there was no war, so the Bat returned to the Birds so wanted to join in the delights, yet they all twisted toward him and he had to take flight. He therefore returned to the Beasts, but they decided to bid an escape soon, or else they'd tear him to bits. "Oh," the Bat stated, "I get it now," He who is neither one nor the other has no mates.

4.29. The belly and the members

This occurred to the leaders of the body one fine day when they were doing all the job and the Belly was eating all the meals and snacks. So they had a conference, and after a long debate, they voted to strike work before the Belly wanted to take their fair share of the job. And the Hands declined to eat the food for a day or two, the Mouth refused to consider it, and the Teeth did not have much job to do. But after a day or two, the participants began to realize that they were not in a really good state themselves: the hands could barely function, and the mouth was all parched and swollen, whilst the legs could not bear the rest. And they realized that only the Belly was performing the required work for the Body in its boring, silent manner, and that it needed to work together or the Body was going to fall to bits.

4.30. The serpent and the file

A Snake walked into an armourer's store in the midst of its wanderings. As he glided over the floor he noticed a file lying there pricked his face. He twisted on it in fury and attempted to stab his fangs into it; but he couldn't do much damage to heavy iron, so he had to give up his anger early.

There is no point in targeting the ignorant.

Chapter 5

Hypnosis Bedtime Stories For Kids

The dreaming and imagination is an important part of the action. A changed state of consciousness is normal, relaxed, and simple to attain for most children. Children like to discover their environments, and feel them. They want to communicate with others and the world around them. We are endlessly curious about the how and why of things, individuals, circumstances and themselves and have an appetite for dominance and mastery. This is from their inner realm of fantasy that infinite possibilities are available to them. A child may use imagination to alter or escape an uncomfortable situation, meet desires that are not fulfilled, recall the past, or imagine the future. The children want joy, safety, warmth and success. A child can develop maladaptive behaviour, either consciously or unconsciously, when physical, emotional, or environmental factors intervene. Hypnotherapy can be a very useful resource for a clinician who is interested in making the child achieve happiness, security and safety in a collaborative relationship. The hypnotherapeutic research stimulates and reinforces the innate interests of the infant for discovery, social interaction, imagination and innovation.

Children seek to explore life to the fullest degree possible; thus, it is not only enticing but successful to develop an imagination of a child with hypnosis. The effectiveness of a hypnotherapeutic treatment strategy depends on many variables which the acronym AH CREAM may recall. The most significant of these is the relation. The effectiveness of the infant-clinician medical relationship is crucial. The child wants to feel comfortable and the specialist optimistic. An accurate assessment, including a detailed history, of the issue is needed. The clinician must not only be knowledgeable and optimistic, but also credentialed, that he or she can help the child. A health care professional should not use hypnosis to cure a disorder without hypnosis which she is not qualified to treat. The child has to expect the hypnotherapy to succeed and to participate actively in the process. Hypnosis is not something that a child does; it is something that the child does for himself or herself, or allows it to happen when he has set the target that he wants to achieve. Another important variable in the effectiveness of hypnotherapeutic therapy is the willingness of the children to improve.

AH CREAM

A: Accurate assessment

H: History

C: Confidence, competence, and credentials

R: Rapport

E: Expectation

A: Active participation

M: Motivation

5.1. Marlene Worry Warthog – Hypnosis story for kids

Marlene was a Pig from Africa. She wasn't sweet, cuddly, or friendly, but she was beautiful. For several months Marlene was able to survive in an environment without any water. She liked taking sand baths, and loved rubbing her bristly body against trees and mounds of termites. Marlene was an extremely fast rider, even backwards. She couldn't see too well, but she would run back into a cave if she saw or sensed an intruder, and shielded herself with her very long tusks. When she was an infant Marlene came to sleep in the Ashland Zoo. She was called a "warthog" for having four big, lumpy warts on her nose. Harry nicknamed her the Hypnopotamus "Worry Warthog," since Marlene was concerned about everything. As she woke up in the morning, all Marlene's fears awoke with her: What if the sun is not shining? What if ashland zoo tourists think I'm ugly? What if the elephant Elkins gets sunburned and becomes rosy? All this imagination made the all-time warthog sound anxious.

Harry found Marlene was so concerned with what-if and thinking at times that she had stopped to have fun and to be comfortable. One day, he asked her, "I used to think over a lot of stuff, you know." "Which stuff?" Marlene asked.

"Ah, the things," Harry said. "I was thinking about all sorts of issues. For eg, I was really stressed when I learned that the zoo was going to move me to a new home." "You don't look worried now, "the worried warthog told me." It's how I've learned to use hypnosis," said Harry. "Hypnosis? What is it? "Marlene asked." This is a means of supporting yourself with your creativity," answered the hypno-potamus.

Marlene was snoring. "I've used my imagination before. I can tell no one likes me. I imagine it could rain on a picnic in the zoo and spoil everything. I imagine a rock landing on my foot and squashing it ... "Harry said," It's like taking an elevator with your imagination. It can take you down to a place you really don't want to be, a place full of worries and doubts, but it can take you up to incredible heights and beautiful places too. You should ride the elevator up to the clouds with your imagination, and fly like the eagles." "You do have a wonderful imagination, "Harry said." You can imagine all these negative things, but why not use the imagination to visualize good ones. You could use your imagination to help with sleeping. "The concerned warthog was worrying about what Harry had said to her. She said, "You know, Harry, sometimes friends are like elevators: they can encourage you and lift you up, or they can push you down." The concerned warthog agreed to use hypnosis and her imagination to strengthen herself after Harry and Marlene talked some more. She decided to push the elevator upwards, not backwards, to be the sort of buddy who raises up your spirits, not one who pushes you down. Marlene was able to take her imagination's elevator up to a marvelous spot. She pulled all her luggage full of fears and what-ifs with her when she climbed into the elevator. All that weight made the elevator so heavy it started to descend, not climb. Marlene had known she needed something to do. She used her dream to envision a WIFT, a What-if Garbage. She wanted the WIFT to be pink, as her dream color was white. She decorated it with daisies, because flowers she cherished. She made the WIFT from steel, because she needed it to be secure and sturdy. WIFT for Marlene looks a little like a mailbox. It had a slot for things to put in so you couldn't pull it back out. Marlene has been bringing all her fears and what-ifs into WIFT. She learned after a while that, if she began getting some anxious feelings ... ZING! They shot in on the WIFT right. That was Marlene's genuinely incredible WIFT, because it never got too loaded to bring things in, but it never let the stuff out again. It kept it secure until the time had passed for what-if, and then ... POOF! ... It WIFTED, and it only vanished mysteriously. After that, Marlene could remember to forget what-if she had put in the WIFT, or forget to remember when. And with the what-ifs in the WIFT before they did WIFT and POOFED, Marlene feels able to enjoy doing fun things. She could take her imagination's elevator up, up, up, up, and down.

5.2. Pediatric Hypnosis and metaphorical approaches

If a picture is worth a thousand words than a million worth of a metaphor. Including parables, myths, and fairy stories, metaphors use abstract words to express a concept in an indirect way. Hypnosis is a valid psychological phenomenon, and a representation of the right brain. Metaphor may well be right brain expression. Metaphors have been used as a means of instruction in history. The Bible's parables, the Grimm brothers' fairy stories, and Aesop's fables are all popular with Western cultures. We learned the lessons of "The Little Machine That Could" and "The Hare and the Tortoise" as youngsters. These stories have much more effect than the "don't give up" mental admonitions and "long and steady race wins" ever could. Metaphors enable the hypnotherapist to interact with both the conscious and the unconscious minds simultaneously. The aware mind absorbs the words, the narrative, and the thoughts while by inference and connotation the motivational meaning is slipping into the unconscious. The unconscious mind examines the metaphor's broader meaning and personalized importance. The greater sense of the metaphor is rarely completely clarified in hypnosis, because the unconscious mind is left to wander far beyond the reach of reason. This pursuit of personalized relevance is what gives its potency to the metaphor. The motivation of the story is never clarified when a hypnotherapist uses metaphors, as it is in the fables of Aesop, allowing the protagonist to work out the meaning by himself — a far more effective experience. A metaphor's effectiveness is generated by a proper brain interaction that connects feeling, symbolic expression, and experience of life. The metaphor's purpose is to extend human consciousness. Since Vogel and Bogen developed a divided brain by transecting the corpus collosum * surgically, researchers discovered a great deal about how knowledge on the two brain hemispheres works. Though knowledge is shared cooperatively by the hemispheres, each has its own specific style or specialty. Logically and practically, the left brain operates to interpret the linear writing of the written word while the right brain actively processes the text in a systemic, tacit, and creative manner. To create the imagery and derive the essence of a plot, right-brain function is necessary. Clearly metaphor is the vocabulary of the right brain. The right hemisphere is triggered when conversation becomes metaphorical, since this is the hemisphere which is most involved in the interpretation of emotional and tactile experiences. Psychosomatic signs are mediated by primarily correct brain functions; psychosomatic

293

disease may be a word in the right brain language. Since the interpretation of metaphors is a valid brain condition, the use of metaphors in hypnosis may be a way of consciously interacting with the right brain in its own words. Because of the right hemispheric interpretation in both symptomatology and metaphorical context, metaphorical approaches to treatment can be even less time-consuming Metaphors enable the hypnotherapist to talk to the unconscious mind in abstract fashion. In a good context, the usage of symbols in the hypnosis results shifts. The audience cannot find the behavioral advice apparent. The idea may be so cleverly woven and ingrained in the narrative that the infant is unwittingly conditioned to improve without being admonished to do so consciously. This will add to a feeling of pride and a stronger sense of self-confidence. The child can be introduced to new possibilities, new viewpoints and different ideologies that metaphors. Metaphors can circumvent resistance, since they are perceived subjectively. The child sees the issue as one that happens to someone else; thus, she doesn't feel affected directly. Bringing constructive feedback to the unconscious is only one metaphoric goal. Metaphors bring the soul in. They also indulge in and strengthen confidence as they are non-threatening, allowing children to extend their minds, expand their horizons and grow knowledge. Metaphors tend to modify behavior patterns by changing the normal way of thinking of the victim. Restating the dilemma of the kid in a non-threatening metaphor allows the parent a clear viewpoint on the situation. Reframing lets the infant take back ownership of the problem to fix it. Throughout reframing, the details of a circumstance or occurrence remain the same, but modify the way the circumstance is interpreted or conceptualized, thereby changing the entire context. Sometimes, the infant has to use senses or experiences that are distinct from those he will usually use to achieve progress. With metaphorical approaches the unconscious mind of the infant is motivated to learn new ways of addressing weaknesses.

5.3. Molly Macaw – A hypnosis bedtime story

Molly was a rainforest macaw in Peru, from the Amazon. A macaw is kind of a parrot — actually, the parrot family's biggest and most stunning member. Molly's feathers were rainbow colors: violet, black, purple, orange and yellow. She was taken to the U.S. Ashland Zoo so everyone could see her stunning rainbow feathers. Everything was kind to Molly in the United States and she loved the zoo, but she missed Peru's tropical forest with its tall trees and beautiful flowers and she missed her friends. Molly had a lot of good friends living near the big Amazon River, with her. Frogs, monkeys, sloths, butterflies, snakes, and lizards were all present. A Toucan was her best friend. He had a big, colorful beak great for ripping open fruit for feeding. One day she was picking out one of her feathers when Molly felt homesick. It had seemed to make her feel better. She took out 2 more the next day. Soon, she learned to be so good at pulling off her feathers that even when she didn't feel bad, she did. It became a habit to take out her feathers, which she did so naturally she sometimes did not even know she was doing it. There were other things Molly did so well that she didn't even have to worry about it — for starters, sailing. That had been a good habit. Molly liked going to her dream spot — a tiny lake in the middle of the Ashland Park. She glanced down one day when she was standing on a tree there, and saw her reflection in the mud. "Two dumbbells! "The macaw screamed. "What happened to my lovely feathers? "The rainbow feather blanket of Molly was ripped and ragged. Most red feathers — her precious ones — had gone out. Molly was really upset. She dipped her beak under her wing to soothe her fears, and took out a thick, blue feather. "Oh, no!" "She kept squawking." I didn't say that I did. I have to stop, but I don't know how. "A friendly voice said," I can help! Molly looked down from her tree branch and, from the middle of the lake, saw Harry the Hypno-potamus swimming towards her. When he hit the beach, Harry said to Molly, "I wasn't listening deliberately, but you've got a pretty loud voice, so I couldn't help hearing what you're doing." Molly was so shocked that she didn't know what to do. "Dr. Dan, the zoo's veterinarian, taught me how I can control things I never thought I could use my imagination, "Harry said." Dr. Dan calls it 'hypnosis.' I am very good at it. That's why the sign over my new home says, 'Harry the Hypno-potamus.'" "I could definitely use some assistance," Molly stated. "If I don't quit drawing my feathers out I'll be as bald as an egg of a duck. Do you think that I should learn through hypnosis? "Yeah," Harry said. "Hypnosis is a lot like deliberate daydreaming. It's a way of thought that makes you come to your rescue. You should continue right now. "Molly sat back and made herself cozy on her tree branch. "Imagine the rainforest jumping away," Harry said. "Notice all the shades of color ... Listen to the sounds of the place — the birds, the monkeys, the insects, so familiar, so safe, so comfortable ... Feel the warmth of the sun and the gentle coolness of the breeze on your feathers ... Breathe in the place's smell, so relaxing, so peaceful ... Maybe you're going to taste your favorite rainforest food." "I should teach Shurcan how to intentionally imagine daydream," Molly said. "Shurcan is a brush but not a true toucan. I imagined him to fly across the rainforest, much as I do. Yet he is my companion and he came to keep me company all the way from the rainforest." "I think Shurcan will help you keep your feathers," Harry said." Every time you feel the urge to take a feather out, see and feel the large, beautiful beak of Shurcan Toucan pulling your bill away from your feathers. Molly kept her eyes closed, and thought. "Sometimes," Harry said, "when you get the need to take a feather you can imagine seeing a giant switch, like the sort that switches on and off a lamp.

You may use the click to turn off the temptation of dragging a feather. You could see a giant stop sign in your mind at certain moments where you felt like tearing your feathers.' Molly did all the stuff Harry said. Then Harry said, "Look into your imagination's mirror and see yourself as you'd like to appear, smell, and be, with all your beautiful, vibrant feathers." "It's easy," Molly said. Each day, she stared into the mirror of her mind and her fantasy feathers started to get prettier and more vibrant. One day, when Molly soared around the lake to her beloved tree, she glanced down from her branch and saw her reflection. "My feathers are thick and lovely too," said Molly. "I see how long my feathers in my tail have grown!" Whenever Molly used hypnosis to support cope with her problem, she felt very positive and proud of what she could do. She understood what she never did and managed what she never thought she could possibly do. She thought to support herself, deliberately hoping about the day. The next time she saw him she told Harry all of this. Harry showed her the wide smile of a hippo. "That's hypnosis," said happily Harry. "I find it the Power of Imagination," said Molly Macaw.

5.4. Harry the hypno-potamus – A hypnosis story

Harry is a hippo. He resides in Zoo Ashland. Harry's got a great creativity. Harry's most favorite spot next to his house is a big mud puddle. There, he likes to run and pretend to be a submarine. Harry seems invisible to all the tourists who come to the zoo when he is all covered up in dirt. Dr. Dan is the doctor who looks after all the animals. He came to give Harry a shot of immunization one day, so that he would not get ill. Harry was scared, because he did not like needles. "I think you've got a wonderful imagination," Dr Dan said. "I'm going to teach you how to use your creativity, so that the shot won't trouble you." "Could you just be teaching me?" He was wondering. "Of course," Dr. Dan said. "Close your eyes, and pretend you're in your favorite place." "I am in a puddle of water," he said happily. "Next," Dr. Dan said, "imagine lying in the rain. No one will see you anyway. You're safe and sound. "Harry thought he was coated in mud all over him. The wet, moist mud felt good to his hands. He was feeling very relaxed. "Take a deep breath now," Dr. Dan said. "Imagine making bubbles in the water." Harry giggled, then breathed deeply. He feigned he was blowing bubbles. He had so much fun dreaming about his mud puddle that when the needle hit him, he had barely registered the slight touch. Harry was suffering a very bad toothache one day. Dr. Dan was going to see him. "Remember when I came to give you the immunization injection, how did your great creativity help?" But my tooth really does hurt," Harry said. Dr. Dan sympathetically smiled. "It will help her to hurt less in the imagination," he said. Harry breathed in heavily. "I'm set." "Close your eyes and pretend that you're having a lot of fun," Dr. Dan said. Harry screamed. "When I was a hippo," he said, "my daddy was telling me tales of Africa. There are big mud puddles, and lots of hippos will get together in the rain. "Harry closed his eyes and thought he was in a giant puddle of mud in Africa. There were plenty of hippos with him splashing and making bubbles in the water. He was so distracted worrying about the puddle of mud that he almost forgot about his toothache. One day, as Harry was playing in the puddle of his water, his friend Pam Penguin waddled up to him, flapping her wings in wonder.

"We're on a run!" She screamed. "The zoo is in the process of creating a new and safer environment for all of us to stay." "Harry feels his stomach ill. He needed it all to stay the same. He liked his very own mud puddle, the cozy, comfortable spot he had. Harry did not think he needed a new home. He felt embarrassed. Then Harry remembered how he had been taught by Dr. Dan to use his imagination to control his emotions and feelings. "I'm calling it hypnosis," Dr. Dan said. "It is about knowing something you did not think you learned. Helping yourself is dreaming.' Harry wondered what his new home would be like. Hippos can't see too well, but they smell amazing. Harry dreamed how his new house would look. He pictured the softness and coolness of his new mud puddle. The puddle of mud made him feel safe and comfortable, just as did the old one. Pretending to think about his new home helped Harry on moving day not to feel so scared. When Harry was taken to his new home by the zoo bus, Dr. Dan was there to welcome him. "You are so proud of me!" He was asking Harry. "When you use hypnosis to help yourself, I brought you a new sign I made for your new home. "HARRY, THE HYPNO-POTAMUS" said the message.

298

Chapter 6

Bedtime Fables To Help With Learning

Fable is, commonly speaking, much more true than reality, since fable portrays a man as he was in his own day, the truth presents him as he is several centuries later to a group of inconsamerable antiquarians. Fable is more historical than reality, as truth informs us about one individual and fable informs us about one million people. "Of all the various forms of counselling, I believe the best, and what pleases the most uniformly, is fable, in whatever type it exists. Whether we find this method of teaching or therapy, it excels all the others, as it is the least surprising and the least arbitrary. For the purposes of the narrative, we peruse the speaker and interpret the precepts rather than his guidance as our own assumptions. Morals imperceptibly insinuate themselves, we are trained by accident, and are oblivious, smarter and stronger. In short, a man is so much over-reached by this approach that he feels he is leading himself as he follows another's orders, and therefore he is not receptive to what is the most awkward situation of guidance.

6.1. Tweety the bird

Once upon a time there was a name for bird Tweety. She really likes messaging. And she's kind of very sweet. And she really likes music. She was the youngest baby bird. But she has been really sweet. She cherished her parents much like she had cherished herself.

She likes to listen to the songs and she wants to perform it.

It was a first day at school for Tweety. Next to her, she stared at the chickens, which were big and smaller. She kept singing each time she was in college. The other birds began teasing her after a while claiming she's nuts and tiny and she'll never be a artist.

She fled to her house from college, and went to her place. She raced for the mountains where she could see the stars. It was her dream place she'd visit every day.

Tweety is dwelling on the stuff they thought about her. She looked sadly at the heavens. Throughout her view, Tweety felt that I don't know what they're doing about me, it just matters what I think of myself. Using a telescope, Tweety gazed at the planets, then exclaimed. She noted that the planets are all the shades of the spectrum as you gaze through a telescope. Yet they were just light, without the telescope. Then, Tweety composed a poem about planets.

It was she who was inspired. So, she began blogging. Tweety asked her mother to send her to a singing festival for a couple days. We stayed in the vehicle and drove home. It was time for the meeting. Tweety went first! Tweety became irritated. Yet Tweety was no longer tense, though. She'd started to record. The magistrates then declared the winners. And it was Tweety who played!

Tweety was the most popular performer, after years and years. Both the songs of Tweety became popular, and the story's philosophy was named "Tweety the Star".

Moral: "Follow your dreams."

6.2. Daisy pumpkin's elephant shadow

A little girl named Daisy Pumpkin woke a dawn with face of a completely developed African Elephant because of a mix up by a very excellently known but rather incompetent shadow seamstress. Daisy stood before a wide wall and waited disbelievingly as the shadow of the elephant mirrored every step. As she raised her back, the face of the elephant shifted her ears, moving from same by same with her tail. As Daisy jumped on one knee to get the reflection made so. She leapt, skip, twirled and repeated her precisely every moment she did the shadow of the elephant. That wasn't what any extent of the possibility expected of Daisy. Eventually, a couple of people arrived to witness why the small belle was running and spinning outsame the building. The instance they witnessed Daisy's elephant shadow the people were surprised.

'That is wonderful,' an old elderly woman.

'That's superb,' an elderly guy said. 'That's witchcraft,' a very old lady said.

A crowd had in very less period and they were all hustling and rushing to get up to the frontend to see Daisy and the sight of her elephant. Daisy was just an average little girl up to that point but she was somewhat different now. Public requested her for signatures and requested that she take pictures for them.

'Run on it,' a tiny boy yelled.

'Go a turn,' another said.

'Hold on your hands,' a small belle yelled.

Daisy followed what they requested of her & she felt dizzy after some time, what to do with obeying the wishes of everyone. That was the peculiars experience. She went to sleep the night before as a normal little girl and was the focus of attention now. She was unable to go outsame anywhere from that day on, without public starring & pointing. Within 24 hours Daisy turned from a simple regular little belle to a celebrity and a superstar. The local press stated her a Gift for Good. It was named a scientific phenomenon by a magazine. Customers have been demanding photos and autographs wherever she goes. People got anxious to see the shadow of the elephant, and would shout at Daisy to make it spin, jump, and twirl. She passed the summer vacations with superstar actors and pop stars attending parties, and premieres. She gave interview to famous magazines, television shows and was a guest for tea with the Queen. Daisy was happiest than anyone who ever claimed he was happy.

Suddenly on a day, at the recess of the summer, Daisy danced at park as a grumbling black cloud drifted across the region and halted facing the light. The park was gone dark, and Daisy's elephant shadow was gone as swiftly as it was surfaced. The crowd hissed & chanted for the image of the elephant to return. Daisy entreated them to sit. She started to dance but in absence of the threat of the elephant copying her steps Daisy was simply an ordinary little belle who loved to perform. The audience got annoyed and started leaving the park letting Daisy to play alone and no one to. It began to rain and to thunder. Daisy squelched home dowsed with sloshy shoes and a streaked face with tears and without any glimpse of the shadow of her elephant. A few weeks passed and the appearance of the elephant just became a vision. It was dark, and gloomy every day. Puddles lined pavements, and abandoned ornaments were park benches. No one called for any more photos, and nobody gave her invitation to premieres and parties. Living was so dreary as to deter Daisy from moving out. Day after day she remained at house in her pyjamas, looking out of her bedroom window, praying and hoping for the sun to rise once more.

6.3 Unity is strength

The Sticks There were two boys called Tom and Robert in a kingdom Once. Live on a cow. The Elder brother was Robert. They will fight forever. If they buy something for Tom from their aunt, Robert would get mad and battle and vice versa.

One day their father had agreed to have a contest. A bundle of sticks was up there. "The one that splits the stick package gets a candy bar" their father said. The former was Robert. He did his hardest but had not been able to crack it. Next was Tom. He did his hardest but still he couldn't. Their father ordered that the boys smash the bunch of sticks. They answered "Giving it a shot is worth it." The boys were stunned. The set was literally split. They were very pleased and each got a chocolate bar. They made apologies one to the other. They recognized that cohesion was power. They agreed they should never fight again, just remain there and support one another. After that they lived together.

6.4 Turtle and rabbit story

A neanderthal named Ug the Thug existed there some five thousands, four hundred and sixty-six years ago. He resamed overlooking a desolate canyon, but was desolate even then anywhere. He used to have a top club and fuzzy shoes and he loved chasing after stuff and most of all scaring them. Ug the Thug had been mean to all he knew. If the stuff he faced was large or small, it didn't really matter if he wanted to give it a shake. He loved to play as hard so he could.

"Raaaar! 'Aaargh!' 'And and' Graah! 'His dream sounds were some of his. In the evening, Ug the Thug retired to his hole. He stood alongsame his blazing fire, eating as much food so he could. He drew images of himself on grotto and even he felt very content with himself.

But no-one really liked Ug the Criminal. All were terrified of him, so remained as far away from it as possible from him. No-one ever headed to, or even moved past, his cavern. They have held to them. And one evening he spotted a falling star when Ug the Thug stood by the bed in the cellar. There was a great white illumination flowing through the skies and he was gasping. It was magnificent. Ug the Thug looked at the skies and he thought he had a mate for first point in his life, so that he could ask them all of what he had witnessed. Ug the Thug felt sad for the first stage in his career. He stepped out the next day in his shoes he would not roar and clatter along. He then came down to the river flowing via the high grass and stood there, painfully staring at his reflections in the water. It happens that even a rodent that had crossed the river higher dropped into the waters at that very instant then started to squeeze and flap its hands in the air so it couldn't swim. Ug the Thug sat down to take a look at the rodent. Without thought, he put out an arm that was as large as a brick and very carefully raised the rodent onto the bank of the river.

However, anything occurred next day. Ug the Thug had only just woke up as he noticed small feet pattering-patter. Everyone walked in. This was the rodent. And thus the rat was holding a rose in its hands. The rodent throw down the rose at Ug's foot then stared up towards him with its wide brown eyes.

The Thug dropped sameways into Ug. He fell beyond his cavern in the desert, utterly shocked. He knew that the rose was a mouse kudos-you. He'd just found a partner! He felt so glad he started singing. He gets up and danced joyfully about the grotto. He felt amazing he was wading over the water, humming again. To all he knew he could not resist grinning. Folks became afraid initially. Is it even conceivable that Ug the Thug will be comfortable and affable? Isn't he just loud and aggressive? However in the ending they started believing that to be real, smiling back and holding palms with Ug and laughing with laughter too.

After a while that no one was anymore scared of him. He left asame his poor lonely house, and came to stay with all the others. He made many friends, and then never felt alone. And he was eventually named Ug the Hug, as this was really what he wanted to do most.

6.5. Geire, the Wolf who tried to flee

"I'm venturing north to live a new future." They were the final phrases his soldier learned from Alpha Zolon. We had lived to difficult periods, so had plenty of soldier Geire. Knowing the danger of becoming a lone man, he chose to leave his clan at the right moment. When he said farewell, much of the group grumbled at him, realizing that the arrogant wolf had abandoned them to quietly willow away. But Zolon politely bid Geire goodbye, and left him to last a week or two with prey. Geire was glad and he took off. Which takes us into the present.

Geire had already begun to regret abandoning his old clan. Another clan who discovered him hidden in the forest not far from their camp had almost killed him, hoping to capture some of their food. He took a mouse, and snarled it down. A group of scouts, however, scented dead mouse but their hunting patrol has not yet been sent out. They had suspected that it was an attacker. To run from their furious clutches, Geire had to scamper up a steep mountain slope. He was watching now, missed their efforts to leap and strike him with their jaws. He barely survived. Geire returned happily to his old home, and discovered that no matter what struggle he had to go through, he had at least members of his home to support him get through. It took them a while to have him recognized again, but he was content in the.

6.6 The Warrior

There was once a guerrilla there. Okay he's been bold for stong and everything just not as widely recognized as he'd expected. And he went down a street one day, and encountered a black smith. He thought of his strengths and his worries. The black Smith told him that we too are one of a kind of his talents. For he was not only able to render the finest weapons on earth but it was also sorcery.

Unfortunately the warrior wasn't very big, but the blacksmith said he didn't care about being willing to compensate him "little by little" in due time. And they partnered up and went on the most exciting and glorious journey across the world, becoming the country's wealthiest and most successful hero. That his enchantment armour rendered him invincible.

So until he had enough of funds he asked the blacksmith again let me pay you. Right now I'm the wealthiest guy in the land ...... the blacksmith said why you've got sir little by little with every spell I've put on your shield that took your existence day. Your mortgage is paid off, and then you will die.

Offer, lend & Take

6.7 The Teddy Bear War

"I am the most slim! "And Baxter Bear asked Billy Bear. He was definitely a beautiful teddy bear. His hair was light gray, and he was sporting a black jumper and a cap with straw.

"I am the most slim! "Insisted by Billy Bear. He was a very pretty teddy bear too. His hair was gray with snow and he put a red jumper over his sweet teddy bear face with little glasses.

We stood on Cindy's bunk. The little girl liked them a lot, and took good care of them still. Per day, she washed them clean with a fluffy cloth and adjusted their sweaters all the way. At night she had them sleep with her in the tent. Every Saturday afternoon she had a tea party for them. She also brought them with her to Grandma's while she was about to play.

After quite some time the two teddy bears were happy with this plan. They both recently felt maybe one would be stronger than the other.

"The way you do, I don't wear yucky lenses," Baxter told Billy, as they relaxed on the bed and wait for Cindy to come back home from kindergarten.

"The way you do, I don't carry a dumb straw hat," Billy commented.

"Wait" said Baxter. "When Cindy gets home from school she'll wake me up first and kiss me. She does so still.'

"No, she isn't," he told Billy. "I am the one who she still picks up first and kisses."

"We are going to talk about it," said Baxter.

"We'll think about that," Billy said. They stayed together on the bed waiting for Cindy to come home. They stayed all afternoon on the fuzzy pink couch and didn't utter a thing to each other. They had been best mates at one point but now they were in the midst of a battle to see who was the slenderest. Everyone thought it was him. Cindy had plenty of toys and dolls but her favorites had always been Baxter and Billy. She received them from her grandpa, who died just before Baxter came to her and Billy did. In reality they were really different.

We remained together in quiet all afternoon and then saw Cindy downstairs. She's been home from college! We saw her come running up the stairs.

"We shall see," muttered Baxter to Billy.

"We shall see," whispered Billy back.

Cindy ran into her bedroom and flung herself down onto her pillow. Her curly pigtails were cute. She had freckles on her cheeks and lost all of her front teeth. When Baxter and Billy placed the teeth under her pillow so the Tooth Fairy might come to see her, she recalled. The Tooth Fairy gave her two cents, and she got Baxter the straw hat and Billy the shoes.

At the same time she picked them both up and hugged them. "What are my two friends doing? "Everyone was granted a kiss on the face. "I've got some wonderful things to say my darlings! My other tooth is loose and that means coming to visit the Tooth Fairy again. I will give you guys, when she does, a sweet little teddy bear bed that you will share with. Mommy says she's going to help me pay for it, because she knows how much I love my children. "I am going to get my milk and biscuits now, darlings. The boys are good and I will come back in a little bit. "She gently set them down on the blanket and rushed downstairs.

Baxter considered Billy. "We both all are special."

Billy looked Baxter. "We're growing just Cindy's cutest teddy bear."

They grinned and rested on the bed waiting for her to finish her snack and returned to play with them.

6.8 The Rabbit's foot and Anna

Anna was called to her senses by a sudden rap at the door and she rushed and watched that who was outsame.

'Hi Anna, where's the Mommy? 'The milkman Mick told, laughing.

'She's been out,' Anna replied, taking the liter of milk gently and setting it onto the kitchen counter, not trying to pay him for it.

Mick frowned at his hairy chin and rubbed it. He patted Anna's thick blond platinum hair, 'Well, I will see her other time, take care smile.' 'Take care, Mick.' Anna absently shuttled the gate and started watching out of the balcony, but despite watching what was going on outsame, she easily slipped into her fantasy universe of fairies and elves dreaming. She leapt as she noticed the opening of the back entrance, and her mum turned up packed with grocery bags and looked cranky.

'Have you paid Mick a milk peddling for that? 'I missed' whoops! "What? I advised you there was some cash in the cupboard. Anna, you're a cynic but you never listen. At minimum, you'd feel I would depend on you. Now you are the only kid in the house so you're 8, not 4! I had enough of it, Anna! If just your dad were always present, but not just at college, he hardly took much obligation for you girls,' she concluded lamely.

Immediately, Anna felt very confused, her mum was constantly reminding her, & just her children. They can get off with something, just for being girls.

'I have just forgotten, mother. It's never my mistake.' Then whose mistake it is consamer that to be? Many times you are being much too sneaky to please me! 'Anna had a withering rub across her thighs with that.

Wise with discomfort, Anna felt that this cannot be a wise thing absent from here for a bit, so she went back upstairs to sleep under the pillow in the guest bedroom. She had something shoved up besame the rear wall in the gritty darkness. This was a small stitching box for mom. Anna stretched out, and raised the top cautiously. There were many jumbled knobs of all shapes and sizes hidden within, combined with pins, black yarn, scissors, tape, a rubber dandelion used for darting socks and some old fading sashes.

She took a bunch of bright buttons then started arranging these for groups of three, layups or occasionally even more. It was the foot of a little bunny on a necklace which caught her attention. o'I recall this, Grandfather brought that to fight but said it helped him secure in the war.' Anna's mom once told her this was a fortunate bunny's foot, but she felt it was funny as Anna stared at this one. He loved seeing the paws of rabbits onto bunnies while they were live, and not deceased! She punched on the rabbit's foot, rubbing it among her fingertips, the soft silky white hair. Erm ... She probably wouldn't, so how could her mother understand if she might just pulled out a bit of the rabbit foot? She will demonstrate it in front of Thumper, who is the grumpy old rabbit of her good friend Jimmy. She realized Jimmy cared nothing for him, and never washed out his cell. Anna has always think it tastes like smoke. She easily shut the stitching box, then slipped back down from below the bed on her bottom. Firmly gripping the foot of the bunny, she pranced down stairs, cautious not to fall on the edge of the wiggly floor. She was able to hear her mom in the dining room, sniffing the sour aroma of boiled brinjal. Nice, at good she was having a rough meal preparing but wouldn't hear her because she went by like a mist.

Anna raced down the paved lane, past the kids rolling the pavement with marbles.

'Hey, sweetie! 'Mr. Fielde, the aged gentlemen at numbered 57, motioned her around and Anna realized he tried to display to her Timmy's budie. Anna's mother told her that he had been a sad old man since the passing of his wife. He loved chatting to people, so his day was livened up. Anna and her dazzling blue eyes particular chatterbox. Anna accompanied the old man into his sitting room, where the door beyond them was locked. His portable Bakelite was spinning 'Broadway's Lullaby' and Anna decided to join along but she was not aware about the whole phrases.

'If you keep out the hand straight, I'll lie down Timmy and you'll be able to caress his belly.' Anna piped and easily put the foot of the rabbit into her purse. In her hands palms Timmy felt odd, so small, but moist and gentle. And as her tiny chest rise and went down, she could feel his heart pounding hard. His dark eyes flew this direction and that when he was startled by Anna. Rather scared than anything, he started chirping and Mr Fielde smiled.

'My feeling is that he enjoys you Anna.' Timmy jumped at the chance to float across the space and instead settled on the forehead of Anna.

'Ooooh! He's got sharpend claws.' 'It's OK, I'm going to lock him in cell, and Jack's just coming.' Jack was a fatty, over-fed ginger cat with a pink nose and a long tail stripes that was rubbing up to Anna's limbs whenever she came to see. She punched it, and he cooed to demonstrate that he was satisfied. Yet she realized that he did not like Timmy, as he just stood by his cages and watched him eat.

'Do you wish seeing my mystery?

What would that be? "See!" 'Anna displayed him the feet of the bunny.

'My God, The owner's name? 'My mother, she claims it's remarkable as it's the whole story she's left to know about my grandparents. He got it in the fight.' 'Do you realize how they are doing regarding the feet of a rabbit? You hold it into your pocket, and if you brush it, it will give you favorable luck, or also anything you've always longed for.' 'And it safeguarded my grandfather in the battle, so it should be nice! I will display it to Jimmy also, so I can't stay.' As Anna reached Jimmy's home, she was exhausted running so fast. She approached the door of Jimmy, and noticed it unlocked. Anna, at the back yard, would find anyone. It's not exactly a garden, just a barren concrete field with a damaged laundry line, an empty bathroom, a coal pit and several plants. Anna went straight to her mom's nursery where Jimmy was spanking out some shoes. Anna, in his enclosure, can see Thumper the bunny. He appeared upset. When his cover was windy white and now it was a muddy brown hue. His eyes had a dark and runny look. As he stuck through the torn metal sheeting, his nose quivered, searching for food.

'I've managed to display for you stuff,' she informed Thumper, bending down before his cell. 'At least you've got all the feet in it! 'She reached into her suit bag, looking for the foot of the bunny but removed her arm in terror. 'O goodness, there isn't one! 'What isn't it? 'So Jimmy called to come in.

'The foot of my dead rabbit' Anna stated regretfully.

'At first, you've never seen one,' Jimmy said, brushing her nostrils on her shirt.

'I might have missed it somehow, of course I did. I've got to find that because then I'm going to be in a major mess, I've only one hit today. I'm going to search for it.' On her journey back, Anna recalled that she was in Mr Fielde's room. 'May I left it in the living-room? 'Then she noticed that Mr Fielde had went out after pounding many times. She stood wretchedly on the road, back, uncertain how to do it. She crawled indoors after a moment, and was shocked seeing her mom leaned against the refrigerator, hands clasped, looking shrunken.

'Oh, where were you? "I had gone to visit alongsame Jimmy.' Anna glanced down at the dinner table and found her four siblings seated.

Getting the entire family together would be uncommon; normally some of them were absent. She found the stitching case, as well. Her heart sunk, particularly as her mom said, 'The foot of your Granddad's bunny has been lost, do anyone of you remember wherever it is? He also pledged lucky, particularly if a bullet skipped off his headset which would have destroyed grandpa in the battle. Given that Granddad's gone, I wear that as a sign of positive luck." 'No,' they all chorted, even Anna, who looked like she was going purple. The eyes of Anna's mom darkened eerily but she kept quiet and took the dinner away. In her mom's face, Anna saw the tragic expression and felt incredibly bad. She will certainly find it later, but also she lost her foot from the bunny where? What if somebody else snapped it up, so they'd keep it?

The next day, while she was going for the class, Anna passed a handful of ladies in a close circle. She saw ring chief Rosy. Rosy was the favorite of the educator who can do nothing wrong, but she still copied positive marks from other students.

'It's mine, I did notice it! 'Rosy kept, waving anything in air with pride.

'Did you notice what? 'Anna stated, as she leaned in to see what she had in her pocket, heart pounding.

'Just mine, my! 'Anna faded away as she saw the foot of her mother's bunny.

'The old cat which belonged to Mr Fielde played with it. Yeah, strikers of finds, nicks of failures! 'Hardly any!' 'The voice of Anna sounded clearly and loudly. 'It's my mom's, I'd give it to Jimmy, yesterday I had to leave it in Mr. Fielde's room. Send it in again! '6 'Shan, don't force me.' Anna consamered for a moment, 'If you don't let me get it, I'm going to put my bigger sibling on you then he's going to kick your face in.' Rosy smirked, 'Wow, do you suppose I care? No. No. I need a nickel for candy for the rabbit's foot.' The children's circle pressed in on Anna shouting, ' 'Anna realized it had not been a good statement. Rosy was a mischievous girl. She gave a slight turn, chewing her lips. 'Ok, I'm going to get the cash after dinner.' 'Ok, then after lunch. I'm going to be standing at the street for your lousy rabbit's foot.' As Anna's mother was talking to the woman nearest door, Anna went through the kitchen and snatched a quarter of the milk cash box. She felt bad, but she realized it was her opportunity to get back the foot of the bunny & make her mother content afterwards. She closely grabbed the penny and dashed into the corner to greet Rosy.

'Here's the quarter,' screamed Anna.

Rosy pulled it down and chuckled. 'My mom said that this was not the foot of a fortunate rabbit. Yesterday she smashed her first tea cup & my sibling knocked over the fire and lacerated his knee. It's not something we want in our home! 'It's fortunate you're a fake. My Grandfather was spared from becoming killed in battle! 'Anna hit Rosy with all of that, caught the foot of the bunny and ran back south. She could not even stop but realize that the foot of the bunny looked muddy and not pristine white any more. Her mum was going to be too mad.

7 Anna noticed her mom quarreling against her dad later that afternoon. 'A cent of the biscuit box has disappeared. You actually took it for you to go into the hotel bar! 'Anna's father's she yelled. Anna stood in the middle on one knee and put the foot of the bunny under her back immediately as her mother turned over

towards her. 'I lose a cent, are you certain Anna didn't take it? 'She stared at him sad, her lips turned off.

'No,' another falsehood, to attach the one from overnight. 'How don't you ever accuse my siblings for this? It is me all the time, it is not reasonable! 'Anna ran straight upwards, she can see her mother cooking, preparing to explode, like luke warm water. She paused to hit the top, and heard.

'Since the foot of the bunny vanished, something went wrong here.' Her mother said her father angrily.

What will Anna do? The first reaction was to do away with it. She will cover the foot of the bunny under the lace curtains in the room of her parents, on the window ledge. This was theirs turn to bear the responsibility. It also just seems to Anna, however, they were able to keep playing in the building and not support. How Anna at that point hoped she might be a child! This will be forgotten quickly like for the cash.

Anna assumed without long that her mother would discover the foot of the rabbit, but that didn't really happen. Anna felt extremely bad every time the idea of a rabbit's foot kept coming up. Very rarely, Anna had seen the light eyes of her mom full of tears when she struggled to find them out where they it could be. 8 'None to know about now, Granddad. After all, not the fortunate rabbit's foot, it was? 'Sorry, her mother used to say.

Just like with Anna, by far the ugly portion, each time she got him at Jimmy's home, she stared at poor Thumper's feet, always buying a feeling of shame to her face.

6.9. Gigantic or super smart

Once upon a time there was a Giant who was so tall that he could see through the tallest mountain of the world.

One day the Giant meets a girl that is really tiny. No, not as tiny as Tom Thumb in the fairy tale but she is not too much taller.

314

"Hello, Mister Giant," says the girl when she sees the Giant: "gosh, you are big, guy!" Hello, little child,"says the Giant: "that is because you are so tiny." The Giant and the little child burst out laughter.

"Say, Big, what can you do what I cannot do?" asks the girl.

"I can move really fast," replies the Giant.

"But, not as quickly as I can," says the kid.

"Oh, no, I must teach you," says the Giant as he plans to take an immense measure of one mile.

Since she is so small, the Giant does not realize that she catches the lace of his boots. Right before he sets down his foot, the girl let go the lace and lands right in front of the Giant.

"What took you so long?" questions the girl to the Giant, who cannot believe his eyes that she is standing in front of him.

"Are you the same kid as before or are you her twin sister?" He's stammering.

"I don't have a mom," the girl says, "but I have a brother who's much smaller than I am because he's just raised." The giant laughs loudly: "He's not as little as you are, but he's a little bitsy boy." "You're sure you can do anything better than me?" The kid questions.

"Of course, little sweetheart, I can see out there the big peak." "Well, go ahead and tell me what you've seen," the girl responds.

"I'm going to put on my cap first, because the light is bright in my hair," the Giant says.

The kid poses next to a large cap for the Giants. She easily places herself at the bottom of the hat right before he lifts it up and place it on its top.

She will gaze up beyond the mountains on top of the Giants shoulders. Much ahead she will see a white lighthouse at the blue bay. A red painted ship with brown sails lies down on the water.

She feels the huge sigh, and she grips the edge tightly as she sees his large hand move for his cap. Luckily the Giant kindly lays his cap down on a plate. He doesn't notice how the girl was sliding down a chair leg.

"Do you go where?" Asks the giant who sees the girl there.

"I'm here, Mister Giant," the girl says: "I'm going to tell you three things you've seen around the range." Laughing embarrasses the Giant's chest. He asks: "Alright, little smart thing, tell me." "There was a very blue sea first of all," says the girl The Giants eyes wide open.

"There was a big white lighthouse second" he now lifts his eye brows.

"Fourth, there was a lovely red-colored ship on the water." Unexpectedly, the Giants mouth falls open.

"Can't do it. That is a bruise, "he babbles.

"Dear my darling Giant, did you note the unusual color of the ship's sails? They were not white as normal but dark. "The Giant did not believe his ears.

"How can this be, it's impossible," he desperately says.

The girl mocks: "Should I offer up something, nice Giant?" Ah, yes, just let me learn how this operates," the Giant begs.

"Oh, Giant love," the girl smiles: "Smart has to be the one who isn't tall!"

6.10 St. Uny Fairy school

There was once a fairy school named St Uny High and the fairies in that school were all exceptionally sweet. There was a very unique community of friends in the classroom, their names were Silvermist who wear a beautiful blue dress and the youngest of them all at the age of 14. And there was Idressa who was twelve and wearing a light sunburst coat. Next was 11-year-old Tinkerbell who wore an emerald green dress. Rosetta then arrived at the age of 10, wearing a ruby red coat. She was second at the age of nine and liked wearing her beautiful purple dress and eventually there was Fawn who was the smallest of all the girls at the age of eight who had an orange ginger jacket.

They played in the woods one weekend and an idea popped into Fawns head. "Oh, you men! Should we be going to Unicorn Meadow? "The friends were not so confident and quite scared but unwillingly decided. So they all went off to the meadow but the Unicorns had mysteriously disappeared before they entered the meadow, but luckily Silver mist could sense where they had gone through her special powers. She said, "Guys, they've gone over the hill to the meadow's Cold Same." Now the Cold Same was an area at Unicorn Meadow's furthest point, and its head teacher, Miss Lopez, strictly forbid any fairies to come near it. But the Unicorns were easily to be seen.

And the confidence was plucked up and they went up and over the slope. Not too far down they found one of the Unicorns, Vidia used the magic dust of her fairy to gather him up and bring him off on the safe hand. Tinkerbell then noticed another Unicorn and gathered it up with her fairy wand and sent him out on his journey. Next Idressa picked up a Horse, then Silver mist, then Fawn, then Rosetta, but only only one more. On they moved more and more to the Freezing Same before they encountered another pal who was the 15-year-old sister of Tinkerbelle, Periwinkle, who was wearing a snowy white dress and standing next to the last remaining Unicorn. Tinkerbelle replied, "Hello Sis," "why are you here? "Last night I had a weird vision," Periwinkle said, "I thought that the Unicorns were in danger so here I am, let's get this one gathered up and off to the safe same of the meadow." So

Periwinkle swept her wand over her head to throw her magic on the Unicorn but ... something unusual occurred.

The clouds darkened, and the wind whispered as the leaves blew away from the trees. The thunder rumbled when a lightning bolt reached the earth just twenty yards from them. Suddenly their Head Trainer, Miss Lopez, appeared before them in the shape of a horrific old troll. Her complexion had a hideous green hue on her lips, and gross rough warts. Her hair was messy and knotty and her dress was nothing but rotting, dusty rags.

"Boys!" Miss Lopez exclaimed," I am angry with you all because I disobey my rules and come to the Cold Same of the meadow! "We didn't mean to come to the Cold Same of the meadow, but we had to get the Unicorns back to their field," Fawn asked, "What happened to you, Miss Lopez? "Miss Lopez said," It's who I am. It is here that I stay. I told you not to come to this location, but you did! And now that's where you're going to have to stay forever since you can't ever return home. Can't really come out of my secret really! "Suddenly in Miss Lopez's hand appeared a thick, bent, magic stick, raising it high above her head to cast her evil spell on the fairies, when Tinkerbelle suddenly screamed," Stop!!! You don't have to do that Miss Lopez. "Idressa added," You can come back with us and still be our Head Teacher.

"There's no need to live out here, Miss." Vidia stressed.

"You can still be a troll and a teacher in the head." Rossetta said, "But be a nice troll and a good teacher in the head."

Once again Miss Lopez's face screwed in anger as she raised her magic staff to cast her evil spell and all the fairies shouted "We love you, please come back with us! "After all," Tinkerbelle said, "we're all special, but we can all be respectful and compassionate." Miss Lopez's scowling face steadily softened as she progressively lowered her employees. Tears began streaming down her cheeks and a huge beaming grin emerged on her lips.

"Thank you for my lovely fairies," Miss Lopez said in a quieter voice now.

In the silver glow, Head teacher emerged from behind the fairies and wrapped like a dazzling twinkling robe around her. A second later the silver light disappeared and there before them sat a stunning young Miss Lopez. The fairies were posing with their mouths open.

Miss Lopez clarified, "You've just broken a 400-year-old curse that a wicked old sorceress put over me. The spell was to transform me into a Troll after the home time bell rang at the end of the school day which then put me back to life the next morning right before school began. I stayed here on the meadow's Cold Same and I couldn't fear all of you, my precious fairies. The spell can only be broken if either of my fairies, while I was in my Troll state, showed me goodness and affection and you did, I'm so thankful to you, my loves. "And with that, Miss Lopez gathered the last remaining Unicorn and turned to her lovely Fairies and said," Shall we go home ladies? "All of them grinned and embraced as they left to head to St Uny Big, where they all stayed happily afterwards!

6.11 The snow mouse

Ears Rodent got up with a shiver, 'Brrrrrrrrrrrrrr' he muttered to himself, 'I'm in my comfortable room and my huge quilt but I'm always cold, my nose particularly.' The nose was nearly as fiery as the head of Ferdinand The Red Nose Reindeer. He placed his night cap over his head to keep his ears dry, and that he had placed many warm clothes over top over his duvet cover, because he figured it would be chilly that evening. He glanced at his watch on his nightstand, which said 8:45 a.m. – but he could n't really see any light coming via his windows as it would usually do at the early mornings.

Ears Mouse numbered one two and three then leapt out of bunk, rushing on to his wardrobe, taking his robe and pulling it in as fast as he should have. Then he moved on to his balcony and the shades raised. What he'd get was white things via his windshield, like very dense fog. He wanted to ignite his flame stronger so his room would be a little hotter. Through the use of an old sock and maybe some stalks, Ears Mouse attempted to have a fire started but a large drop of water will fall down the chute and put out the flames any time a strong fire traveled up to the ceiling. Ears Mouse felt he had to go there to explore. So he went equipped very rapidly, putting on his hottest jacket, his wellies, his gloves and his scarf. He raised his main gate and stepped through mist – or at best he was trying to do so. Ears Mouse jumped back to his house then fell to the floor on his middle. It hit him then-it wasn't rain, this was ice. He remembered that really transpired last night, 'it should 've snowed really significantly and blocked my chimney, gate and walls,' he said to himself.

So Ears Mouse became really concerned, 'how do I get out of here? 'He asked,' because I was preparing to pick a little more food for lunch, I don't have any stuff left throughout my pantry. He figured he had best start digging itself off just in scenario the ice won't melt for a couple of days, so he took his sled out of the kitchen drawer and lodged it in the ice at his doorstep. 'Hold on,' he said, 'where I position the ice I pull out.' He knew he was going to need to place it in his room. Ears Mouse had ice all over him for a little while, and looked like he was stuck in a cellar. He had always begun to feel really cold.

Stuff just looked a bit better outsame. That day, Jerry Jermie had already been searching for some sweet, nutritious caterpillars and sounded the alarm when he saw what has done to Ears Mouse's home. The ice had drifted down the lane throughout the night, as well as the strong wind made a cloud of ice around the property of Ears Mouse. Several of Ears Mouse's buddies are dreaming about what they can do to support get him into his freezing rain-covered home. There was so much ice to move the livestock using only aces and pickaxes. 'To make it look better, we should ask Bernie Pony to stomp on the ice,' Jerry Jermie stated. 'No, it could be too bad,' Sam Squirrel said, 'Heads Mouse might dug his path out to get stepped on.' "I get a notion," Lucy Mole said, "via the ice I might try to make a door." 'Did you ever burrow under snow before, Lucy? 'Dezzie Frog inquired. 'No,' Lucy replied, 'but it's supposed to be the same just a little colder. 'I think this is a brilliant idea,' Sam Squirrel said, 'is everybody in agreement? '. All decided that until now this was the right idea.

Lucy organized itself for her snow-walk. Sam Squirrel lent her his beanie hat that she was carrying on her nose to aid keep it dry. Jerry Jermie lent her his jumper despite the fact that it was made of gaps through his pointy beaks.

Lucy began digging via the freezing ice so fortunately it wasn't that difficult. In the meantime it was really chilly now down in Ears Mouse's house as Ears Mouse began looking a little dark. He hadn't tried to get through snow too much until the trigger of his sled snapped. Then he used his hands to reach via the ice and it was so chilly he couldn't reach his fingertips. Looking away from the ice and taking a break, Ears Mouse began to see stuff too. He could see a red dot in the air, and it became larger and larger. This was the red knit beanie that was sticking via the ice on Lucy Mole's nose then shortly afterwards Ears Mouse saw Lucy's eyes. 'I'm happy seeing you Lucy? 'I was really just about to freeze because I had to sit here for more,' Ears Mouse stated. He took a hug from Lucy and instead led Lucy back through the door.

When Lucy Mole & Ears Mouse each came out of the snow pipe there had been a large round of cheering. All mates of Ears Mouse have gathered over and given him a hug and a kiss. Sam Squirrel placed a nice warm cover over the shoulder of Ears Mouse and Jerry Jermie offered him a glass of hot water, becoming careful not to leave a gap in it from its points. They all returned to the location of Jerry Jermie, because he had lit a great fire.

321

Ears Mouse stood by the stove enjoying a delicious cup of vegetable broth, and quickly felt much colder.

The home of Jerry Jermie had been so cozy that other pets wanted to get out and create a snowman – a snowy mouse likes the buddy Ears Mouse.

6.12 The Glittery Easter's Eggs

There was once a family who had worked on a dairy. They didn't make ends meet. Whenever the farm starts earning money it seemed many crops might be destroyed or several animals might catch a disease.

Joe & Louise had been the farm owner's daughter & son, Mr. Patrick.

An early Easter dawn, Joe & Louise played down the stream near the field. They were looking for rocks that would carry them away to the creek to seek to avoid the river. This has been most preferred pastimes. Joe looked around an ancient tree's base, As he saw a small white bunny. The rabbit went in a hole, and was gone. Joe & Louise waited about for an hour for the bunny, but he did not come out from his burrow.

When they were almost close of finding rocks to jump into the sea, they found a basket which was green and bright full of sweets and eggs which were golden lying in the base of the huge exanimated tree log. They rushed over, then picked up the tub. They raced home and showed that to their brother.

Mr. Patrick was seated on the porch and he was on the front side with depressed facial expressions, as they got back to the house. All its crops seemed to have ruined this year again. He wasn't a good shepherd.

Mrs. Patrick said: "Hi guys. What was it you were you up to? We were searching for skipping rocks down by the stream and we noticed this tub," Anna said. "What's in same a basket?" Mr.

Patrick inquired. "Some dumplings, some golden chickens," Joe said. "Looks like a pretty interesting material," Mr. Patrick said. "Did you suppose it put Easter's Bunny here for you? He inquired the Kids. He was pretending to be interested although he was disappointed at the prospect of going back to the city and finding a factory job. He has always hated life in the area. This is why 3 years earlier, he actually decided to move back to the farmland to try his luck at agriculture.

"You may take brunch for the kids?" Mr. Patrick inquired. "Yes, we're really starving," Joe said. "Let's see what mum wants to cook for lunch," Mr. Patrick said.

They went home, and noticed some new bread made by Mrs. Patrick. "Freshly baked bread, delicious," Louise said. "Do you want any sandwiches, guys?" Then Mrs Patrick inquired. "It sounds terrific to me," Joe said. "And me too," Anna said.

As they started to eat sandwiches the phone bell rang it was Mr Devy, the person in charge of running the bank in locality. He told he had to come along & get several funds from Mr. Patrick to compensate on the farm for the loan that he had.

"What is it we should do? Mr. and Mrs. Patrick confronted one another. They realized they hadn't got the cash that Mr. Devy wished they'd obtain. "I guess we're about to auction the property," Mr. Patrick said.

"Maybe we should send any of the Easter basket golden eggs to him," Joe said. "What sort of basket of Easter?" Then Mrs. Patrick inquired. This got Mr. Patrick's eye because he figured Mrs. Patrick was the individual who that place the Easter basket in the farms that the kids find. "Come on have a glance at those shells," Mr. Patrick said. Joe & Louise went up to the porch and took the container out. Their mother and father stared at the shells. Every picked up one. They'd been enough strong as gold, Mr. Patrick figured. Would they have been gold?

323

They accomplished to offer Mr Devy one egg in exchange for loan payment which was due on the fields. They knew that he should ask whether or not the egg were genuine gold, because it was believed that Mr. Devy understood between the quality of original gold and false gold.

They rang the doorbell. It was Devy, Mr. All became apprehensive. Will he approve of their egg offer? Will the egg become real gold?

"Hi Mr. Devy," Mr. and Mrs. Patricksaid as Mr. Devy walked through the threshold. "Hey people. I'm sorry I had to be here to ask for support, "Mr Devy said. Everyone suspected that he was not telling the truth.

"I don't have to compensate you with some money but I will sell you those magnificent eggs which are made of gold," Mr. Patrick said. "One golden shell. Are you mad? There is nothing exist which we may call a golden egg, "Mr. Devy said. Everybody seemed concerned.

"I'm asking you what," Mr. Devy said, "provide me the egg & I will bite it in & let you know if it has some original gold present in it." If it has some gold, I'll send you the gold worth of your pocket. "Mr. Patrick gave the egg to Mr. Devy. Mr. Devy held it in his hand, bringing it close to his lips. He fucks the shell. The pupils, as he was, seemed bigger and clearer than anybody else had before. "It's just gold!" Mr. Devy said, seems really enthusiastic. Where did you bring it to in the world? "We had it in basket from Easter," Joe & Louise said with a wide grin on their lips.

"I'm going to send you one thousand dollar cash for that," Mr. Devy said, realizing its worth even much greater than this. "This is a contract," Mr. Patrick said. It would absolutely pay back my debt and give everyone some more money to enjoy. "Everybody in the Patrick family was really pleased as they realized they had a bowl full of golden eggs.

The farm became classified as Luckiest Farms in lieu of Patrick Farms from this day forward.

Each Easter the Patrick's using quite a bit of fortunately discovered riches to put all the l children of their locality in the town down by the stream for a yearly Easter egg hunting.

They weren't fortunate enough to have another golden eggs basket full although they still look like the basket tale with the Easter eggs of gold isn't just a legend, it's real.

6.13 Water In The Desert

Once, a boy was raised in a family called Bodhisatva, baptized Vaishya. The family has had a thriving business. When Bodhisatva grew older, he began to assist in the family company. Often he had to travel to other cities to search for water in the desert for company. When Bodhisatva and some five hundred entrepreneurs went on a business tour, we all had their carts of the bullock. The leader cart was leading upfront, and others followed him. The caravan came gradually to the mountains. None to be seen everywhere but sandy desert. After traveling such a long distance through the desert, they all felt exhausted. It was impossible to go on since the sun was too bright.

Seeing all of this, the caravan leader said, "Let's stop here for the day. We'll start our trip in the evening, and then the conditions will be pretty good." They parked their carts in bullock, gave the bulls fodder and water, and went to rest. The caravan leader yelled out in the evening, "O guys get ready for the ride. They're not that far out. We're going to get there in the morning."

Everyone got ready, and one after the other Bullock carts made a long queue. Weight reduction on the bullock carts. They drained the vessel of water to fill the containers with fresh water in the area. They were hoping there would be no more land. Bullock cart caravans continued forward. The carts had accompanied each other tightly. The chief led the caravan into town. Throughout the night, they continued their journey into the dark without realizing whether it was in the right direction or not.

At dawn, they realized they'd lost their way. After a long trip, they finally agreed to go back to the very same spot. As the caravan searched for the place, the sun was getting hotter. They finally reached the same spot where they had been the previous day. The water they brought given them has already been cast out. Already getting so hungry, they searched desperately for water but could not be found anywhere. The carts were stopped in a loop. They 'd died because of cold. Seeing no other option, Bodhisatva agreed to dig across the desert for water. He had been so determined he needed to drill a water well. But his quest continued in vain. Then he began searching for an suitable location where water could be discovered on digging. He went ahead, and discovered some cactus. It occurred to him that it was an appropriate place to dig, as cactus would not grow without underground water. He then told a cart owner, "Mate, dig over here. Water would possibly be found at this location." He started digging. His spade hit a rock when he digged deep! He quit digging and yelled, "There's a block!" Bodhisatva saw the digger, and went down into the hole. He 'd moved back to the block. Suddenly its lights were glowing. Beneath the rock he could detect a rush of motion.

He went out of the pit then said to his companions, "If we don't do anything, we're sure to die of thirst. I've heard water running underneath the rock. Let's try to break the rock at any cost. We 're sure to get water. We're going to have power and courage. Let's try again with confidence." Bodhisatva was saddened to see that none of them had the bravery to go forward to search. Suddenly a young man stood up and managed to pick up the spade, and went down the pit. Seeing the Bodhisatva youth was optimistic for water. At last they found the water in the desert. The youth started to strike the stone with all his strength and the destroyed and a small, pleasant water fountain came up. Seen this, the crowds ran toward the fountain and started joyfully dancing. They quenched hunger. Bulls were given water, too. Both of them praised Bodhisatva, and went on their way. They soon reached the town. Thus Bodhisatva could save the lives of his friends with his courage and determination. In addition, the water fountain was a spot for the tourists to quench their thirst and relax. Strength and bravery are the key to success.

6.14 Water In The Desert

His wife once worked a woodcutter. He used to cut and sell wood in the mountains. It was the only way of his lifespan—a woodcutter chopping wood. One day, he went to destroy forest timber. On the road, he sang a poem, praising nature and beauty. He noticed a really large tree before him. He figured chopping the entire tree for more timber. As the tree was growing, the wood from it will be enough for his entire life. As the woodcutter picked up his axis to cut the tree, he heard a voice, "Please don't cut this tree." The woodcutter stopped to look but found none. He figured it's an idea. Again he picked his axis and aimed at the tree, but again he heard the same words, "Please be kind to me. Don't cut this tree." The woodcutter stopped and looked around. But he could see none. He was perplexed. And a fairy talked from the tree, "I am a fairy and reside in this tree. I stay in the root throughout the winter, and I reside on the roots during the remainder of the year. When you kill this tree, I would be poor, winter is quickly coming, and I will die of cold. Please don't ruin my house. Then, I will satisfy your three wishes." Now he could be rich without any work. He welcomed the bid of the fairy and rushed home to inform his wife about it. His wife awaited him as well. She was shocked to see the woodcutter back too early and asked, "Why did you come too early today? You 're looking so excited. What's the matter? Please let me know." The woodcutter responded, "I've got a huge fortune today. I 'm going to get the fortune shortly." His wife couldn't understand anything, saying, "What's the matter? Tell me. I can't hold my patience anymore." The woodcutter portrayed his companion. His wife hopped joyfully. The woodcutter said,

"I'm starving. Give me anything to eat." His wife said, "Because you arrived late, I haven't cooked something till now. Wait, I'll only prepare anything for you." The woodcutter said, "No, don't cook something. I can satisfy any three wishes. Now, as the first, I want candy and hot pudding." He ate to his enjoyment, loading the plate again and again. Then he begged his wife to finish the pudding. Yet she became really mad, claiming, "You've lost one blessing, and now I want the pudding to be placed on your nose!" The pudding quickly stuck to his nose. The woodcutter got angry and said, "Oh, what a fool you 're! What did you do?" He attempted to clean the pudding from his nose, but the pudding kept trapped. He scolded his wife and said, "You've lost the second blessing, so we should call for loads of revenue." The woodcutter got annoyed, so replied, "God, you 're a huge fool. There's hot pudding sticking to my nose, and you're looking for money! I wish my nose's pudding will disappear instantly!" The woodcutter breathed satisfaction. The woodcutter and his wife wasted the golden chance to become wealthy. Their luck would have knocked at their gate, but the opportunity was missed and remained poor as before.

6.15. The Ugly Duckling

The tale starts at a field in which a duck sits on an egg clutch to help them hatch. One after another, the eggs start to hatch, and then there will be 6 yellow-feathered ducklings, singing in excitement. The last egg needs longer to develop, and a weird duckling with black feathers grows from it. All, including his mum, considers the grey feathered duckling disgusting. The sad duckling tries to get away and stays in a marsh by itself before winter arrives. When a farmer sees the duckling hungry in the winter, he takes mercy on the poor duckling and offers him food and protection at home. The duckling, though, scares the loud children of the family and flees across an icy lake towards a cave. A herd of stunning swans descends on the lake as spring arrives, and the small duckling, now well grown but alone, reaches to the swans, hoping that he will be rejected. But a big shock! He is greeted by the swans. He looked at his own reflection into the water and realizes he is no longer an ugly duckling but a pretty swan. The swan decides to join that flock and flutters off along with a new and lovely family.

6.16. Dinosaurs In My Bed

Andrew lay in his room, shivering. Only beyond his house, the sky was filled with loud noises and bright lights.

He asked fifteen minutes ago, "Mother, will the tempest last long?

"Don't stress please," she added. "The weatherman said Truro would easily cross through. Have more relaxation now.

Except that they didn't; so he couldn't.

Andrew saw his alarm clock. "Tick ... Tick ... Tock." Evidently the night lasted indefinitely. Seconds give way to minutes.

And for what seemed as hours. Loud lightning bolts over the house caused him crawl deeper under the covers. His glass also rang out noise.

Does he have to move into his parent 's room? But now, he was a big kid. And he has had to be courageous. Father helped him prepare for that poor weather.

It lasted the whole night just in case. Now he'd covered my bag under the covers. Made with childhood gadgets, cards, and comic books. He 'd already seen "Panda" bear when he was two years old.

Mom made sure there were a few treats for Andrew too. On his right hand was a large bag of popcorn. Then on the other, there was one packet of rippled chips.

His family was tenting last weekend in Cape Breton. And instead, he was a kid with experience camping. stYet he had learned how to stay brave.

Which jumped on the toes? "Ouch that hurt," whispered his shivering voice. There was a much noise outside Andrew could hardly speak.

A dim night filtered the stars out of the glass.

The kid immediately became excited. What was the pillow beneath? He's been wondering, rummaging in his bag.

"OMIGOSH!" said Andrew. "I just forgot about my torch."

He rolled out of bed, and ran across the floor. Andrew searched about in the top dresser drawer before he discovered it.

Jumping back into bed easily, he pulled freezing feet down to the very edge. Bare toes laid loosely on something hard. Now it seemed to creep around his ankles. Yikes ... Yikes! He hadn't been in bed yet!

He looked under the coverings where it was black as tar, just as outside. Rather of showing up gleaming stars, highlights appeared much like eyes.

From behind his left knee came Roaring. Andrew chewed at his left hand, looking at the torch. "It couldn't be that scary sound ...? "He wavered.

Yeah, you dinosaur! Yet that was unlikely, was it not? Dinosaurs couldn't fit beneath a little boy's bedcovers, residing within his room. Exactly right?

Incorrect. This was a Stegosaurus to star right at him. Then they tried his vinegar chips from Hostess, the only little packet left only a few morsels.

"Go your way, you! "Andrew bellowed, then attempted to be courageous. Someone rumbled back underneath the blanket-sky and dashed into a dark corner.

New sounds catched the eye of the child. His flashlight helped pick out shadows that were moving. What happened? He marvelled. A Triceratops and a Deinonychus were in there.

And another Tyranosaur!

"Start off! "Andrew yelled. Instantly he felt as if he were the only one on earth alive. But he was still under his blanket, which appeared to be expanding in the distance and even above him.

He was searching for places to run.

Cold feet just couldn't move. Beneath the blankets it was like another world. His core marched to drum rhythm. Lightning zipped then zapped beneath his cloak.

Large animals had started chasing smaller ones.

Racing a Dicraeosaurus toward him. It was a friendly eater of plants that did not harm him. But, Andrew was not able to take any chances.

He took his bag off a fire truck. Jumping on the front seat, Andrew turned the siren to maximum power. All he did was ears hurt.

An Albertosaurus and Ceratosaurus bounded after him. We were like those big nice dogs that liked to play. But Andrew hadn't wanted to get crushed. He pushed on the throttle button. And the fire engine sprang forward. The road soon became a narrow lane, led straight into the trees. Andrew parked fast. Then he laced his backpack on new sneakers. He brought in his whistle, too. Shrill blowing warned us all to get out of his way. A flurry of feet fled down the trail, pounding hard at every step. One arm clung straight to 'Panda.'

The wind blew off his cap and sent it down the road. Branches to his neck grabbed. He did not want any dinosaurs to be squashed or eaten. Compared to the wild animals following him under his blanket, the storm outside was nothing. Why did it all happen anyhow? Growls and feet speeding kept focus behind him. Reaching Andrew grabbed his roller blades into his backpack. Now, he figured, Skating away safely should be fast. That is, before he was driven to the mud by a sly tree root. Now it was time to climb a tree in a hurry. "Mom, where are you? "Andrew screamed. "Daddyyyy! " Skinny legs were scrambled the trunk. And like a monkey, from branch to branch climbed up higher.

The head of a Brontosaur was unexpectedly between two arms. Smiled as he chewed a leafy mouthful. "What is your problem with that? "It seemed to be said. "Andrew, ANDREWW! "someone shouted. Voices were like waves going back and forth, running around. Yes, his name was shouted by the people!

The boy hurriedly threw his blankets off, sat up, and stared at his mother and father. He gazed in between Venetian blinds while the morning sun peeked. "Panda" was now tucked under his arm, safely. "Beneath your blankets I see you found our surprises," Mom said. Andrew stared at his mother blankly.
"You know. Do you remember the dinosaur models that you have asked last week?"

"I'm proud of you," daddy said. "see how tidily you set them all on your dresser."

When dad found out, Andrew looked strange. A group of vibrant dinosaurs stood in a tidy row. We chased a sweet Dicraeosaurus, and at the end of the line a fearsome looking Tyrannosaurus Rex. Leading the party as a whole was a little boy guy. So he hugged closely to a teddy bear.

Both the dinosaurs in this Fantasy story are accurately named. My wife, Esther and I have visited Drumheller in the area of Calgary Alberta where they roamed once.

6.17. The Boy Who Cried Wolf

The narrative comes from the Fables of Aesop, which impresses on the value of being real. It's the tale of a shepherd boy who saw herd of sheep near to his village. The region was reported to have a wolf notorious for attacking the herd of sheep and doing away with a hundred goats. Every villager knew about the threat and was always willing to help anyone who had a trouble. But the boy ignored, and in turn mocked, this friendly aspect of the villagers. He pulled out the villagers for his entertainment, three times, by pleading for support, saying "Bear! Man, dog! ". He was quickly supported by the ever-vigilant farmers, only to see the shepherd boy enjoying a good laugh. They were obviously offended when he chuckled at them for having them tricked. However, one day a wolf actually came and started killing his sheep and eating them. None of the villagers came to his assistance this time when he screamed for support, because they assumed he was playing a joke on them again. As a result the wolves killed the flock of the farmer. The morale of the tale is that, no-one trusts a liar even though he says the truth.

6.18 Little Albert and White Fluffy Bunny

Little Albert is a baby. He's got one mate, Richard. Robert is a fuzzy white rabbit. His eyes are red and wonderful like flame, his fur white and fluffy like snow, soft and cozy like a bed hugging.

Little Albert and Robert are great mates, they play together all day, they feed together and they sleep together. There's one evil man, though, his name is Dr. Watson. Dr. Watson is a bad guy, and to k ids he's pretty much evil. He said to his mates, "Let's catch up with 12 guys, I can turn them into anything."

Dr Watson went to the garden one day, and little Albert played in the orchard with Robert. Dr. Watson stared at little Albert and said, "Look at this kid and his bunny buddy, they look so joyful, I'm going to make him scared of this rabbit," Dr. Watson made a pit, and sadly little Albert was caught. Robert has been worried and had been wants to assist out. But Dr. Watson helps make a scary sound whenever Robert approaches little Albert. The tone was so terrifying that Robert was terrified away and little Albert busted in tears.

It has been occurring over and over and little Albert became afraid of Bob. Little Albert cries and breaks in anger every time Robert enters, even when Dr. Waston has already departed.

Robert wanted to console little Albert again, but little Albert screamed, "Go ahead, I 'm scared of you, just go now."

Robert was really angry, but he was also eager to support little Albert. So Robert went out to the street, sneaked into the house, and discovered Jerry, a fuzzy rodent, in the house corner.

Robert asked, "Jerry, little Albert, you can help, he's scared of me."

Happily Jerry decided. Then Jerry went to the garden and attempted to console little Albert, but little Albert always cried, "Go away, please go away, I 'm scared of you, you're fuzzy."

Jerry has always been angry. And Robert and Jerry went to the roof and discovered a white cat called Tom. "Tom, you should help little Albert, he's frightened of me," Robert said. Tom enthusiastically accepted. So Tom went to the garden and wanted to console little Albert, but little Albert again pleaded, "Go away, please go away, I 'm scared of you, you're dark."

Robert discovered that little Albert isn't only frightened of him; he's terrified of something like him, so Robert's got a different concept. Robert went to the living room, and discovered old Tony, a hound dog, in his armchair. "Yeah, let me help you" was glad to support old Tony. Old Tony went to the garden, and the little Albert approached. "Don't be afraid, I'm going to help you," said old Tony in a calm voice.

"I'm not frightened of you, you're not white nor fuzzy," this time little Albert didn't whine.

Old Tony guided little Albert out of the hole, "You are all right now, go and play with your mates, little Albert"

"No, they're too scary," is terrified little Albert. "Little Albert, they're not frightening, they're your friends, they support you," said old Tony, smiling at Robert, Tom and Jerry.

"Ph.D. we're going to protect you, Watson is gone.

Little Albert listened to the words of old Tony and surmounted his fear, he is no longer afraid of his friends.

6.19. A Queer Friendship

His closest mates were Max puppy and Lucy crow. Yet it was a strange relationship, because Max was deaf and Lucy boring. Lucy did not fly after injuring her left arm and hip, which had been smashed beneath the wheels of a motorcycle. She stood on Max 's back all day and the dog brought her to areas where food was available, including the waste bins and parks on the countryside.

The two mates in the business were content and enjoyed each other and appreciated each other.

The other animals in the community always loved and also welcomed this Queer relationship. But, one day, with the arrival of the monsoons, tragedy hit. The entire field was overflooded. As a consequence, all people and livestock perished, homes ruined and crops burned. Sick and cold, Lucy and Max wanted to quit the city, heading to a new location. Having to carry Lucy on his back, Max trudged along the lane, and only paused to rest at night.

They finally moved to a new place, where the inhabitants were wealthy and food was still polluted with dustbins and roadsides. Max and Lucy both agreed to stay, making it their permanent house. We were happy but not the others. The two men were angry. Leo a street dog called Max a idiot and said, "You're a mad dumb guy." How else would you be wearing the lame crow on your back? Which use would you make of the

Worthless bird? "Lucy was branded a worm by Chinni sparrow and rebuked her for taking advantage of a vulnerable deaf puppy. The locality's crows did not speak to Lucy because she chose to be nice with Max instead of their business. The street dogs for their part ignored Max, as he had lowered himself by holding company with a local crow.

Max just smiled as he learned all this so Lucy was sad. "She thought, I'm worthless." "I just let Max do it all for me, but I never did anything at all for him, nor did I support him in some way." As the days went by Lucy was steadily sad. "I have to do everything for Max to remind him I value him so much and enjoy his friendship."

One day Max was staying on one side of the lane, it was afternoon. Lucy, who sat near Max, instantly spotted a large meat bone from the butcher's shop on the opposite side of the street that had fallen on the ground. Her eyes gleamed. "Let me bring Max the slice of meat. Assuming so, she walked across the ground and pulled her left knee. Bending picked up the slice of bone with her beak and crossed the path when she noticed a vehicle coming at high pace to serve left and right. She even saw Max turning in his sleep and now, stretching halfway across the lane. "I've got to alert him." Lucy was panicking, and wondering. Acting on an whim, at Max, Lucy tossed the bone with all her strength. Startled, Max opened his eyes and looked up at the car. Instantly behaving, he jumped over to safety.

Lucy had rescued Max's career, and now all the animals and birds were starting to value Lucy.

6.20 The Picnic (Ears mouse)

On the edge of a very small country village in England there is an old road called Pollies Lane. This lane leads to a small but beautiful forest called Oak View, which is not visited very often by people. All along this lane, if you were to look very carefully, you would find lots of holes – some big, some small and some very small. All of these holes are homes to various creatures – some big, some small and some very small. If you were to look even more closely you might see that just insame these holes there are doors – just like those on your house. And if you were very lucky to see into the holes, when the doors were opened of course, you might be very surprised to see that insame they are very like houses, just like the ones that you and I live in.One of the smallest houses in Pollies Lane belonged to a field mouse who's name was Ears Mouse. Ears Mouse was a very ordinary mouse except for one thing. . . . he had rather large ears for a mouse. All mice have very good hearing, but Ears Mouse's hearing was so good that he could hear a pin drop a mile away even with the door shut. Ears Mouse lived in a hole at the bottom of a very large, beautifully shaped, old oak tree. He built his house with the help of his many friends, most of whom lived in the lane or the nearby forest. It had taken about a week to build the house and then about another week to make all of the furniture. The front door was made from a few hazel twigs which were tied together with string. The windows were made from some broken glass that Ears Mouse found in the laneway near an old broken down cottage.Over the years Ears Mouse had made this house a very cozy place and it even had a fireplace and chimney to heat the house in the winter and to boil a little pot of water to make his favorite drink – nettle leaf tea.The old Oak tree that Ears Mouse lived under was also the home to one of Ears Mouse's friend, Sam Squirrel. Sam's house was a hole about halfway up the tree where a large branch had dropped off a few years ago during a terrific gale. When it broke off it had left a hole into part of the tree, which had died about fifty years ago when it had been hit by lightning. This had left a hollow in the dead part of the tree and had made an excellent place for a house.

There was lots of room for Sam to be able to store his hazel nuts each year before the winter set in. There were lots of other trees in Pine View forest and there was nothing that Sam enjoyed more than jumping from tree to tree in search of more nuts. He was vary daring and if you saw him jump you would sometimes think he had wings as he would appear to fly from one branch to another. Next door to Ears Mouse's house was a very big house which belonged to his friend Jerry Jermie. Harry's house was not quite as tidy as Ears Mouse's house as he was always picking up bits of grass and leaves on his spikes and then bringing them into his house where they would fall onto the ground. However it was a very cozy house with a lovely carpet of soft straw which made you feel like you were floating on air. Jerry Jermie was very proud of his garden where he grew some very tasty vegetables. He never had any problems with slugs or grubs, which would normally make holes in the vegetables, as they were his favorite type of food.

The next building along road was more of a pool rather than a home. Here stayed Dezzie Frog who became the greatest sprinter among all lane-living species. He is also the greatest and fastest jumper, that proved useful to get there quick. Dezzie used to stay underneath a big daisy plant at the bottom of a lake which was like his shades to block out the sun. He will leap out of the pool throughout the day and run though the tall grass throughout the pasture area of peasant Gill in search of bugs lying on the mossy rocks. He will eat any kind of bug he might catch but he enjoyed blue flies particularly since they were so tasty.

Only a bit later on was fellow Louise with Ears Cat. Hammy was probably the best buddy of Ears Mouse since they had matured with each other and both enjoyed a lot of the same stuff like cheese and grain. Hammy had a really comfortable room, but since it was lined with straw that was just as Hammy wanted to be, this was difficult to go into. That kept it a really pleasant home throughout the year, even throughout the coldest temperatures.

He would open his front door and then climb into the straw and vanish and if you tried to draw his attention, you just had to yell loudly. Throughout the day Louise was a fitness fanatic, he'd sit near the line of traffic for hours to ensure he didn't put on that much poundage – because he would never fit in to his apartment if he appears to have done.

After that was Lucy Mole whose room, because the gate became flat on the floor, was indeed a bit strange. Lucy stayed deep underground and now once more pushed her home across the road, starting a new doorway every moment. She won't have very poor vision or just a very nice sense of balance, which supposed she ran into stuff once in a while and had an achy nose. She never went too far but she was only a little bit small and that was hard to reach beneath the dirt. Lucy usually came out only at dark, and if she ever went out all day she would almost hold her eyelashes shut to shield her delicate eyes against getting sunshine.

Lastly, Ears Mouse's best pal Suzaine Owl stayed just within the Pine View tree. Suzaine was housed in a really tall elm tree that was one of the tallest plants present. She typically took a nap, and only headed out to eat when it was dusk. Suzaine was a really special Owl since she was a vegan and had spared Ears Mouse from ever being killed by some other Owl, in which he was only a mouse for kids. He had already been running with his mom as it was getting dark and not seeing behind the form of a massive owl. Before the owl got to Ears Mouse Suzaine Owl barged or brought him home and dropped him next to his mum. The mom of Ears Mouse had never seen anything like this, nor felt she wouldn't see Ears Mouse ever. They also expressed their gratitude to Suzaine Owl and have become good friends.

Ears Mouse had several other colleagues, all of whom were Drip Donkey, that crossed the path now and then again. Drip stayed in the farm but at the other part of Peasant Gill's shed but when it was time to harvest he generally helped push the harvest cart out.

Often Drip will come down the pitch seeing his buddy if anyone had left the gate opened to his area.

The Picnic Ahhhhhhh – Ears Mouse released a really long breath and raised his arms after he awoke today. He got up, put on his bathrobe and headed on to the opening for the shades to open. And once he raised his shades, he saw the sun rising, but to his shock the horizon was entirely black with no cloud in view. He gave a massive smile, because that was just what he was doing. This was just the perfect day for a lake-side picnic he figured for sure.

Ears Mouse consumed his cereal as quickly as he can and, when doing a shower and at same time pushing ready. He would be out the gate under no moment and he makes his way across the lush green road to his mates' homes. He then call in at the house of Jerry Jermie. 'Jerry,' Ears Mouse yelled, scratching at his door, 'you've seen how beauuuuuuuu. It's tiful now and great for a pond picnic? Jerry cautiously opens his eyes still partially shut, already in his pyjamas. As he was so vivid that was he have to roll his eyes and went straight back home to grab his shades.

'Wow,' Jerry Jermie said, 'yeah, great conditions for an Ears Mouse picnic, I'll be prepared right away.' His closest colleagues, Dezzie Rat, Louise , Lucy Mole and Sam Squirrel, headed in seeing Ears Mouse instead. Everyone decided that only a picnic was a great idea, and planned to meet in half hour at Ears Mouse's place.

Ears Mouse immediately went back to his home, making some good chocolate sticks and a half of an apple that he would have picked that day in an apple tree. The slices tasted so good that he had been almost compelled to instantly eat it all. He put all his food wisely in his backpack and got his wool beanie hat then headed outside for a while in line to have all his buddies arrive at his house.

'Prepared? 'Ears Mouse asked, 'Up,' then everyone replied, so they went through the farms to Woodside Lake, some of the beloved picnic places. As it seems, Woodside Lake was really nearby to the forest named Woodside but was in which Suzaine Owl, another friend of Ears Mouse, stayed. Ears Mouse understood Suzaine was going to be sound asleep at such a time of day because she was staying up most of the night so needing her bed, so he didn't ask her if she wished to go out to the party for such a purpose.

Woodside lake wasn't that far away but Lucy Mole was a little sluggish and her vision in the daylight wasn't so nice. Thus Sid Squirrel had her rest almost all of the way on his neck. On the route they all conversed about certain wonderful times they got last season at Woodside Lake. They reached at the reservoir after around nearly an hour then Jerry Jermie laid a large kilt blanket over the surface. Each of them laid their backpacks on the ground, then brought their beverages outside and put them in a nearby pond that flowed into the lake to hold them cold. It was too soon to start feeding and that they all goes down to the lakeside then threw their heads across the edge and through the water – all that apart from Dezzie Frog who jumped right in with a huge plunge in.

Dezzie vanished for a few moments below the waters but suddenly reappeared on his head with a wide smile – 'mind-blowing' he said, 'come on, it's about the perfect temperature.' Even the participants rolled their eyes, none of those could dive, and they won't even want to get soaked with the exception of their foot, or even when they needed to shower.

They both felt a little woozy for a moment, and ran back to the picnic blanket. Ears Mouse pulled out his waffles from his lunch stall and had a quick whiff while taking a chunk – Mmmmmmm, that tastes wonderful he stated. Sid Squirrel had carried several red currants during winter which he had left over. Louise used to have some nice grain which he had picked in the hay field of Rancher Gill the week before. Jerry Jermie had delivered several grubs that he have picked up that day - 'good new delicious ones' that he said to himself. Dezzie Frog hadn't had to bring any food, because he picked plenty of bugs along the lake's rim and was nearly finished before the others began feeding.

Ears Mouse stared at Lucy Mole then found that she felt a bit ashamed. Lucy had a very vivid imagination as well as poor vision, and had neglected to carry some milk. All others proposed 'Do you want some of our fresh produce?.' 'No, thanks so much,' Lucy Mole replied, there's only one thing that I want to consume and this is insects. 'My caterpillars resemble worm,' Jerry Jermie said. 'Ugh, how do you consume such awful things,' Lucy Mole replied, 'shameful – good thanks, I have to go to find some new worms.' Then Lucy started digging a pit, something she had been very effective at doing, and she had vanished beneath the earth in no time. Here, Lucy was really weak at the others and it was guidance, sadly. She digged really quickly then dove headfirst for the water.

There has been a very loud hissing sound and then a huge water pipe shot out from where Lucy Mole had begun digging the pit. Everybody glanced around when a drinking fountain fired up into the sky then they realized it was just on surface of the water gun - it was Lucy Mole'Help, help-get me back from there, hurry, I can't bear pressures or water,' Lucy said. 'What are we doing' retorted Mouse of the Ears? 'We may try and stop the liquid apart,' Sid Squirrel retorted. 'We might do,' Dezzie Frog answered, 'so after that, without a major bounce, Lucy will fall would be really upset at us.' 'Fix, assist,' Lucy Mole screamed out once again. All others yelled 'we are trying to think."Think faster please,' Lucy Mole said, 'I get really damp over here.'

When it was over the sky changed, and a darkness fell over them both, like a storm. Swhooosh, Lucy vanished from those in the rim of the pool. It was Suzaine Owl that flew in Pine View forest from her shrub as well as pulled down, softly picking up Lucy Mole in her clutches.

Suzaine put Lucy Mole softly on the outdoor rug, and afterwards perched nearby. "Suzaine" Ears Mouse stated, "Why are you here? I figured at this moment of day you'd be deep asleep.' 'I was enjoying a really good night,' Suzaine explained 'before I realized Lucy Mole's screaming so I decided I'd best know whatever was going on.' 'Thanks Suzaine,' Lucy said, 'and you're sorry to get up.' 'I might as well get anything to eat now i'm up,' Suzaine added. And everybody gives Suzaine some of the food for a picnic.

They wanted to play a game of tag because they had just finally eaten the meal. Dezzie accepted not to disappear in the water, Sid decided not to climb a mountain, Suzaine accepted not to go in the skies so Lucy decided not to get under the field, particularly while she was still dripping off and didn't want to break up at the peak of a well. They all had a wonderful time searching for each other it'sn't long when they all got wiped out and chose to take a sunny sleep. The sunlight began to set at first and then Ears Mouse feel it's time to begin their way back home. They assembled the picnic, and headed back to the apartment of Ears Mouse through the plains. Suzaine Owl kept Lucy Mole in her paws and fortunately due to her weak vision, Lucy did really not see that far she was flying.

As they all returned to the apartment of Ears Mouse he welcomed them in for pizza as well as tea. They spoke of the great day they had as well as the silly stuff which had occurred for years, or even Lucy Mole felt her trip on tops of the waterfall may have looked weird. They had loved the beautiful lake picnic and were now thinking forward to see more.

6.21.Mommy

There resamed a Monarch in a glorious fortress on the sea coast. In pregnancy the poor bloke had lost his wife even because she had given life to the first daughter, Duchess Selena. The King did never let his tiny girl, Selena, from under view after that terrible day, because he realized he wouldn't be capable of living to himself if something occurred to her, also.

One afternoon, Princess Selena told her father: "Papa, couldn't you put my arm if later today we go to the seafront?"For all this, dear girl, you're very little." "Oh, Father, just for a while! "You could slip and injure yourself." "No, Dad, if you're holding my arm, the children do not want to interact with me." "I advised you, sweet darling, now you are too little." The Ruler hugged his baby farewell fell asleep. But, Royal Selena had been so depressed that she wasted practically the whole night weeping.

"If I could interact with the children for a bit ..." plagued her feelings.

The girl woke ill the day after, and was unable to get off of bed the whole day. Its status remained constant one day after. And a whole week elapsed. Poor Selena's cough wouldn't crack with the finest medics in the realm taking better care of them. At about the same period the two deities, Violet and pinky, began doing hide-and-seek between the clouds of paradise.

"Run, it's your time," Pinky screamed.

"I no longer intend to play," Violet responded.

"What, then? "Since playing for only the 2 of us is tedious." "Not so! "Replied Pinky, annoyed.

"And so, it is! "At that point God's word reverberated:" Shouldn't battle, girls." "Kindly, Lord, please send us a buddy to have joy of, "Violet begged with zeal.

"Purple, understand me. Two are only a handful but three are far too many! "God's word replied.

"But only the 2 of us are lonely," Violet persistently kept on.

"There is always error with all that," screamed Pinky.

344

"I'm just no longer talking to anyone! "Bitten by his argument, Violet interjected.

"As though it was I who cared! "Pinky wept, upset much more, until he sailed south.

"Violet, two are very few yet three are enough," echoed God's sound.

"Blablabla-blah-blah ...." teased Violet.

"Well maybe. And let it be! "The word of Christ reflected through the heavens. The sickness almost instantly overwhelmed Royal Selena back on earth, and she turned her head feebly.

The unfortunate King was not able to get over her fragile body in his embrace.

"rise up, Selena," he called out. Yet the fairy didn't raise her face, because she was still playing with Pinky in the clouds at the time.

Eventually, the dream of the young girl had come to pass, and she did not have enough of the fun and mutual laughter with her best pet, Pinky.

"Pinky, in just a short period you clearly forgot so much about me," Violet proclaimed with frustration the next day.

"You didn't tell me you didn't play alongsame me? When I was too dull. What, still, is tedious? "As he proceeded to interact with Little Selena, Pinky's conceited answer arrived.

Violet has said nothing. She is about to shift away of everyone, until she overhead God's speech.

"Won't you inquire to get a buddy playing? What else are you screaming, right today? "And I've lost my mate." "If you don't listen to me, that's what happens." "I need Pinky back," the angel began crying more.

"Alright, Violet, I'm making your fantasy come true, but unless you convince me whatever the motivation of it all is." "Two are so few, but 3 are too many." "Yes! "So the word of God answered. But by then, Beauty Selena in her dad's arms raised her face.

Gladly the King whisked, but his grin quickly wavered.

"Papa, I was having a blast in the sky. We were doing anything we liked. So you weren't anywhere, so I needed you. ".." "It is all my responsibility," howled the King. "You fell ill because of me, my kid. I just about lost everything ... My dear girl, I am never going to discourage you from doing whatever. I'll tell you! "When we're at the pool, you won't take me by the same? ""This is right. I'm not going to." "Thank you very much, Father, "marveled the princess.

Everybody was free, finally.

At a shore, Royal Selena made several new mates, whereas the 2 angels, Pinky & Violet, became together than ever before.

And the years went by.

Future queen Selena grew even more, till the the moment she wed Prince Kodor, the courageous and lovely.

But while they lived in peace and joy, for a number of years their cradle stayed barren of a descendent.

It wasn't much until the empire's people began to fear there was no successor to the crown, although Prince Kodor & Princess Selena were ill of despair.

This was then that Violet drifted around clouds to clouds in paradise, searching of Pinky.

"Ha, you're back. I was searching for you." "Why did you ask me? "Pinky questioned.

"What would you say, how do you think? 'Playing, of course.' "Violet, I no longer want to play." "Pinky, why do you not want to play? "And I've been playing with Princess Selena for so long. She was so kind and sweet. I just want her! "And the word of God rang across the skies: 'Want to meet her again? "Yeah, indeed! "Pinky shouted happily.

"Alright, I'm going to give you over to her, so you're going to call her 'Mommy.' Would you agree? "Yes. Yet what's 'Mum?' '"You're going to have to find out," God's word replied, as Violet began crying.

"Pinky, what will I do without you? "Who said you're going to be without him? Hehe-ha-ha ... "The 2 angels discovered themselves in the heart of Princess Selena, as long as God began to chuckle. 09 months after the King traveled to see her when the girl finally gave life.

"Dear girl, you're going to always be twice as careful now as you're taking good care of your spouse & your first child."

"What is so humorous about that? "The King inquired. "Move with me into the nursery and you can see for yourself," he was told by Mistress Selena.

Upon reaching the crib, the King have not see one but two crèches.

"Do you now see why I smiled, Papa? This is that I have 2 sons. The duchess happily declared that this is Pinky in the pink cradle, and Violet — in the purple same.

First the King was dumbstruck with gladness. Yet shortly afterwards, he returned with himself and began to worry about his child once more.

"Dear child, two kids offer joy double but still double the obligations." "Avoid thinking about me so much, Papa. I am an adult and a Mama! "The Finish

3.22. WOODY THE WOODPECKER

Julie hen went to the house of her aunt Mira located at the end of wood. She had told her good friend Diana duck to take care of her Gigi baby before she left. It was a dozing afternoon when small Gigi stepped out into the daylight from underneath the wings of the duck and started catching bugs.The fox named Johnny, who'd been awaiting for such a golden chance for several days, and particularly that day, because he knew Gigi 's mother was trapped in his tight grip by the chick. However he noticed his name was being called from far before Johnny could feast on Gigi. It was Sam fox his buddy who came to visit him. Johnny said to himself, "I would not like to share you with others." He placed Gigi in a box placed in front of his house, banging the door.

Woody the woodpecker observed the hearings seated on a rock, and heard the cry of pain from the chicken. 'In the wooden shell, the poor creature will die of oxygen deprivation,' thought Woody. After Johnny had gone to visit his buddy Sam, Woody flew from the tree, seated on the crate, and with his beak created holes on it. Air began to flow in the box and Gigi could breathe again.

Meanwhile, Diana duck in Gigi 's quest learned of the entire Roma butterfly incident, and Tuna porcupine, Ruby Giraffe, all had learned of Gigi 's troubles. This is Charlie monkey strutting from one tree to the other who first tried to enter the wooden box and pull the lid open. Julie hen was joined with Gigi on her comeback and she was very thankful to Woody the Woodpecker, without his help and effective treatment, her child would have expired. Henceforth the two were best friends.

Fearing of the animals' vengeance, Johnny decided to leave the jungle for better

Chapter 7

Greek Mythological Stories

The Greeks of antiquity told legends regarding their gods. Such tales are called myths (summary for mythology, or legends about gods). Tales are still being told today about the ancient Greek gods. Every narrator told the stories in their own way, and was clear from story to story whatever strength and character a god had. Zeus, for instance, was the lord of all supernatural beings and only Zeus was able to fire thunderbolts.

The ancient Greek gods' fictional world was a world full of squabbling and fighting but also genocides, and compromise and fear and fun and punishment and love. Many myths were based on the fact that gods could be punished or praised for their acts just like mortal men.

7.1. Zeus, King of the Gods

There was a very high mountain called fort Olympus in the northern part of Greece; so high that it's top was covered with snow during almost the whole year, and often wrapped in clouds, too. I sides were very steep, covered in thick oak and beech trees forests. The Greeks thought their gods' stately homes were above the top of this hill, far out of men 's reach and hidden by the clouds from their sight. Here they thought the gods were going to meet in a grand council hall, traditions feasts, talking about the world's affairs. Zeus, who ruled the world and the sea, was the king of the gods, and was among them the greatest and most strong. He could not be defeated by the power of all of the other Gods and put together. It was he who formed the clouds, and sent the precipitation to refresh the thirsty earth. The thunder bolt was his great weapon, which he carried in his right hand. But the thunder bolt was rarely used, because Zeus's frown and angry nod was enough to shake the gods' palaces themselves. But while Zeus was so strong, he was king and generous to those who enjoyed him too. The people that lived on the earth both loved him and feared him, and called him father. Of all the gods he was the most just. Once when there was a great war between the Greeks and another people, all the other gods took sides, trying to help those whom they favored whatever they could. But Zeus has not. He tried to be honest, and eventually gave the victory to the side he felt he deserved. The oak was held sacred to Zeus because it was the strongest and biggest of all trees. There was a forest of these in one region of Greece, called the Dodona range. It was so thick and the sunbeams hardly found their way to the moss on the ground through the leaves. Here the wind made strange low tones amongst these tangled branches, and people quickly began to think that this was their sky god Zeus speaking to men through the leaves of his favorite tree. So they set this forest apart as holy to him; and only his servants, who were named priests, were allowed to live in it. People from all parts of Greece came to this place to ask the God's advice; and the priests would consult with him and hear his answers in the wind murmuring among the branches. For their gods, however, the Greeks built magnificent temples, as we build churches. We brought rich gifts of gold or silver and other valuable items to these temples, to prove how thankful they were for the support the gods provided them. There was a good block of marble in each temple called the altar, and the priests always had a small raging fire on it.

When someone tried to get the aid from one of the gods, he would bring to the temple dove, or goat, or horse, so that the gods could destroy it and burn part of his flesh as an offering. For they felt the gods were satisfied with the scent of a burning body. Even though Zeus was the gods' greatest, many of Greece's most beautiful temples were built in his honour. Part of one of these temples to Zeus still stands, and if you ever go to Greece, you can see this. These were made of the finest white stone, and finely carved rows of tall columns lined it on all sides.

Even though Zeus was the gods' greatest, many of Greece's most beautiful temples were built in his honour.Part of one of these te mples to Zeus still stands, and if you ever go to Greece, you can s ee this. These were made of thefinest white stone, and finely carv ed rows of tall columns lined it on all side.There was a huge statu e of Zeus in another temple, made of ivory and gold.Itwas over 6 0 feet high, and showed the god sitting on a large throne covered with carving. The god's robe was in solid gold. But it was the stat ue's face that was most beautiful to the Greeks though. It was so amazing and wonderful that they said: "Either the sculptor shoul d have disappeared up to heaven and seen Zeus on his throne, or the god must have descended to earth and showed the artist his face." In addition to constructing temples for their gods, the Gree ks also held great festivals in their honor. The biggest of these fes tivals was that which took place at a place called Olympia in Zeus ' honor. Messages would go about from town to town every four years to notify it. Then all wars would cease and people would co me to Olympia from across Greece to worship the god. They wou ld find the fastest runners racing there as a prize for a wreath of olive leaves. Those who would just even consider chariot racesbo xing tournaments, and other sports there. The people believe tha t Zeus and the other gods were fond of seeing men using their co nfidence and ability at their festivals to honor them. But people t rained for these games for months and months beforehand; and t he onewho won the win in them was known as ever after gods a nd man's favorites.

7.2. Poseidon, God of the Sea

Poseidon was Zeus' brother, and even as Zeus ruled over the earth and the heavens, Poseidon ruled the rivers and the oceans. He was often depicted as bearing three points of a trident, or fish-spear. With that, as he reached the sea, fierce winds would arise; then, with a word, he might ease the dashing waves and make the water surface as smooth as a bay. Poseidon's temple has been said to be on the seabed. It was made of shells and coral and fastened with silver and gold. The walls were pearl and all the kids were adorned with precious stones. There were large gardens full of lovely sea-plants and vineyards around the temple. The flowers were the lightest and most delicate shades, and they were much more exquisite than the ones emerging under sunshine. The leaves were of the most wonderful sea-green color, not the deep green we see on land. Whether you should ever go to the sea-shore and look down through the water, you might also see Poseidon's gardens lying on the bottom of the ocean among the rocks.

Poseidon rode over the sea surface in a chariot made of a massive sea-shell drawn with golden hoofs and manes by great sea-horses. The waters would get still at the god's arrival, and mysterious fish and massive sea-serpents and sea-lions would rise to the fore to play with his chariot. Magnificent animals called Tritons were blowing on shells like trumpets before and beside his chariot. These hyper had green hair and eyes; their body parts were like those of men, but rather than their legs they had tails like fishes. Also emergers swam along by the chariot of the sea-god. A few of them, like the Tritons, were part human and good portion fish. Others were like beautiful maidens, having fair faces and hair. A few lived in the depths of the sea so much that their soft blue eyes could not carry the light of day. And they never left the water except at night when they would find a quiet spot on the shore and dance to the music they made on fragile shells of the fish. Once upon a time, Poseidon had a dispute with one of the goddesses over a parcel of land she wished to own and eventually begged the other gods to resolve the dispute for them. So at a conference on Mount Everest the gods decided the land should have the one who should make the most helpful gift to the people.

Whenever the trial came, Poseidon thought it would be an awesome gift to have a spring of water. He struck a big blow with his trident on a rocky hill willing to stand in that property, and a stream of water gushed out. But Zeus had lived so much at sea that he had forgotten that only fresh water could be intoxicated by men. The spring he had decided to make was as salt as salt could be and it was of no use whatsoever to people. Then, in turn, the goddess caused an olive-tree to spring from the earth. When the gods saw how much fruit and oil men could make use of it, they decided the goddess had won. So Poseidon didn't get the property, but the people are showing the salt spring and the olive tree on the top of the hill as evidence of the trial.

The people who lived by the sea shore adored Poseidon the most. Every town along the coast had a temple in front of Poseidon, where people came to pray for the fair weather and happy trips for themselves and friends.

7.3. Hades, King of the Dead

Hades, the god of the underworld, was also Zeus' brother; yet the Greeks, like the other gods, did not think of him as brilliant and majestic. They claimed, too, that he helped to sprout the seeds and lift their leaves over the earth's crust, and that he brought people the gold and silver they had mined from their mines. But they thought of him more often as the god of the gloomy land of the dead; so they imagined that in appearance he was dark and stern and they feared him as much as the other gods.

The Greeks thought his soul or shade went to the Kingdom of Hades at once when every one died. The path to this afterlife lies by the side of a still lake, through a cave that was in the center of a deep and dim forest. The shades came to a deep, swift stream of black water after they had passed down through this cavern. There they found a bent old man named Charon, in a small, leaky boat, whose duty was to take the shades across the stream. But only those spirits could cross whose bodies in the world above had been properly burned or buried; and those whose funerals were not properly attended to were compelled to wander on the river bank for a hundred years before Charon would take them across.

They came across a hideous beast after the shades had crossed the water, protecting the road so that no one who had once fallen into the land of the dead might ever come forth again. This would be the great dog Cerberus, who had 3 siblings, and who barked so fiercely that all the lower world could hear him.

Throughout the world of the dead the shades that had lived bad lives throughout the world above were dreadfully punished. Once upon a time there was a King named Sisyphus, cruel and wicked all his life. The judge told him that his punishment would have been to roll a wonderful stone up a steep hill and down the other side when john died, and his shade went down to the underworld. Socrates at first thought this would be an easy process to do. But when he had almost reached the top of the stone, and it seemed as if one more push would send it over and finish his task, it slipped out of his hands unexpectedly and rolled back to the hill 's foot. So it happened several times; and the Greeks believed that as long as the world lasted, Sisyphus would have to continue to work in this way, and that his task would never be complete.

Once upon a time there was another king, named Tantalus, who on earth was wealthy and fortunate and loved by the heavenly gods. Zeus even invited him to sit at his table once, and told him about the gods' secrets. Tantalus, however, had not proved worthy of all this dignity. He couldn't keep the secrets he had been trusted with, but had told them to the whole world. And he, too, was given a terrible sentence as his shadow fell before the judge of the dead. He was chained in the middle of a sparkling little lake where almost the water came up to his lips. He was always going to burn with thirst; but every time he bowed down to drink from the lake, the water sank before him into the ground. He was always hungry, and branches loaded just above him with delicious fruits. And when he raised his hand to gather them, they were just swung out of his reach by the brise. And the Greeks believed Tantalus was to be punished permanently because he had revealed the gods secrets.

354

Hades, King of the Dead - A Myth with a Moral

Most of the other oldest myth legends, such as the myth of Hades, King of the Dead, contain tales of morality that offered the old story-tellers of brief illustrations about thrilling tales about how to live and behave and represent valuable life lessons for children. In this type of fable the characters of the heroes demonstrated the qualities of courage, absolutely adore, commitment, strength, persistence, leadership and self-reliance. While the villains proved all the vices, and the gods killed or punished them. The story and fable of the old, famous misconception, like Hades, King of the deceased, were meant to motivate, thrill and motivate their young listeners.

7.4. Hera, Queen of the Gods

Zeus' wife was the tall and pretty goddess Hera. Even as Zeus was the king of all gods, so was she their queen. She sat next to him in the gods' council-hall, on a throne just a little less splendid than her own. She was the world's best of all priestesses, and she was incredibly proud of her own power and beauty.

For her favorite bird Hera chose the peacock, because her plumage was so beautiful. The priestess Iris has been her servant and messaging service, and upon her errands flew quickly through the air. The rainbow, which with its beautiful arch appeared to join heaven and earth, was thought to be the road Iris traveled along.

Not only was she proud of her own beauty here, but she too was very jealous of anybody else's beauty. She would even punish women who she thought were too gorgeous, like they've just done something quite wrong; she often did so by reshaping them into mammals or bird species. There was one woman Hera turned into a wild bear and turned out to wander through the forest even though she hated her pretty smile. Among the fearsome animals of the jungle, the poor girl was desperately scared; for even though she herself now had the body of a beast, her spirit still was human. At last Zeus, who was heartless than Hera, had pity on her. He pulled her well above the earth, and positioned her among the heavenly stars; and so, ever afterwards, the Greek people known as the great Bear a group of stars.

Thereby for quite some time there was a wood-nymph called Echo, who misled Hera, and made her very sad. Echo was a beautiful, merry girl whose tongue always went away and who was never completely comfortable except if she can have the last word. Hera took away her voice as a penalty for her deception, leaving her only with the power to continue the last word she should be spoken to. Echo now did not care to join her playmates in their merry games, and thus wandered all alone through the forests. But she sought to speak, and often hid in the woods, repeating the words of the hunters and others who managed to pass that way.

Finally she learned to take pleasure in mystifying and mocking the people who were listening to her.

"Who are you?" they'd scream at her.

"You" her reaction will come.

"So, who am I?" they would ask, even more perplexed.

"I," Echo would reply in her sweet, teasing way.

One day Echo met a young man named Narcissus in the woods, and he loved him. But he was very cruel, and would not notice her except to tease her for her voice loss. She was very sad, and began to waste away with sorrow, until eventually little was left of her except her lovely teasing voice.

When the gods learned what happened to the beautiful Echo they became really furious. They transformed him from a powerful young man to a small, fragile vine, to punish Narcissus for his meanness, which is now still called by his name.

Hera, Queen of the Gods - A Myth with a Moral

Several of the old myth stories, such as the mythology of Hera, princess of the Gods, integrate tales with moral principles that supplied the old storytellers with brief examples of future " of how to act and act and reflect important life lessons for children. In this type of fable the protagonists of the heroes proved the qualities of bravery, absolutely adore, commitment, strength, persistence, governance and self-reliance. Whereas the protagonists proved all the vices, and the gods killed or punished them. The ancient, familiar myth tale and fable are built to amuse, impress and motivate their young listeners, including Hera, Queen of the Gods

7.5 Artemis, Goddess of the hunt:

Athena was Apollo's twin sister and she was very skilled with the arrow and bow like him. She ended up going to her father, Zeus, when she was very young, and begged him to allow her to live on the beautiful mountains a free and happy life. Zeus granted her wish, and so she became the fields and forests' great hunting goddess.

As Athena was sun god and daylight bright, so Artemis was the moon goddess. She loved hunting by light of the moon; and when the Greeks made her sculptures they always portrayed her with a torch in one hand held high and a weapon in the other.

Athena always had with her a band of maidens, who ran beside her, cared for her dogs, and managed to carry her arrows. She could run so fast that she'd be able to catch the hunt's fleetest deer. With crying and merry laughter, she and her maidens would dash thru the forests and then, when the hunt was over, they would bathe in the pure mountain streams.

Athena so dearly cherished the forests and mountains that she never left them for men's settlements. Yet in her passion for them she was very greedy, and in her pleasure she did not want to be interrupted.

7.6. Artemis, the huntress

For the first and only time there was a young man named Actaeon, who had been a voracious eater, and often wandered alone with his dogs through the forests.

Just then he came upon the greek goddess, playing on the banks of a stream with her maidens. He remained very still and watched them, rather than running quickly at once, as he would have done. This made Artemis so furious that she turned him into a wolf, and then turned his own dogs on him and cut him to parts.

Artemis loved all the forest mammals but the deer was her favorite. Once a great Greek king killed a doe Artemis was very fond of. This king was just beginning a great war and he had plenty of warships ready to sail in the harbour. Yet day after day passed, and the wind was continuously blewing from the opposite direction, and the boats were unable to set out to sea. The Greeks became anxious, and inquired the priest why the gods didn't give them a reasonable cold wind.The priests then approached the gods and informed the public that Artemis was furious that the king had destroyed her doe, and that goddess would not let the correct winds blow until the president offered up his innocent child to be sacrificed on the goddess' altar. As first the king declined to do so, that he loved his child greatly; but at final he had for submit to it. Then the pretty girl was taken to the crucifix, and the priest lifted his long knife to kill. But a cloud dropped over her before anything fell upon her breast, and hid her from sight. The girl was not to be seen when it floated away; only a white doe stayed in her place, and the priest prepared to sacrifice this in her place. This same priestess had taken pity on the maiden and carried her far away to a distant country in the midst of that huge fog. There, she served as a priestess in one of Artemis' temples for a long time. But at last, her brother found her after many years, and once again she was expected to come to her own nation and friends.

Artemis, Goddess of the hunt - A Myth with a Moral

Several of the prehistoric myth stories, such as the mythology of Artemis, the hunting goddess, integrate tales with moral principles that supplied the old scriptwriters with simple illustrations of illusion" for children about how to act and start behaving and reflected valuable lessons from life. In this type of fable the protagonists of the heroes proved the qualities of courage, absolutely adore, commitment, resilience, persistence, governance and self-reliance. Whereas the protagonists proved all the vices, and the gods killed or punished them. The old, famous story of myth and fable, like the hunting goddess Artemis, were meant to motivate, thrill and excite their young viewers...

7.7 Apollo, The God of Light:

Apollo was Zeus' son, and was one of Mount Olympus's greatest gods. He was often called the sung-god, for the Greeks thought he brought the light and warmth of the sun to men. They assumed that Apollo was also the god of health and masculine beauty, since these are so necessary to every living thing. Thus the Greeks always represented him as a strong and beautiful young man in their pictures and statues.

Apollo liked music very much and was in the history of running on the lyre at the gods' feasts, to the delight of all those who noticed him. He was quite appreciative of his ability, and would often have competitions with the other gods, and even sometimes men. King Midas had been present at one of these contests. But rather than deciding, as usual, that Apollo was the more skilled player, he was happier with another player. Apollo was very upset at this and he turned his hands into those of a donkey to demonstrate his view to Midas. This was then Socrates' turn to get vexed. He wore a cap that covered his big, ugly ears; and he wanted nobody to understand what actually happened to him but the man who shaved his head. Midas made a vow to this man that he would not reveal any of his misfortune, but the man tried to state that he could no longer bear it at all. He ended up going to the brink of a stream, dug the hole in the planet, and muttered the secret into it. Then he filled the hole, and went satiated away. But a bunch of reeds sprang up from that spot, which soon started whispering on every breeze, "king has donkey's ears; king has donkey's head." And so the story soon became known to the entire world. The Greeks believed Apollo was causing death among people by firing swift bows that never missed their intent. He punished the bad in this manner, and made the decent who were hurting and desired

to die happy death. The people believe that Apollo caused death among humans by trying to fire swift gauntlets that never missed everyone's desire. In this way, he punished the poor, and made the good people who were suffering and trying to die happier death.

Apollo, the God of Light - A Myth with a Moral:

Many of the ancient myth legends, such as the legend of Apollo, the God of Fire, include tales of morality that provided the ancient storytellers of brief illustrations about thrilling tales about how to behave and act and represent valuable life lessons for children. In this type of fable the characters of the heroes proved the qualities of testicular fortitude, absolutely adore, commitment, resilience, persistence, governance and self-reliance. Whereas the villains proved all the vices, and the gods killed or punished them. The old, famous myth story and fable was meant to motivate, thrill and inspire their young listeners like Apollo, the God of Light ...

7.8. Hephaestus, God of Fire and the Forge:

The god of fire and metal-working, Hephaestus was the son of Zeus and Hera. As a child he worked in an underwater cavern with the sea-nymphs. He was capable of creating all manner of useful and beautiful things from his very babyhood and it was his daily joy to prepare a fantastic creation. He took his place with the other gods on mount Everest when he was born, and was always occupied with creating things for himself or for them. He made magic feet, among other marvelous items, that could tread water or air as effortlessly as the earth; caps that made invisible the people that wear them; and gold and silver dishes that would take away from the table, without the aid of staff. Hephaestus had his own forge and workshop on Mount Olympus, in his own house. He trained many servants to help him in his work, and he planned twenty great bellows for his forge, which would blow his fire at a word from him into a fierce heat. He had other workshops on earth; and wherever there was a volcano coming from its summit with smoke and fire, the people said Hephaestus was busy with his giant helpers doing wonderful things for the gods. The gods and goddesses, as you have learned, were not all nice and loving. One day Hera angered her husband; and Zeus glued hannah hands and feet together to punish her, and ended up hanging her in the air among heaven and earth at midway. That was a very mean way of treating the lovely and stately athena and she was scorned by all the gods. Hephaestus had been so apologetic for his mom that he tried to free her. This made odin even more furious, and in his fury he hit him so severely that poor Hephaestus was hurled headlong from the heavens, down he fell for a whole day, and struck the earth at last upon a beautiful island The fall did not kill him, for he was one of the immortal gods, and could not die; but he fell with such force that he was lame ever afterwards. Down, down he fell for a whole day, and struck the earth at last upon a beautiful island The fall did not kill him, for he was one of the immortal gods, and could not die; but he fell with such force that he was lame ever afterwards.

Chapter 8

Inspirational Bedtime Stories:

Milton Erickson believed that every child has a motivating desire to know and explore, that any stimulation is an opportunity for the child to react in a new way (1980), through which we may infer that the purpose of pediatric psychotherapy is to promote and enhance these learning opportunities. Knowing how to read is one of the basic skills in adulthood, equipping the infant with information, exchanging memories, coping mechanisms, purpose, happiness, and living well-being. Our concept of schooling, however, extends beyond the three Rats that are the foundation of our educational programs to involve building on and using the innate interest of the infant and the ability to learn as a framework for the development of beliefs, pro-social habits, problem-solving approaches, and other essential qualities that are incorporated — or not — during childhood.

We also included stories in this chapter about inspiring children to make a change, cultivating optimistic attitudes to life conditions and learning to be self-reliant. There are tales of how to leverage a child's talents, tools, and ability, as well as how to adopt a practical path to happiness (Burns & Lane, 2003; Seligman, 2002).

8.1. Look after yourself – Five little chickens

Have you heard the story of the Five Chickens? Okay, once in a while there were five little chickens residing alongside Daddy Rooster and Mommy Hen. One morning the five little chickens woke up feeling hungry, as most of us do first thing in the morning or afternoon when we get home from school. The first said, "I'm tired. I wish someone would send me a big fat worm. "He began to think about a big fat worm, he wanted to peck it in his beak and hear it slithering in his gut, as if you were a starving little chicken,

I suppose you should. Not quite what I'd want for tea! What's up with you?

No matter how badly anyone might like the first little chicken to send him a big fat worm, no worm came and the hunger he looked.

Even the second little chicken was thirsty, so when she heard her brother speak about a big fat worm, she replied, "I am now famished. I wish there was a huge fat slug here in front of me right now. "In excitement, she stared at the table. She glanced about and stared back. And they got ever more hungry.

The third little chicken, like his brother and girlfriend, felt as hungry. "Cheep, cheep," he said, anticipating that someone might notice. "I wish the farmer would bring us a big bowl of those delicious chicken pellets he sometimes delivers." With that thought in his head he was watching the gate in the coop, hoping the farmer would appear. And felt like he was thirsty.

"And," said the fourth, following her brothers and sisters wishes, "that the farmer's wife should carry out from last night's meal, like she always does, one of those large bowls of food scraps." Like her dad, she stood watching the gate in the coop, hoping and hoping a big bowl of scraps. And grow tired.

All this discussion of food got become ravenously hungry the fifth chicken feeling he felt he was going to faint. "What I would not give for a large crunchy grain tub," he said. "I wish I had some 52 curing tales, maize, oats, or barley teaching tales." His eyes were focused on the tin tray where the farmer often scattered some food. He gazed at the tray and looked away, growing hungry by the second.

Overhearing the desires of the five little chickens, Daddy Rooster said, "Come here." Collecting the five little chickens around him, he said, "Do you see what Mommy Hen and I do when we're hungry? Help us out into the garden patch if you decide to have coffee. You will learn to hack and peck your own food there, much as we do.

8.2. Kids can make a difference – Goldilocks and four bears

A long time ago, when Goldilocks visited, there were just three bears. Now there are four — Little Bear, Mama Bear, Big Brother Bear, and Papa Bear. Grandpa Bear had come to live with the Bear family even after Goldilocks' tour. He was a poor old bear whose hair had turned grey. As he attempted to chew, his hands moved, and his head leaned down as if he were sick of standing.

Little Bear cherished dog Grandpa. Grandpa Bear still listened to Little Bear while everyone else was getting too far to gather honey or something. If Little Bear tried to rest peacefully on his lap and be told a story, Grandpa Bear would never tell "No." And there were other fantastic tales about Grandpa Bear.

Grandpa Bear, whose hands rattled so badly at times that his spoon could skip his mouth and spill porridge all over his head, was always sorry for Little Bear too. He will also drop his bowl on the concrete floor, crack the bowl and create a huge mess.

He'd have mother bear and dad bear upset. Besides destroying the all bowls that Goldilocks had made popular in her novel, they had to clean up after him. "As if we don't still have anything to do," they would complain. Big Brother Bear will say something like, "Grandpa Bear has the plague of CRAFT — He Can't Recall a Burning Thing," and laugh loudly. Little Bear realized she was mocking Big Brother Bear but it always hurt and she despised him for it. She tried to support Grandpa Bear so what was she supposed to do?

One day, once again, when Grandpa Bear lost his mug, Little Bear got down on the floor and took all the bits. Afterwards she asked Papa Bear if he had some adhesive.

"Why would you want some glue?" Papa Bear inquired.

"And, after I've grown up, I will tie the bowl of Grandpa Bear back together and hold it for you and mum," Little Bear answered.

Silently, Papa Bear leaned back in his daddy-bear chair and stared at Mama Bear in her mom-bear chair. They both stared at each other for a moment. We became kinder to Grandpa Bear after that, Little Bear said. They got him a special plastic grandpa bowl that wouldn't fall too quickly off the table, and wouldn't crack if he dropped it. When he poured porridge down his hair or created a mess on the tablecloth, they didn't appear to mind too much. We talked more to him, and listened to his stories, even though they had read them before.

And this is a happy conclusion to our plot. Mum Bear and Papa Bear became happy, due to Little Bear. Big Bear Pal. Okay, he was the same as he'd always been. No wonder Grandpa Bear was happy. And Little Bear too was happy.

8.3. Seeking happiness – an inspirational bedtime story for kids

There was once a princess who had it all. Ok, pretty much everything. She lived in a magnificent palace. She was the most significant person in all 58 Healing Tales, Teaching Tales Nation, after the king and queen. She was of course the queen, she had everything she could possibly think of.

Can you work it out? If she wanted it, so all she needed to do was inquire, and she was given it. She was a modern queen, who got the best in new toys. She had a specially designed toy palace packed with dolls from Barbie and Ken, and all their accessories. She had the best in video games played on a huge plasma screen in her playroom, which occupied a whole wall. And her playroom alone was as large as some houses where some of her kingdom's families lived. And she still lost interest, got bored or felt alone amid all of this. The princess will often open her playroom window and gaze out at the streets below. There she saw other kids play hopscotch or tag, laugh, talk and sing. "How do the kids make all those sounds?" The princess one day told her kingly nanny. "I guess that is because they are satisfied," the royal nanny responded.

The princess looked down at the kids again, and said, "I just want to be happy. What are they going to make me happy? "The kingly nanny had never before found herself in such a difficult position. If she could just let the princess out onto the streets to play with the other kids, the princess might start learning to laugh and having fun too. If only the princess had some friends she could share stories with, chat about her thoughts or even do some of the stuff that a friend is good to do. The nanny also started to talk of certain ideas that would have been too evil for a royal nanny to have. She wondered if the princess would like playing a fun snowball battle with other kids on the sidewalks, or if she'd joke about paddling barefoot in the mud along the side of the river and maybe making one of her cute little dresses dirty. How would it be for her not to care about her looks, or what other people were feeling of her? But these were of course not things a royal nanny might tell to the princess and yet keep her work. Besides that, no matter what the nanny thought, the princess would never be allowed to do these.

So what was that royal nanny saying? She needed to think of something for addressing the query of the queen. She glanced down in contemplation, and saw her socks. Perhaps that was the solution. She eventually said, "If we could find the happiest child in the country, you could stand in that child's shoes, or even walk in her footsteps, and realize what it's like to be happy." Immediately, the princess insisted that the king send off a whole battalion of his guard to search out the happiest child in the country. "If you've found him or her," the princess said, "show me the children's shoes right away." Scanned and scanned the king's guard. The princess became irritated as the hours were days, and the days turned into weeks. He asked several times a day, "Did they find their happiest child yet? Where are the shoes that you told me? "The princess was worried about the waiting. Which would the happiest child's shoes look like?

Will they be trendy jeans, work shoes or brand-name sneakers? Which color would it be? Pink, red, yellow, blue? Happy shoes must definitely have been colored. Will it decorate them with roses, bows or bells? Will they have blinking lights like those she'd seen on television selling shoes? She just couldn't resist.

Yeah, day in and day out, the princess kept telling her royal nanny, "When are they going to bring me the shoes?" The day eventually came. The royal nanny came rushing into the princess' chamber with the news, "Your Highness, I've got some good news and some bad news," the little princess excitedly screamed, "Give me the good news first." "Well," the royal nanny said, "I am proud to say that we find the happiest kid in the entire country." "Where are my shoes then?" The princess asked, impatiently.

"This is the bad news," the royal nanny answered. "In the kingdom the happiest boy had no socks."

8.4. Feed what you want to grow – An inspirational bedtime story for kids

A grandfather and his grandson settled down on a rock in the sunlight next to a babbling lake.

"Tell me one story," the grandson said.

"This is a two-wolf tale," Grandfather said. "As we develop it often seems like two wolves are fighting to gain power inside of us. The first wolf with soft gray fur, a loving look in his eyes, and maybe even a friendly smile on his lips, you might imagine. It is a wolf who barely ever bars his teeth and is able to stand back and let feed the little ones. We might name him the wolf of harmony, compassion and goodness, because the wolf believes that if we can work alongside each other in harmony, every animal and every human being would be far happier.

"Love is more important to this wolf than everything else. You see, she thinks our animal and human existence will cease to exist without affection. It's because a mother loves her baby that she takes care of her, cooks her, dresses her, covers her and saves her from danger. We come into the world as an act of affection and we learn from the affection parents give us. If we love and are cherished in exchange, we hope to be accepted, and our souls are nurtured and filled.

"Apparently the wolf always understands that goodness is part of that affection. When we are compassionate to someone they are apt to display compassion back to us, if not always. Smile at someone and they can smile back with a fair chance. Go off to be helpful and the one you are helping is more likely to help you when you need it. Wolves are a little like dogs, who work in packs. They blend together, and usually feel happier when they combine in a dry, harmonious way.

"But," the grandfather added, "lets say that the group includes another wolf that doesn't think the same way. This wolf has a really mean, mischievous face. Often it draws back its lips to threateningly show its teeth against other species. Typically they experience terror more than affection and reverence as it happens, because that is the wolf of anger, greed and hate. Maybe it's afraid or nervous, and so it's just on watch. Unfortunately, it hasn't realized that it creates a lot of negative emotions among itself and in the other wolves by being too frustrated or violent toward others, by thinking about who or what it hates more than who or what it loves. This wolf is looking for number one while the wolf of harmony, compassion, and goodness watches out for the joy and well-being of others as well as for his own.

"As you may guess, there might be two these wolves in a group fighting to see which one is heading off on its path. The wolf of goodwill, compassion, and goodness wishes to express those ideals with everyone, but the wolf of greed, covetousness, and hate cares only about himself. It feels terrible about itself and leaves it feeling worse for those around it.

"Let's carry on dreaming," the grandfather said, "that two such wolves are in a fight inside you." The little boy stared up at his grandparents, wide-eyed. "Which one wins? "He inquired anxiously.

The grandfather looked down, compassion in his eyes, gentleness in his expression, replying, "The one you feed."

8.5. Kids can make a difference – Trevor a boy in early teens

Trevor did what a lot of other 13-year-old kids might do that night: he watched tv. He noticed on the television a report of some homeless people living out on the sidewalks in the rain, in a trendy section of Philadelphia where he worked. Trevor never once quit talking about how fortunate he was to stay in the same city's relatively well-to-do neighborhood. His heart was moved by the stories of homeless people and he began asking what he should do to support these men.

Trevor might possibly have known about it. There are so many tragic things you can see on Television. That may have been yet another aspect he overlooked.

Perhaps Trevor felt too, Ok, what should I do with it? I am a child, but he wasn't. Then, he began asking if he could support and this prompted him to recall that there were some unused, spare blankets in their workshop. So he went to his friend, wondering if he could take them to the downtown citizens who had no homes to go to the night.

Maybe Trevor's father thought the request was a bit weird. It's natural for children to try to cling on to the stuff we've got, good for adults to believe they've been working hard to earn what they deserve and why would they offer it away? I suppose it's pretty much the same as a kid thinks, it took me a long time to save my pocket money to help purchase this new ride, so why would I gift it to a buddy who wants to get home quickly?

Now, Trevor's father had been a kind-hearted kid. He rode downtown Trevor to help out some of the residents on the streets with a few leftover blankets. When it came time to curl up and sleep that night, I think the citizens were pretty satisfied with the new blankets providing comfort.

Trevor, too, was pleased. He felt nice to give out the blankets. He sensed an intense fire, almost as though he himself had been enveloped in an emotional blanket. But he knew that there was a risk — it might feel so amazing that you would like to do it again.

Trevor went the next day to his nearby grocery store and other public areas in his area where notice boards were placed. He put up posters asking that citizens contribute whatever extra blankets or food they didn't use. The outcome was outstanding. Kindness was universal. Trevor saw so many people eager to support he packed his father's workshop with food and blankets within a week.

What had started with Trevor's generosity developed and spread across the group? It wasn't long until the kindness of the citizens overflowed from the garage of his father and Trevor and his father needed to search for a better building to accommodate all the presents that were donated. Will you know that there are already a variety of different warehouses all over Philadelphia that store food and blankets to feed and shelter the homeless? They are both named "the place of Trevor."

8.6. It's in the way you do it – An inspirational bedtime story:

One day the breeze, the heat, and the sun spoke about how they should convince us to adjust what they were doing. Often it may be a huge challenge because you are performing something that you just don't want to do, or doing something that don't benefit you or anyone. Yeah, that's what the breeze, rain, and sun is thinking about. "Let's just play a draw," the sun said. "See the man with a jacket over there? Let's see who can convince him to cut it off. "The breeze said enthusiastically," Let me try first. The wind began rushing by the ear of the child, at first softly saying, "Take off your jacket. Take off your jacket. "If the boy didn't take off his jacket, the wind began roaring a bit harder towards his face, but the stronger it screamed, the warmer the boy got, so the more snugly he wrapped around his jacket. The wind in his ear started to hurl harder. It was no longer pressing him for instructions but roaring: "Take off your shirt!

Take the jacket off! "The more the boy defied the breeze screamed the louder. So the more the man overlooked. The wind blew out, screaming and spinning, but the boy snuggled tighter into his blanket, pulling it more closely around his chest.

"Grant me a try," the rain said. "What you're doing clearly isn't effective. There's no use in yelling at him, and the sooner you try, the more he's wearing his sweater. "The rain continued to do what it does best. It started to roar quietly, calling as it dripped through the ears of the kid, "Take off your jacket. Taking off your hat. "But then the boy pulled the cap around his head and zipped the hat to keep out the rain on his body. Frustrated, it was determined the storm should not give up. It seemed to ignore the strong wind advice it had provided. "If he's not going to listen to me, I'm going to beat him to take off his jacket," the rain said angrily, and started pouring heavily with that. Raindrops pelted the boy: "Take your jacket off! Take the jacket off! "But the child declined to listen anyway. The storm changed to hail and flew at him, yelling loudly at him to take his jacket off. Instead, the boy decided to cover whatever aspect of him the jacket was able to conceal and search about, searching for protection to grab.

"It has got to be my time," the sun said softly. It began to shine off, drying the boy and his jacket without saying a word. The sun started caressing the boy in water, only slowly increasing the air temperature without having it too high. The kid slid the hood behind at first. When the sun kept warming the day softly, the kid pulled off his jacket zipper. Carefully, the sun lifted the temperature to another degree or two, all the while caressing the boy warmly, and it wasn't long before the boy stripped out of his sweater to fully appreciate the sunshine's soothing warmth.

8.7. Do what you can do.

It's easy enough to find yourself in turmoil even because you don't want it to be. Often we don't know what to do when we are facing a new situation, probably because we never had to experience it before. That's what got Mrs. Teresa Frog. Everyone had used to name her Little Tessie Tadpole when she was little. She favoured Ms. Teresa Frog now, because she was smaller. Ms. Teresa Frog had been working on a farm in a field. She was an imaginative young frog who loved to go and play. Others characterized her as nosy, or a "sticky beak." She was always told by her mother that she stuck her nose where she should not. "Mark my name," he would say to her mother. "You're going to be in big trouble one day." But Teresa needed to discover. She just wanted to figure out things she didn't know. After all, leaving her pond and going running across the farmyard was enjoyable. Seeing the comical chickens scratching busily and pecking their way through the coop was always enjoyable. She didn't want to be confined much like them, she said to herself.

She had found that almost all visiting the pigpen gave her the ability to catch a plump fly or two. There were so many around her that her long tongue's fast flick almost always ensured a meal. This specific day, after smelling the new scent of milk, Ms. Teresa Frog (formerly known as Little Tessie Tadpole) was running by the dairy. She found the tempting smell coming up from a bucket on the floor after her nose. She climbed to the top of the pot, trying to try the sugar, but did not reach nearly far enough. She tried again, putting all of her effort into this. She overdid it this time, leaping straight over the rim and landing with a soft plop in the lush cream.

The cream was moist, and dense. In her frozen pool it felt so much better than swimming. Perhaps better, drinking had tasted fine. She flicked out her long tongue, and lapped a few rich mouthfuls. But after playing and drinking her fill for a bit, Ms. Teresa Frog felt it was time to go back into her pond house. That was when the trouble began. You know, Ms. Teresa Frog hadn't been looking too far ahead. She would have been thinking about getting into the bucket but she hadn't given any thought to get out of the bucket. The walls were high, her feet coated in cream were too slick for a grip so she couldn't just hop off the top. She was trapped, feeling powerless and knew what to do.

She should just move on, she said to herself. But even though she might have enjoyed herself for a bit, this would not fix her dilemma. She might wait for someone to come and save her, but it might be a long time, so if the farmer found her, he would not be too happy to discover a frog in his cream that had just visited the swimming pigpen. If she surrendered and stopped, she could drown.

Oh my little Ms. Teresa Frog it all felt so rough. She did the only thing she could do, not knowing what to do: She stopped swimming. She swam in the cream round and round, doing the frog jump, as frogs prefer to do. She sat back, then screamed. She sat back, then screamed. She then threw out a couple more. Ms. Teresa Frog has been adamant she will not give up and drown. She had to carry on, so she kicked and kicked a few more. As she did, she began to notice that swimming through the cream was becoming increasingly difficult. She thought she was just getting sleepy at first, but then noticed that the cream itself was getting thicker. Her kicking turned the milk into butter!

In that, her faith was renewed and she swam faster and deeper, going round and round in the bucket until the butter was so strong that she could stand on it and run. Fair over the bucket top. Tired, she joyfully jumped back into the pool. When she washed the butter off her body in the bath, Ms. Teresa Frog said to herself, "I have liked cream but I love butter best.

8.8. Make the most of what you have been given

Once upon a time there was a farmer not far from a country town, who had a small farm. He owned very little but he was able to support his family from this small farm. Of the few items he had, one had been an elderly mule. The old mule had helped him plow his field for years, bring his produce into the village and push his family to church every Sunday, harnessed to a horse.

The village near where the farmer lived loved to stage all the yearly festivities, and planned to have a fireworks display for the coming New Year. No one stopped to think about how an old mule in a neighboring paddock could impact that.

The mule stood in his paddock, head dropped to the ground, eyes closed, sleeping peacefully on New Year's Eve when unexpectedly the sky filled with odd streaks of light and cannon-like bangs that could have heralded the beginning of a war. Thinking the world was coming to an end, the poor mule fled in panic, racing desperately across the paddock. There was an old well inside the paddock as it occurred. It was empty and neglected, not having been willing to maintain its water flow for several years. The mule would normally have evaded it very carefully. But the mule staggered in the pitch black of the night and was overcome with fear, and dropped the small well. Luckily he arrived at the bottom unharmed.

The farmer was surprised to find his mule missing the next day, and started searching around his house. It wasn't long until he heard a soft, ringing bray coming from the well's depth and finding his mule at the bottom to his dismay. There was no way he could comfortably get to the mule by slipping down the old well. There wasn't a large enough ladder in the village to reach the bottom and how would he get the mule out, even if he'd been able to get down? He called to help his peasant friends. They figured they should set a winch up to lower the farmer down to the mule, but the well's walls were too rusty and decaying. It had been too dangerous. How should he add a brace to raise the mule out of such a limited room, even though they had lowered anyone down?

The farmers sat peering down across the well and rubbed their ears. "That is impossible," one said. "Unthinkable," said another. "He'll probably die a long, horrible death down there," a third said. "Better put him out of his misery." So the farmers picked up some shovels and started to bury the mule by pouring dirt down the well.

The mule noticed this strange stuff, like dry rain, dropping on his back at the bottom of the well; he gave himself a shake, and the dirt dropped through his hooves. The mule staggered a bit, and the dirt beneath its hooves became rough. Further dust was falling down on his legs. He brushed it off, and then rolled even more once again. He was shocked to note that the bottom of the well had risen by an inch or two after doing so for a bit. He stood a bit further up at the wall than he had been farmers kicked in the dirt, the more the mule shook it off and trampled it deeply beneath its hooves — and the further it climbed bit by bit upward to the top. Yeah, the mule finally found its way to the brink, as you suspected, and was saved before. The harder the farmers kicked in the dirt, the more the mule shook it off and trampled it deeply beneath its hooves — and the further it climbed bit by bit upward to the top.

Yeah, the mule finally found its way to the brink, as you suspected, and was saved.

References

What Is ADHD?

https://www.psychiatry.org/patients-families/adhd/what-is-adhd

ADHD in Kids

https://www.helpguide.org/articles/add-adhd/attention-deficit-disorder-adhd-in-kids.htm

Treatment for Kids with ADHD

https://www.helpguide.org/articles/add-adhd/treatment-for-childhood-attention-deficit-disorder-adhd.htm

What Causes ADHD?

https://www.health.com/condition/adhd/what-causes-adhd-12-myths-and-facts?slide=b1a01d31-5836-427a-a74d-ce3dd7ada810#b1a01d31-5836-427a-a74d-ce3dd7ada810

7 ADHD Mindfulness Exercises for Kids, Teens, and Adults

https://www.themindfulword.org/2019/mindfulness-exercises-adhd

Your Child's Brain on Mindful Meditation

https://www.additudemag.com/mindfulness-meditation-for-kids-with-adhd/

Natural Remedies for ADHD: ADD Treatment Without Medication

https://www.additudemag.com/slideshows/treating-adhd-without-medication/

7 Reasons to Consider ADHD Hypnotherapy

https://www.addvantagehypnotherapy.co.uk/7-reasons-consider-hypnotherapy-adhd/

CPSIA information can be obtained
at www.ICGtesting.com
Printed in the USA
LVHW080236121220
674003LV00006B/187